5TH Edition

COLLEGE
ACCOUNTING

Study Guide and Working Papers

Chapters 1–12

Paradigm PUBLISHING

St. Paul · Los Angeles · Indianapolis

Senior Developmental Editor: Christine Hurney
Copy Editor: Susan Free
Proofreader: Nancy Ahr
Production Editor: Amy McGuire

Cover Designer: Leslie Anderson
Production Specialists: Jaana Bykonich, Matthias Frasch, Ryan Hamner, John Valo
Cover Image: © Robert Marien/Corbis

ISBN 978-0-76383-491-3

© 2010 by Paradigm Publishing, Inc.
875 Montreal Way
St. Paul, MN 55102
E-mail: educate@emcp.com
Web site: www.emcp.com

CONTENTS

The Nature of Accounting

Chapter Summary

Interactive Summary in English and Spanish

Every individual involved in any kind of work practices **accounting**, which is the process of recording, summarizing, analyzing, and interpreting financial activities to permit organizations and individuals to make informed judgments and decisions.

Organizations need accounting in order to measure success (or failure). One form of organization is the private **business**, which is organized with the objective of earning a profit. Three common forms of business are the **service business**, the **merchandising business**, and the **manufacturing business**.

Users of accounting information include owners, managers, investors, lenders, and the government. Ownership of business can be in the form of a **sole proprietorship** (owned by one person), a **partnership** (owned by two or more persons), a **corporation** (owned by stockholders), or a **limited liability company (LLC)**, which combines features of a corporation and those of a partnership or a proprietorship. In financial terms, accounting is used to communicate to those who have a need or legal right to know about the financial activities of a particular business. Thus, accounting has been called *the language of business.*

The **business entity concept** states that the owner of a business and the business are two separate accounting units. Personal items of the owner should be excluded from all business documents and records.

The accounting system that we use today is deeply rooted in history and is based on three elements: assets, liabilities, and owner's equity. An **asset** is an item with money value that is owned by a business. Common examples of assets include **cash**, **accounts receivable**, **equipment**, and **supplies**. Equipment and supplies are **tangible**, or physical, assets. A **liability** is a debt owed to a **creditor**. **Accounts payable** is the major type of liability, and another is **notes payable**. **Owner's equity** is the dollar value of the financial claim of the owner to the assets of the business. The accounting elements are combined into the **accounting equation**: Assets = Liabilities + Owner's Equity, or A = L + OE.

The value of the accounting elements changes constantly as transactions take place. A **transaction** is any event or condition that changes the value of a firm's assets, liabilities, or owner's equity. The **cost principle** is used to value assets.

All business transactions affect one or more of the basic accounting elements. The effect of business transactions can be stated in terms of increases and decreases in the accounting elements. To maintain the accounting equation in balance, all transactions are recorded as having a **dual effect** on the accounting elements. One type of transaction involves a **shift in assets**, in which one asset increases and another asset decreases. Other transactions affect two accounting elements, such as an increase in an asset and an increase in a liability.

There are two ways to increase owner's equity: (1) an owner investment of cash or other assets into the business and (2) **revenue**—income from carrying out the major activity of a firm. The **realization principle** states that revenue should be recorded when it is earned. There are two ways to decrease owner's equity: (1) an owner **withdrawal** of cash or other assets from the business and (2) an **expense** incurred in operating a business. Expenses are the costs of operating a business.

The summarizing function of the accountant is shown by the preparation of **financial statements** at the end of an accounting period. An **accounting period** is a period of time, usually a year, for which accounting records are kept. The **income statement** summarizes revenues and expenses, showing **net income** or **net loss** for an accounting period. When revenues exceed expenses, there is a net income. On the other hand, when expenses exceed revenues, there is a net loss. The **statement of owner's equity** shows changes that have occurred in owner's equity during an accounting period. The **balance sheet** is a list of assets, liabilities, and owner's equity on a specific date, usually the last day of an accounting period.

Business **ethics** are the standards of conduct that lead to fair, honest, and reliable financial reporting. Ethical considerations affect accounting because effective and accurate financial reporting depends on sound ethical behavior. While we never hear about them, the vast majority of accountants do their jobs professionally and ethically. It is, unfortunately, those who get caught cheating that make the headlines. In the early 2000s, there were accounting scandals, the likes of which our nation has not seen since the 1920s. Congress responded quickly by passing the **Sarbanes-Oxley Act of 2002**, which made it a criminal offense to falsify financial statements.

True/False

Please circle the correct answer.

T   F   1. Recording means making written records of events.

T   F   2. Accounting is a narrow, specialized field that serves only a small part of society.

T   F   3. Accounting is often called *the language of business.*

T   F   4. A merchandising business is one that performs services for customers in order to earn a profit.

T   F   5. The three accounting elements are assets, liabilities, and owner's equity.

T   F   6. An account payable is usually an informal debt that is based on a spoken promise made to a creditor.

T   F   7. The cost principle states that when purchased, all assets are recorded at their actual cost regardless of market value.

T   F   8. The effect of every business transaction can be stated in terms of increases or decreases (or both) in the basic elements of the accounting equation.

T   F   9. When business transactions are recorded, the accounting equation must always be left in balance.

T   F   10. Owner's equity is increased by revenues and expenses and decreased by owner withdrawals and investments.

T   F   11. An accounting period is usually one year, but it can be any length of time.

T   F   12. In determining net income, withdrawals by the owner of the business are deducted as business expenses.

T   F   13. Other names for the income statement include operating statement, earnings statement, and profit and loss statement.

T   F   14. A statement of owner's equity is a listing of all the assets, liabilities, and owner's equity of a business.

T   F   15. A balance sheet is rather like a financial snapshot of a business because it shows the firm's financial position at a specific point in time.

T   F   16. Business ethics only apply to larger companies.

Matching

Please match each of the following terms with its definition.

a. accounting
b. accounts payable
c. accounts receivable
d. assets
e. balance sheet
f. business entity concept
g. cash
h. creditor
i. equipment
j. expenses

k. financial statements
l. income statement
m. liabilities
n. net income
o. note payable
p. owner's equity
q. revenue
r. supplies
s. transaction
t. withdrawal

_____ 1. The asset that includes currency, coins, checks, and money orders made payable to the business.

_____ 2. The asset that includes physical items such as copy paper, staples, pencils, and other items needed to run the business.

_____ 3. The process of recording, summarizing, analyzing, and interpreting financial activities to permit individuals and organizations to make informed judgments and decisions.

_____ 4. Debts owed by the business.

_____ 5. Any activity that changes the value of a firm's assets, liabilities, or owner's equity.

_____ 6. Costs of operating a business that do not provide future benefit to the business.

_____ 7. A summary of the revenues and expenses of a business for a period of time, such as a month or a year.

_____ 8. A listing of the firm's assets, liabilities, and owner's equity at a specific point in time.

_____ 9. A removal of business assets for personal use by the owner.

_____ 10. The liability that results from purchasing goods or services on credit.

_____ 11. The principle that a business is separate from its owner and other businesses.

_____ 12. Summaries of financial activities that are prepared on a regular basis at the end of each accounting period.

_____ 13. The difference between assets and liabilities.

_____ 14. Income that comes from carrying out the major activity of a firm.

_____ 15. The excess of revenue over expenses.

_____ 16. The physical assets, such as desks and computers, needed by a business in order to operate.

_____ 17. Items with money value that are owned by a business.

_____ 18. A formal written promise to pay a specified amount at a definite future date.

_____ 19. A person or business to whom an account payable is owed.

_____ 20. An asset arising from selling goods or services on credit to customers.

Fill in the Blanks

Please complete each sentence with the correct word or words.

1. A(n) _____ is an organization that operates with the objective of earning a profit.

2. A(n) _____ is a business owned by one person.

3. A(n) _____ purchases goods produced by others and then sells them to customers in order to earn a profit.

4. _____ means examining reports by breaking them down in order to determine financial success or failure.

5. Combining written records into reports at regular intervals is the process of _____.

6. A business owned by more than one person is a(n) _____.

7. A(n) _____ is a business owned by stockholders.

8. _____ are items with money value that are owned by a business.

9. The asset arising from selling goods or services on credit to customers is called _____.

10. The liability that results from purchasing goods and services on credit is called _____.

11. The difference between assets and liabilities is the part of the business that the owner can claim. It is called _____.

12. The accounting equation can be stated as _____ equals _____ plus _____.

13. The purchase of supplies for cash is a transaction in which a(n) _____ occurs.

14. In order to maintain the balance of the accounting equation, it is necessary to record transactions as having a(n) _____ on the basic accounting elements.

15. When expenses are greater than revenues, a(n) _____ results.

16. The _____ Act made it a criminal offense to falsify financial statements.

Multiple Choice

Please circle the correct answer.

1. The term *accounting* includes which of the following activities?
   a. Recording
   b. Summarizing
   c. Analyzing
   d. Interpreting
   e. All of the above

2. A form of business that is owned by investors (called stockholders) is a
   a. sole proprietorship.
   b. partnership.
   c. corporation.
   d. None of the above

3. The items with money value that are owned by a business are its
   a. liabilities.
   b. assets.
   c. expenses.
   d. revenues.

4. The debts owed by a business are its
   a. liabilities.
   b. assets.
   c. expenses.
   d. revenues.

5. Examples of assets include
   a. cash, accounts receivable, accounts payable.
   b. accounts receivable, equipment, supplies.
   c. equipment, accounts payable.
   d. None of the above

6. Owner's equity is defined as
   a. the things owned by a business.
   b. the revenues produced by a business.
   c. the difference between assets and liabilities.
   d. cash.

7. If a business has assets of $50,000 and liabilities of $15,000, the owner's equity is
   a. $65,000.
   b. $35,000.
   c. impossible to determine. There is not enough information given.

8. Which of the following transactions would affect only the assets of the business?
   a. Purchase of supplies for cash
   b. Purchase of a computer on credit
   c. Investment of cash by the owner
   d. Withdrawal of cash by the owner

9. Which of the following transactions would affect both the assets and liabilities of the business?
   a. Purchase of supplies for cash
   b. Purchase of a computer on credit
   c. Investment of cash by the owner
   d. Withdrawal of cash by the owner

10. The business entity concept states that, for purposes of accounting, the owner of a business and the business itself are
    a. the same.
    b. separate only if the business is a corporation.
    c. two separate units.
    d. None of the above

11. The statement that shows a summary of a firm's revenues and expenses for a specific period of time is the
    a. statement of owner's equity.
    b. balance sheet.
    c. financial statement.
    d. income statement.

12. Which of the following statements are called "period" statements?
    a. Income statement and statement of owner's equity
    b. Income statement and balance sheet
    c. Balance sheet and statement of owner's equity
    d. All are period statements.

13. What is the equation for the balance sheet?
    a. Revenue minus expenses equals net income.
    b. Beginning capital plus investment plus net income minus withdrawals equals ending capital.
    c. Assets equals liabilities plus owner's equity.
    d. None of the above

14. In which order should the financial statements be prepared?
    a. Balance sheet, statement of owner's equity, income statement
    b. Statement of owner's equity, income statement, balance sheet
    c. Income statement, statement of owner's equity, balance sheet
    d. Preparation order does not matter.

15. If the statement of owner's equity is prepared before the income statement, what information will be missing from the statement of owner's equity?
    a. Revenue
    b. Beginning capital
    c. Investment
    d. Net income

Writing/Short Answer

1. **Reflect** Make a list, in words or simple phrases, of the most important and meaningful points in this chapter.

2. **Question** Think about the most confusing points or the material you do not understand in this chapter. Write down two or three questions that remain unanswered.

3. **Connect** Explain, in one or two sentences, the connection between the main points of this chapter and the major goals of the entire course.

4. **Summarize** Review this chapter's Joining the Pieces visual summary, and explain the concept(s) illustrated in a few sentences.

This page intentionally left blank.

Skills Review

Quick Practice

QUICK PRACTICE 1-1

(a) _____

(b) _____

(c) _____

QUICK PRACTICE 1-2

	Correct	Incorrect
(a)	_____	_____
(b)	_____	_____
(c)	_____	_____
(d)	_____	_____
(e)	_____	_____
(f)	_____	_____

QUICK PRACTICE 1-3

	Assets		= Liabilities		+ Owner's Equity	
	+	−	−	+	−	+
Example	✔					✔
(a)						
(b)						
(c)						
(d)						

QUICK PRACTICE 1-4

QUICK PRACTICE 1-5

QUICK PRACTICE 1-6

QUICK PRACTICE 1-7

QUICK PRACTICE 1-8

Appears on Balance Sheet

	Yes	No
(a)	_____	_____
(b)	_____	_____
(c)	_____	_____
(d)	_____	_____
(e)	_____	_____
(f)	_____	_____
(g)	_____	_____
(h)	_____	_____
(i)	_____	_____
(j)	_____	_____

QUICK PRACTICE 1-9

Item	Classification	Financial Statement
1. Cash	_____	_____
2. Jeff Gordan, Capital	_____	_____
3. Jeff Gordan, Drawing	_____	_____
4. Revenue from Services	_____	_____
5. Accounts Payable	_____	_____
6. Salaries Expense	_____	_____
7. Equipment	_____	_____
8. Rent Expense	_____	_____

Exercises

EXERCISE 1-1

(a) _____

(b) _____

(c) _____

(d) _____

(e) _____

(f) _____

EXERCISE 1-2

	A	=	L	+	OE	
	+	−	−	+	−	+
(a)						
(b)						
(c)						
(d)						
(e)						
(f)						
(g)						
(h)						

EXERCISE 1-3

	Assets				= Liabilities +		Owner's Equity		
	Cash	+ Accounts Receivable	+ Supplies	+ Equipment	= Accounts Payable	+	Tracy Corrigen, Capital	+ Revenue	− Expenses
(a)									
(b)									
(c)									
(d)									
(e)									
(f)									
(g)									
(h)									

EXERCISE 1-4

EXERCISE 1-5

EXERCISE 1-6

Appears on Balance Sheet

	Yes	No
(a)	_____	_____
(b)	_____	_____
(c)	_____	_____
(d)	_____	_____
(e)	_____	_____
(f)	_____	_____
(g)	_____	_____
(h)	_____	_____
(i)	_____	_____
(j)	_____	_____
(k)	_____	_____
(l)	_____	_____

EXERCISE 1-7

EXERCISE 1-8

1. _____

   _____

   _____

2. _____

   _____

   _____

3. _____

   _____

   _____

4. _____

   _____

   _____

5. _____

   _____

   _____

6. _____

   _____

   _____

Case Problems

PROBLEM 1-1A OR 1-1B

	Cash	+	Office Supplies	+	Office Equipment	=	Accounts Payable	+	Capital	+	Revenue	−	Expenses
Assets						**= Liabilities +**			**Owner's Equity**				
(a)													
(b)	_____		_____		_____		_____		_____		_____		_____
Bal.													
(c)	_____		_____		_____		_____		_____		_____		_____
Bal.													
(d)	_____		_____		_____		_____		_____		_____		_____
Bal.													
(e)	_____		_____		_____		_____		_____		_____		_____
Bal.													
(f)	_____		_____		_____		_____		_____		_____		_____
Bal.													
(g)	_____		_____		_____		_____		_____		_____		_____
Bal.													
(h)	_____		_____		_____		_____		_____		_____		_____
Bal.													
(i)	_____		_____		_____		_____		_____		_____		_____
Bal.													
(j)	_____		_____		_____		_____		_____		_____		_____
Bal.													
(k)	_____		_____		_____		_____		_____		_____		_____
Bal.													

This page intentionally left blank.

PROBLEM 1-2A OR 1-2B

	Assets				= Liabilities +		Owner's Equity		
	Cash	Accounts + Receivable +	Supplies +	Equipment =	Accounts Payable	+	Capital	+ Revenue	– Expenses
(a)									
(b)	_____	_____	_____	_____	_____		_____	_____	_____
Bal.									
(c)	_____	_____	_____	_____	_____		_____	_____	_____
Bal.									
(d)	_____	_____	_____	_____	_____		_____	_____	_____
Bal.									
(e)	_____	_____	_____	_____	_____		_____	_____	_____
Bal.									
(f)	_____	_____	_____	_____	_____		_____	_____	_____
Bal.									
(g)	_____	_____	_____	_____	_____		_____	_____	_____
Bal.									
(h)	_____	_____	_____	_____	_____		_____	_____	_____
Bal.									
(i)	_____	_____	_____	_____	_____		_____	_____	_____
Bal.									
(j)	_____	_____	_____	_____	_____		_____	_____	_____
Bal.									
(k)	_____	_____	_____	_____	_____		_____	_____	_____
Bal.									
(l)	_____	_____	_____	_____	_____		_____	_____	_____
Bal.									

This page intentionally left blank.

PROBLEM 1-3A OR 1-3B

	Assets					=	Liabilities +		Owner's Equity		
	Cash	+ Accounts Receivable	+ Office Supplies	+ Store Supplies	+ Equipment	=	Accounts Payable	+ Capital	+ Revenue	– Expenses
(a)										
(b)										
Bal.										
(c)										
Bal.										
(d)										
Bal.										
(e)										
Bal.										
(f)										
Bal.										
(g)										
Bal.										
(h)										
Bal.										
(i)										
Bal.										
(j)										
Bal.										
(k)										
Bal.										

This page intentionally left blank.

PROBLEM 1-4A OR 1-4B

1.

2.

PROBLEM 1-4A OR 1-4B (continued)

3.

1.

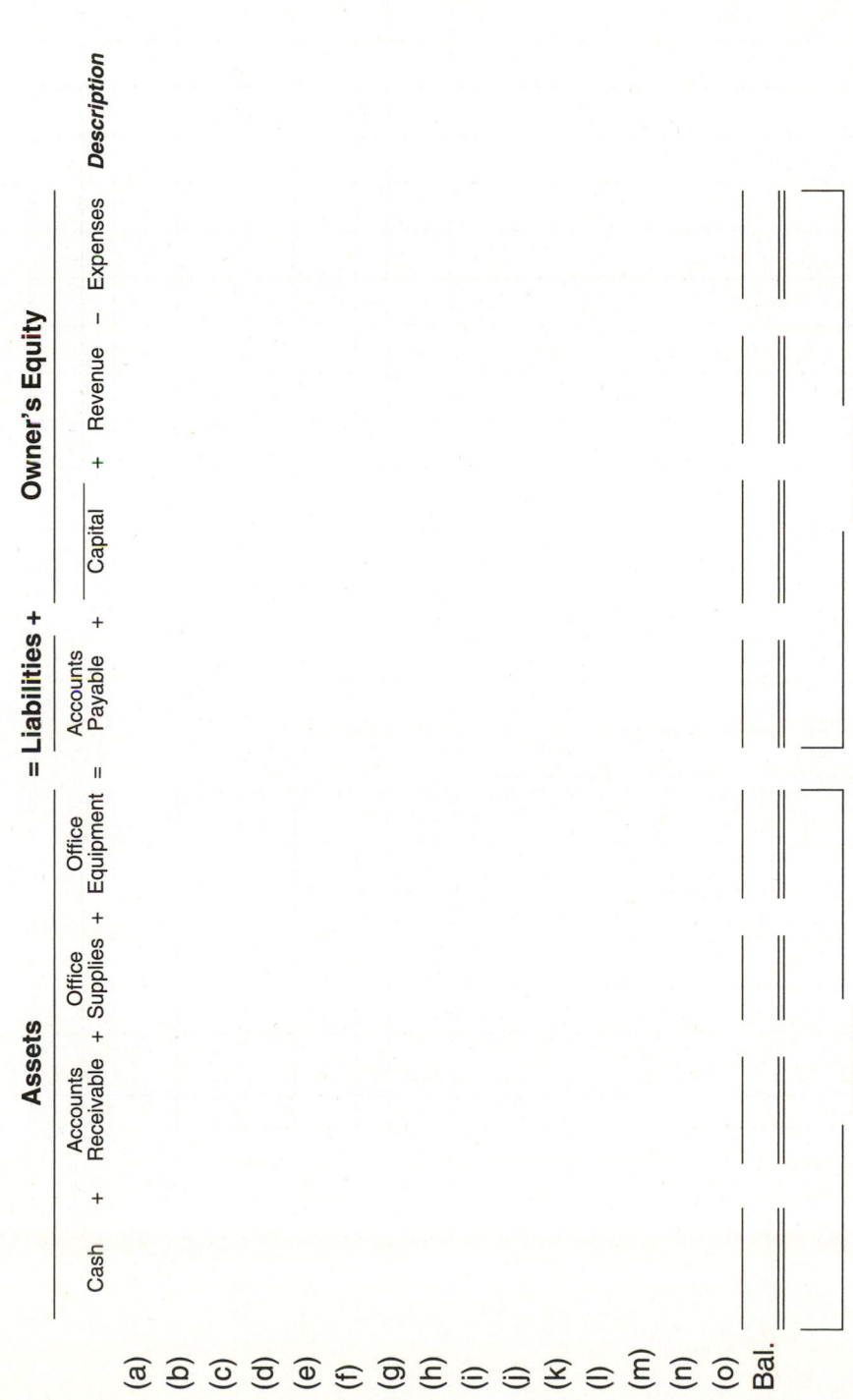

PROBLEM 1-5A OR 1-5B (continued)

2.

3.

PROBLEM 1-5A OR 1-5B (continued)

4.

This page intentionally left blank.

Critical Thinking Problems

Challenge Problem

January Transactions

1., 2.

	Assets						=	Liabilities			Owner's Equity				Description
	Cash	+	Accounts Receivable	+	Office Supplies	+	Office Furniture	+	Office Equipment	+	Land	=	Accounts Payable	+	Notes Payable	+	Andi McWhorter, Capital	+	Revenue	−	Expenses	
Bal.																	
(a)																	
(b)																	
(c)																	
(d)																	
(e)																	
(f)																	
(g)																	
(h)																	
(i)																	
(j)																	
(k)																	
(l)																	
(m)																	
(n)																	
(o)																	
(p)																	
(q)																	
(r)																	
(s)																	
(t)																	
(u)																	
Bal.																	

Challenge Problem (continued)

3.

Challenge Problem (continued)

Challenge Problem (continued)

4.

February Transactions

	Assets					=	Liabilities		+	Owner's Equity			
Cash +	Accounts Receivable +	Office Supplies +	Office Furniture +	Office Equipment +	Land	=	Accounts Payable +	Notes Payable	+	Andi McWhorter, Capital +	Revenue −	Expenses	Description
Bal.													
(a)													
(b)													
(c)													
(d)													
(e)													
(f)													
(g)													
(h)													
(i)													
(j)													
(k)													
(l)													
(m)													
(n)													
(o)													
(p)													
(q)													
(r)													
(s)													
Bal.													

Challenge Problem (continued)

5.

Challenge Problem (continued)

Communications

_____
_____
_____
_____
_____
_____
_____
_____
_____
_____
_____
_____
_____
_____
_____
_____
_____

Team Internet Project

_____
_____
_____
_____
_____
_____
_____
_____
_____
_____
_____
_____
_____
_____
_____
_____
_____
_____
_____

Ethics

_____

_____

_____

_____

_____

_____

_____

_____

_____

_____

_____

_____

_____

_____

_____

In the Real World

_____

_____

_____

_____

_____

_____

_____

_____

_____

_____

_____

_____

_____

_____

_____

_____

Practice Test Answers

True/False

1. T
2. F
3. T
4. F
5. T
6. T
7. T
8. T
9. T
10. F
11. T
12. F
13. T
14. F
15. T
16. F

Matching

1. g
2. r
3. a
4. m
5. s
6. j
7. l
8. e
9. t
10. b
11. f
12. k
13. p
14. q
15. n
16. i
17. d
18. o
19. h
20. c

Fill in the Blanks

1. business
2. sole proprietorship
3. merchandising business
4. Analyzing
5. summarizing
6. partnership
7. corporation
8. Assets
9. accounts receivable
10. accounts payable
11. owner's equity
12. assets, liabilities, owner's equity
13. shift in assets
14. dual effect
15. net loss
16. Sarbanes-Oxley

Multiple Choice

1. e
2. c
3. b
4. a
5. b
6. c
7. b
8. a
9. b
10. c
11. d
12. a
13. c
14. c
15. d

Writing/Short Answer

Answers will vary. Please discuss questions with your instructor.

Recording Business Transactions

Chapter Summary  Interactive Summary in English and Spanish

Every business transaction has at least two effects on the elements of the accounting equation. Since there are at least two effects, this has come to be known as the dual effect. Recording both effects of a transaction is called **double-entry accounting**. Double-entry accounting is the foundation of modern accounting.

The dual effect of a transaction can be recorded in terms of changes in the accounting equation. However, it is considered a better practice to have an individual form to record and store financial information concerning each component of the accounting elements. An **account** is an individual form or record used to show changes in each asset, liability, and owner's equity item. There are various types of accounts. Usually, accounts are bound together in book form, are kept in loose-leaf binders, or are part of a computer system. Such a grouping of accounts is called a **ledger**.

The **standard form of account** is a basic account form with two amount (or money) columns. A **T account** is a skeleton version of the standard form of account. The left side of an account is the debit side. The right side of an account is the credit side. **To debit** an account means to enter an amount on the left, or debit, side. **To credit** an account means to enter an amount on the right, or credit, side.

Changes in the various accounts are recorded by entering debits and credits. A debit can signify *either* an increase or a decrease, depending on the type of account. Likewise, a credit can signify *either* an increase or a decrease, depending on the type of account. Asset accounts are increased on the debit side and decreased on the credit side. Liability accounts and the owner's capital account are increased on the credit side and decreased on the debit side. Having opposite increase and decrease sides for accounts on the left side of the equation (assets) and accounts on the right side of the equation (liabilities and owner's equity) maintains the accounting equation in balance.

Revenue increases owner's equity. Expenses and owner withdrawals decrease owner's equity. These changes in owner's equity could be recorded directly in the owner's capital account, but this would clutter the account and make it necessary to analyze the owner's capital account in order to determine the amount of net income or net loss for an accounting period. Thus, increases in owner's equity due to revenue are recorded in revenue accounts; decreases in owner's equity due to expenses and owner withdrawals are recorded in expense accounts and an owner's **drawing account**.

The rules of debit and credit are applied to revenue, expense, and drawing accounts based on their relationship to owner's equity. Because revenue increases owner's equity, increases in revenue accounts are recorded on the same side that shows increases in owner's equity—the credit side. Because expenses and owner withdrawals decrease owner's equity, increases in these accounts are recorded on the same side that shows decreases in owner's equity—the debit side.

At the end of an accounting period, the balances of all revenue accounts, expense accounts, and the owner's drawing account are transferred to the owner's capital account. Therefore, these accounts are referred to as **temporary owner's equity accounts**.

There are customarily more increases in an account than decreases. For this reason, the **normal balance** of an account is always on the increase side. Thus, asset and expense accounts and the owner's drawing account have normal debit balances because these accounts are increased on the debit side. Liability and revenue accounts and the owner's capital account have normal credit balances because these accounts are increased on the credit side.

In a double-entry accounting system, total debits must always equal total credits. To check this equality, a trial balance is periodically taken of accounts in the ledger. A **trial balance** is a listing of all ledger accounts with their balances, usually prepared at the end of each month.

The **balance** of an account is determined by adding (**footing**) the debit side, adding the credit side, and calculating the difference between the two sides. A **debit balance** occurs when the debit side is larger; a **credit balance** occurs when the credit side is larger.

We can summarize the rules of debits and credits in this chapter as follows:

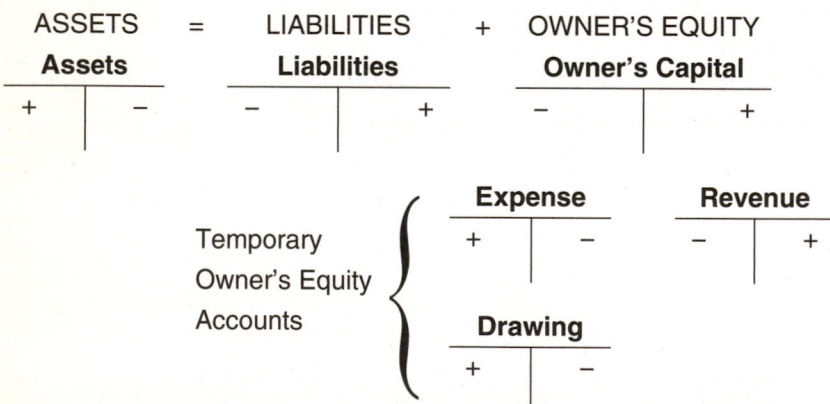

True/False

Please circle the correct answer.

T F   1. Double-entry accounting means that each transaction has at least two effects, both of which are recorded.

T F   2. In double-entry accounting, each transaction is recorded twice.

T F   3. An account is a separate form or record used to record and summarize information related to each asset, each liability, and each component of owner's equity.

T F   4. Debit is the name given to the right side of an account.

T F   5. Credit is the name given to the right side of an account.

T F   6. A grouping of accounts is referred to as a journal.

T F   7. The word *charge* is sometimes used as a synonym for debit.

T F   8. When we debit an account, we make an entry on the left side of the account.

T F   9. When an account is credited, it is decreased.

T F   10. Asset accounts are increased with debits and decreased with credits.

T F   11. Liability accounts are increased with credits and decreased with debits.

T F   12. Entering equal debits and credits keeps the accounting equation in balance.

T F   13. Revenue and expense accounts are temporary owner's equity accounts.

T F   14. Revenues and expenses are increased with credits and decreased with debits.

T F   15. The trial balance is one of the formal financial statements.

Matching

Please match each of the following terms with its definition.

a. account
b. balance
c. credit
d. credit balance
e. debit
f. debit balance
g. double-entry accounting

h. drawing account
i. footing
j. ledger
k. normal balance
l. T account
m. temporary owner's equity accounts
n. trial balance

_____ 1. A collective grouping of accounts.

_____ 2. An entry on the right side of an account.

_____ 3. A listing of all ledger accounts with their balances.

_____ 4. The balance that one expects to find in an account; the balance on the side that increases an account.

_____ 5. The balance that occurs when the debit side of an account is larger.

_____ 6. Recording both effects of a transaction on the accounting elements.

_____ 7. A skeleton form of the standard form of account.

_____ 8. The expense and revenue accounts and the owner's drawing account.

_____ 9. An amount determined by footing the debit and credit sides of an account and calculating the difference.

_____ 10. The total of the debit or credit column of an account.

_____ 11. An entry on the left side of an account.

_____ 12. A separate form or record used to record and summarize information related to each asset, each liability, and each aspect of owner's equity.

_____ 13. The account used when the owner withdraws cash or other assets from the business for personal use.

_____ 14. The balance that occurs when the credit side of an account is larger.

Fill in the Blanks

Please complete each sentence with the correct word or words.

1. To _____ an account means to enter an amount on the left side.

2. To _____ an account means to make an entry on the right side.

3. The terms *debit* and *credit* do not mean _____ or _____.

4. Debit and credit can each mean either _____ or _____, depending on the type of account.

5. If Pam Jones invests $10,000 cash in a new travel agency, both the _____ account and the _____ account will be increased.

6. If Pam Jones purchases supplies for cash, the _____ account will be decreased and the _____ account will be increased.

7. Revenue and expense accounts are subdivisions of _____.

8. Revenue accounts are increased on the _____ side.

9. Expense accounts are increased on the _____ side.

10. Withdrawals decrease _____; therefore, the drawing account is increased on the _____ side.

11. In analyzing a transaction, we must decide which _____ are affected by the transaction.

12. A(n) _____ is a listing, as of a certain date, of all ledger accounts with their balances.

13. The first step in preparing a trial balance is to find the _____ of each account.

14. Footing means _____ the debit and credit columns of each account.

15. The normal balance of an account is on the _____ side.

Multiple Choice

Please circle the correct answer.

1. A grouping of accounts is referred to as a
   a. journal.
   b. ledger.
   c. book.
   d. file.

2. To debit an account means to
   a. increase the account.
   b. decrease the account.
   c. make an entry on the left side of the account.
   d. make an entry on the right side of the account.

3. To credit an account means to
   a. increase the account.
   b. decrease the account.
   c. make an entry on the left side of the account.
   d. make an entry on the right side of the account.

4. An asset account is decreased by
    a. debiting the account.
    b. crediting the account.

5. The owner's capital account is increased by
    a. debiting the account.
    b. crediting the account.

6. In order to make a proper entry for each transaction, a careful analysis is made to determine
    a. the titles of the accounts affected.
    b. whether the accounts affected are increased or decreased.
    c. how to record the increase or decrease.
    d. All of the above

7. The purchase of equipment on account would be recorded as a
    a. debit to the Equipment account and a credit to the Accounts Payable account.
    b. debit to the Equipment account and a credit to the Cash account.
    c. debit to the Accounts Payable account and a credit to the Equipment account.
    d. debit to the Equipment account only.

8. Owner's equity is increased by
    a. revenues and expenses.
    b. revenues and investments.
    c. expenses and withdrawals.
    d. revenues and withdrawals.

9. Owner's equity is decreased by
    a. revenues and expenses.
    b. revenues and investments.
    c. expenses and withdrawals.
    d. revenues and withdrawals.

10. An expense account is increased by
    a. debiting the account.
    b. crediting the account.

11. A revenue account is increased by
    a. debiting the account.
    b. crediting the account.

12. If Pam Jones' Travel Agency pays rent on office space for the month,
    a. the Rent Expense account is debited and the Pam Jones, Capital account is credited.
    b. the Cash account is debited and the Rent Expense account is credited.
    c. the Rent Expense account is debited and the Cash account is credited.
    d. None of the above

13. If Pam Jones collects revenue for services performed,
    a. the Revenue account is debited and the Cash account is credited.
    b. the Cash account is debited and the Revenue account is credited.
    c. the Cash account is debited and the Pam Jones, Capital account is credited.
    d. None of the above

14. If Pam Jones withdraws cash for personal use,
    a. the Personal Expense account is debited and the Cash account is credited.
    b. the Pam Jones, Capital account is debited and the Cash account is credited.
    c. the Cash account is debited and the Pam Jones, Drawing account is credited.
    d. the Pam Jones, Drawing account is debited and the Cash account is credited.

15. The first step in preparing the trial balance is to
    a. put the heading at the top of the page.
    b. list all accounts in the ledger with their balances.
    c. determine the balance of each account.
    d. foot the trial balance and check for equality of debits and credits.

Writing/Short Answer

1. **Reflect** Make a list, in words or simple phrases, of the most important and meaningful points in this chapter.

2. **Question** Think about the most confusing points or the material you do not understand in this chapter. Write down two or three questions that remain unanswered.

3. **Connect** Explain, in one or two sentences, the connection between the main points of this chapter and the major goals of the entire course.

4. **Summarize** Review this chapter's Joining the Pieces visual summary and explain the concept(s) illustrated in a few sentences.

This page intentionally left blank.

Skills Review

Quick Practice

QUICK PRACTICE 2-1

(a) _____

(b) _____

(c) _____

(d) _____

(e) _____

(f) _____

(g) _____

(h) _____

QUICK PRACTICE 2-2

1. _____

2. _____

3. _____

4. _____

5. _____

6. _____

7. _____

8. _____

QUICK PRACTICE 2-3

	Increase Side	Decrease Side	Normal Balance
Asset	Debit	Credit	Debit
Liability	_____	_____	_____
Owner's Capital	_____	_____	_____
Revenue	_____	_____	_____
Owner's Drawing	_____	_____	_____
Expense	_____	_____	_____

(a)

(b)

(c)

(d)

(e)

(f)

QUICK PRACTICE 2-4 (continued)

(g) _____

_____

_____

_____

_____

_____

_____

_____

_____

_____

_____

QUICK PRACTICE 2-5

Cash			Accounts Payable	
300	100		100	400
700	400		300	100
200				500
Bal._____			Bal._____	

ACCOUNT TITLE	DEBIT	CREDIT

Exercises

EXERCISE 2-1

	Type of Account	Increase Side	Decrease Side	Normal Balance
Cash	Asset	Debit	Credit	Debit
Equipment				
Gene Hopkins, Drawing				
Accounts Payable				
Service Revenue				
Accounts Receivable				
Gene Hopkins, Capital				
Taxes Payable				
Fees Earned				
Rent Expense				

EXERCISE 2-2

		Recorded on Debit Side	Recorded on Credit Side
(a)	Increase in Cash account	✓	
(b)	Decrease in Accounts Payable account		
(c)	Increase in owner's drawing account		
(d)	Increase in owner's capital account		
(e)	Increase in expense account		
(f)	Decrease in owner's capital account		
(g)	Increase in revenue account		

EXERCISE 2-3

Equipment		Accounts Payable	

Cash		Service Revenue	

Rent Expense	

EXERCISE 2-4

(a) _____

_____

_____

_____

_____

_____

_____

_____

_____

(b) _____

_____

_____

_____

_____

_____

_____

_____

_____

_____

EXERCISE 2-4 (continued)

(c) _____

(d) _____

(e) _____

(f)

(g)

(h)

EXERCISE 2-4 (continued)

(i) _____

(j) _____

EXERCISE 2-5

Cash	Accounts Receivable
	Supplies

| Equipment | Accounts Payable |

| Ray Ingram, Capital | Ray Ingram, Drawing |

| Revenue from Commissions | Rent Expense |

| Utilities Expense | |

EXERCISE 2-6

ACCOUNT TITLE	DEBIT	CREDIT

This page intentionally left blank.

Case Problems

PROBLEM 2-1A OR 2-1B

1., 2., 3.

Cash	Accounts Receivable	Office Supplies

	Truck Supplies	Equipment

Truck	Accounts Payable	_____, Capital

_____, Drawing	_____ Fees	Rent Expense

Salaries Expense	Truck Expense	Utilities Expense

3.

ACCOUNT TITLE	DEBIT	CREDIT

PROBLEM 2-2A OR 2-2B

(a) _____

_____

(b) _____

_____

(c) _____

_____

(d) _____

_____

(e) _____

_____

(f) _____

_____

(g) _____

_____

(h) _____

_____

(i) _____

_____

(j) _____

_____

(k) _____

_____

This page intentionally left blank.

PROBLEM 2-3A OR 2-3B

1., 2., 3.

| Cash | Accounts Receivable | Office Supplies |

| Office Equipment | Accounts Payable |

| _____ , Capital | _____ , Drawing | Revenue from Fees |

| Rent Expense | Salaries Expense | Advertising Expense |

| Telephone Expense | Utilities Expense | Miscellaneous Expense |

3.

ACCOUNT TITLE	DEBIT	CREDIT

PROBLEM 2-4A OR 2-4B

1., 2., 3.

Cash	Accounts Receivable	Office Supplies

	Office Equipment	Automobile

Trucks	Accounts Payable	_____, Capital

_____, Drawing	Service Revenue	Rent Expense

Salaries Expense	Gasoline and Oil Expense	Telephone Expense

Utilities Expense	Miscellaneous Expense	

3.

ACCOUNT TITLE	DEBIT	CREDIT

PROBLEM 2-5A OR 2-5B

ACCOUNT TITLE	DEBIT	CREDIT

This page intentionally left blank.

Critical Thinking Problems

Challenge Problem

1., 2., 3.

Cash	Accounts Receivable	Office Supplies

	Truck Supplies	Equipment

Truck	Accounts Payable	Notes Payable

David Payne, Capital	David Payne, Drawing	Delivery Revenue

Challenge Problem (continued)

Rent Expense	Salaries Expense	Gasoline and Oil Expense

Utilities Expense	Telephone Expense	Repair Expense

Miscellaneous Expense

Challenge Problem (continued)

3.

ACCOUNT TITLE	DEBIT	CREDIT

Challenge Problem (continued)

4.

5.

Challenge Problem (continued)

6.

This page intentionally left blank.

Communications

Team Internet Project

Ethics

_____
_____
_____
_____
_____
_____
_____
_____
_____
_____
_____
_____
_____
_____
_____
_____

In the Real World

_____
_____
_____
_____
_____
_____
_____
_____
_____
_____
_____
_____
_____
_____
_____
_____
_____
_____

Practice Test Answers

True/False

1. T
2. F
3. T
4. F
5. T
6. F
7. T
8. T
9. F
10. T
11. T
12. T
13. T
14. F
15. F

Matching

1. j
2. c
3. n
4. k
5. f
6. g
7. l
8. m
9. b
10. i
11. e
12. a
13. h
14. d

Fill in the Blanks

1. debit
2. credit
3. increase, decrease
4. increase, decrease
5. Cash; Pam Jones, Capital
6. Cash, Supplies
7. owner's capital
8. credit
9. debit
10. owner's equity, debit
11. accounts
12. trial balance
13. balance
14. adding
15. increase

Multiple Choice

1. b
2. c
3. d
4. b
5. b
6. d
7. a
8. b
9. c
10. a
11. b
12. c
13. b
14. d
15. c

Writing/Short Answer

Answers will vary. Please discuss questions with your instructor.

Starting the Accounting Cycle for a Service Business

Chapter Summary  Interactive Summary in English and Spanish

The **accounting cycle** for a service business consists of the steps involved in the recording and summarizing processes of accounting. The first four steps in the accounting cycle for a service business are:

Step **1** Analyze transactions from source documents.
Step **2** Record transactions in a journal.
Step **3** Post from the journal to the ledger.
Step **4** Prepare a trial balance of the ledger.

A **source document** is a business document or paper that proves a business transaction occurred. Examples of source documents include checks received, bills received, receipts, check stubs, and invoices. The accounting **principle of objective evidence** states that source documents should form the foundation for recording business transactions.

A **journal** is a form in which transactions are recorded in chronological order (by order of date). Since the journal is the first place in which transactions are formally recorded, it is referred to as the **book of original entry**. There are many forms of journals in use today. The most basic form of journal has two money (or amount) columns and is referred to as the **general journal**.

The process of recording transactions in a journal is called **journalizing**. Recording transactions in a journal follows the same analysis and uses the same account titles as recording transactions in T accounts. Recording transactions in a journal, however, is considered a better practice because both the debit and credit parts of an entry are shown together in the same record.

Most journal entries involve only one debit and one credit, but occasionally, more than one debit or credit will be needed to record an entry. An entry requiring three or more accounts is called a **compound entry**.

The journal provides a complete record of each transaction in chronological order. However, the ledger is still needed to provide a summary of data relating to each account. Entries in the journal are transferred to the ledger on a regular basis, usually at the end of the month. The process of transferring amounts from the journal to the ledger is called **posting**. The ledger is usually called the **book of final entry**. After all postings have been made to the ledger accounts, the equality of debits and credits is proved by preparing a trial balance.

Since most businesses have many accounts in their ledger, a directory of the accounts available in the ledger is needed. A directory of the accounts in the ledger is called a **chart of accounts**. The numbering system for the chart of accounts depends *on the needs* of the individual business. In this chapter, we used a three-digit, five-category plan, with the first digit indicating the category of an account and the second and third digits indicating the position of the individual account within its particular classification. Journal page numbers and account numbers are used as a **cross-reference** after posting.

We also showed a more functional form of ledger account called the **balance form of account**. The balance form of account resembles the standard form of account; however, balance columns are added that display the balance of the account after each posting.

A trial balance that does not balance is said to be "out of balance." An unbalanced trial balance means that there is an error somewhere in the system. Errors are of three types: math, recording, and posting. A **math error** results from incorrect addition or subtraction and is corrected, if made in pencil, by erasure and recalculation. If made in ink, a math error is corrected by lining out the wrong figure, initialing the correction, and entering the correct figure in ink.

A **recording error** is an error made in a journal entry. If the recording error is discovered before it has been posted to the ledger, a correction can be made by lining out the incorrect information and entering the correct information. If the recording error has been posted to the ledger, a **correcting entry** is needed. A good technique for making correcting entries is to set up two sets of T accounts. One set shows the incorrect entry that was made. The other set shows the correct entry that should have been made. By analyzing the two sets of T accounts, a proper correcting entry can be made.

A **posting error** results from an incorrect transfer from the journal to an account or from the ledger to the trial balance. A posting error should never be corrected by erasure. Instead, such an error is corrected by lining out the incorrect information and inserting the correct information. For future reference, the correction should be initialed by the person who made the correction.

Common posting errors include transpositions and slides. A **transposition** is the reversal of digits, such as entering 240 for 420. A **slide** is an entry with an incorrectly placed decimal point, such as entering 100 for 1,000 or 24.50 for 245. An imbalance that is divisible by nine indicates that a slide or transposition error may have occurred.

Some errors that are very small in amount may not be corrected. This follows the **principle of materiality**, which states that proper accounting procedures have to be strictly followed only for events and transactions that would have a material effect on a business's financial statements. A material effect is an effect that involves a significant dollar amount.

True/False

Please circle the correct answer.

T   F   1.   The sequence of steps or procedures used by a business to record and summarize accounting data is known as the accounting cycle.

T   F   2.   The first step in the accounting cycle is to record transactions in the journal.

T   F   3.   A source document is a business paper such as a check or a sales slip.

T   F   4.   The journal is referred to as the book of original entry.

T   F   5.   The process of recording transactions in the journal is called posting.

T   F   6.   When a transaction is recorded in the general journal, the name of the account to be debited is written on the first line at the extreme left of the Account Title column.

T   F   7.   A compound entry is a journal entry requiring more than one debit or one credit.

T   F   8.   The ledger provides a chronological record of the transactions of a business.

T   F   9.   A journal entry records all of the important information about a transaction in one place.

T   F   10.   The process of transferring entries from the journal to the ledger is called journalizing.

T   F   11.   The chart of accounts is a directory of all the accounts in the ledger.

T   F   12.   Posting reference numbers make it easier to trace an item in the ledger back to the journal entry in which the transaction was originally recorded.

T   F   13.   The trial balance shows that debit balances equal credit balances in the ledger.

T   F   14.   Recording a transaction twice will cause the trial balance to be out of balance.

T   F   15.   Failure to record a transaction will cause the trial balance to be out of balance.

Matching

Please match each of the following terms with its definition.

a. accounting cycle
b. book of original entry
c. chart of accounts
d. compound entry
e. correcting entry
f. general journal
g. journal
h. journalizing

i. posting
j. posting error
k. principle of materiality
l. principle of objective evidence
m. recording error
n. slide
o. source document
p. transposition

_____ 1. A business document or paper that proves a business transaction occurred.

_____ 2. A form in which transactions are recorded in chronological order (order by date).

_____ 3. An entry requiring three or more accounts.

_____ 4. The principle that states that source documents should form the foundation for recording business transactions.

_____ 5. A reversal of digits, such as entering 480 for 840.

_____ 6. A directory of the accounts in the ledger.

_____ 7. The journal.

_____ 8. An error made in a journal entry.

_____ 9. The basic form of journal.

_____ 10. The process of transferring entries from the journal to the ledger.

_____ 11. An entry with an incorrectly placed decimal point, such as entering 10.5 for 105.

_____ 12. An error resulting from an incorrect transfer from the journal to an account or from the ledger to the trial balance.

_____ 13. The process of recording transactions in the journal.

_____ 14. The principle that states that proper accounting procedures have to be strictly followed only for events and transactions that would have a significant effect on a business's financial statements.

_____ 15. An entry used if a recording error has been posted to the ledger.

_____ 16. The steps involved in the recording and summarizing processes of accounting.

Fill in the Blanks

Please complete each sentence with the correct word or words.

1. The third step in the accounting cycle is to _____ from the journal to the ledger.

2. The accounting principle of _____ states that source documents should be used as a basis for recording transactions.

3. The journal in which any business transaction can be recorded is called the
_____.

4. _____ is the process of recording transactions in the journal.

5. If Sue Smith invested $5,000 to begin a new business, the Cash account would be debited and the _____ account would be credited.

6. When transactions are recorded in the general journal, the name of the account being credited is written on the line below the debit entry and is _____ one-fourth to one-half inch.

7. If Sue Smith purchased office supplies for cash, the _____ account would be debited and the _____ account would be credited.

8. The journal provides a(n) _____ record of transactions; it is a diary of the company's transactions.

9. Transferring information from the journal to the ledger is called _____.

10. The order of accounts in the ledger usually follows the order of accounts on the financial statements, beginning with the _____ accounts.

Multiple Choice

Please circle the correct answer.

1. The first step in the accounting cycle is to
   a. record transactions in the journal.
   b. take a trial balance.
   c. analyze transactions from source documents.
   d. post to the ledger.

2. Which of the following is *not* found in a journal?
   a. A Date column
   b. An account for each asset, liability, revenue, and expense of the company
   c. An Account Title column
   d. Two money columns

3. If Sue Smith paid rent for one month on her office, the transaction would be recorded as
   a. a debit to Rent Expense and a credit to Cash.
   b. a debit to Cash and a credit to Rent Expense.
   c. a debit to Sue Smith, Capital and a credit to Cash.
   d. a debit to Cash and a credit to Sue Smith, Capital.

4. Which of the following are advantages of using a journal?
   a. The journal provides a chronological record of the transactions of the company.
   b. The journal provides a place to record an explanation of the entry.
   c. The journal decreases the possibility of recording errors.
   d. All of the above are advantages.

5. The second step in the accounting cycle is to
   a. journalize the transactions.
   b. post from the journal to the ledger.
   c. take a trial balance.
   d. foot the accounts.

6. The chart of accounts provides a directory or table of contents of the ledger. Which of the following types of information is *not* found in the chart of accounts?
   a. Account titles
   b. Account numbers
   c. Page numbers where the accounts are located
   d. Categories of accounts

7. The posting reference recorded in the journal after posting an entry to a ledger account is
   a. the account name.
   b. the account number.
   c. the journal code and page number.
   d. None of the above

8. The posting reference recorded in the account during the posting process is
   a. the account name.
   b. the account number.
   c. the journal code and page number.
   d. None of the above

9. The first step in preparing a trial balance is to
   a. write the name of the company, Trial Balance, and the date at the top of the trial balance form.
   b. write the account titles and balances on the form.
   c. determine the balance of each account in the ledger.
   d. foot the debit and credit columns and check for equality.

10. When is it proper to erase an error?
    a. When the error is written in pencil
    b. When the error is written in ink
    c. When the error has been posted
    d. It is never proper to erase an error.

11. What is the proper procedure to follow when correcting an incorrect amount posted to the correct account?
    a. Use correction fluid to cover the error, and write over it.
    b. Make a new journal entry and post.
    c. Line out the incorrect amount, initial it, and write in the correct amount in ink.
    d. None of the above is correct.

12. Which of the following errors would require a correcting journal entry?
    a. A $200 debit to Cash posted as a credit to Cash instead
    b. A debit of $255 posted as $225
    c. A credit of $15.00 posted as $1.50
    d. A debit to Supplies recorded in the journal as a debit to Salaries Expense and posted

13. Sue Smith purchased supplies for $200 cash and recorded the debit to Salaries Expense by mistake. The error was posted. What correcting entry must be made?
    a. Debit Supplies and credit Salaries Expense for $200.
    b. Debit Salaries Expense and credit Cash for $200.
    c. Debit Cash and credit Salaries Expense for $200.
    d. No correcting entry is needed.

14. Which of the following errors would cause the trial balance to be out of balance?
    a. Failure to record a transaction
    b. Failure to post an entire entry
    c. Posting the wrong amount to both the debit and credit sides of the correct accounts
    d. Posting a debit or credit to the wrong account
    e. None of the above

15. The principle that states that proper accounting procedures have to be strictly followed only for events and transactions that would have a significant effect on a business's financial statements is the principle of
    a. objective evidence.
    b. materiality.
    c. accounting.
    d. cost.

Writing/Short Answer

1. **Reflect** Make a list, in words or simple phrases, of the most important and meaningful points in this chapter.

2. **Question** Think about the most confusing points or the material you do not understand in this chapter. Write down two or three questions that remain unanswered.

3. **Connect** Explain, in one or two sentences, the connection between the main points of this chapter and the major goals of the entire course.

4. **Summarize** Review this chapter's Joining the Pieces visual summary, and explain the concept(s) illustrated in a few sentences.

This page intentionally left blank.

Skills Review

Quick Practice

QUICK PRACTICE 3-1

1.

2.

3.

4.

QUICK PRACTICE 3-2

General Journal Page 1

	Date		Account Title	P.R.	Debit	Credit	
1							1
2							2
3							3
4							4
5							5
6							6
7							7
8							8
9							9
10							10
11							11
12							12
13							13
14							14
15							15
16							16
17							17
18							18
19							19
20							20
21							21
22							22
23							23

QUICK PRACTICE 3-2 (continued)

General Journal

	Date	Account Title	P.R.	Debit	Credit	
1						1
2						2
3						3
4						4
5						5
6						6
7						7
8						8
9						9
10						10
11						11
12						12
13						13
14						14
15						15
16						16
17						17
18						18
19						19
20						20
21						21

QUICK PRACTICE 3-3

ACCOUNT **Cash**   ACCOUNT NO. 111

DATE	ITEM	P.R.	DEBIT	CREDIT	BALANCE DEBIT	BALANCE CREDIT

QUICK PRACTICE 3-4

General Journal

Page 1

	Date		Account Title	P.R.	Debit	Credit	
1							1
2							2
3							3
4							4
5							5
6							6
7							7
8							8
9							9
10							10
11							11

QUICK PRACTICE 3-5

General Journal

Page 1

	Date		Account Title	P.R.	Debit	Credit	
1							1
2							2
3							3
4							4
5							5
6							6
7							7
8							8

QUICK PRACTICE 3-6

ACCOUNT Cash

ACCOUNT NO. 111

DATE		ITEM	P.R.	DEBIT	CREDIT	BALANCE	
						DEBIT	CREDIT

QUICK PRACTICE 3-7

Account Title	Increase Side Debit	Increase Side Credit	Normal Balance Debit	Normal Balance Credit
1. Accounts Payable				
2. Accounts Receivable				
3. Cash				
4. Owner, Capital				
5. Owner, Drawing				
6. Rent Expense				
7. Rental Revenue				
8. Service Revenue				
9. Supplies				
10. Utilities Expense				

QUICK PRACTICE 3-8

Killingsworth Electronics

Trial Balance

December 31, 20XX

ACCOUNT TITLE	DEBIT	CREDIT

QUICK PRACTICE 3-9

1.

2.

3.

4.

5.

QUICK PRACTICE 3-10

General Journal

	Date		Account Title	P.R.	Debit	Credit	
1							1
2							2
3							3
4							4
5							5
6							6
7							7
8							8
9							9
10							10
11							11
12							12
13							13

Exercises

EXERCISE 3-1

General Journal

Page 1

	Date		Account Title	P.R.	Debit	Credit	
1							1
2							2
3							3
4							4
5							5
6							6
7							7
8							8
9							9
10							10
11							11
12							12
13							13
14							14
15							15
16							16
17							17
18							18
19							19
20							20
21							21
22							22
23							23
24							24
25							25
26							26
27							27
28							28
29							29
30							30
31							31
32							32

EXERCISE 3-1 (continued)

General Journal

Page 2

	Date		Account Title	P.R.	Debit	Credit	
1							1
2							2
3							3
4							4
5							5
6							6
7							7
8							8
9							9

EXERCISE 3-2

General Journal

Page 1

	Date		Account Title	P.R.	Debit	Credit	
1							1
2							2
3							3
4							4
5							5
6							6
7							7
8							8
9							9
10							10
11							11
12							12
13							13
14							14
15							15
16							16

EXERCISE 3-3

Account Title	Increase Side		Normal Balance	
	Dr.	Cr.	Dr.	Cr.
1. Supplies				
2. Tim Green, Drawing				
3. Accounts Receivable				
4. Truck				
5. Service Revenue				
6. Payroll Taxes Payable				
7. Tim Green, Capital				
8. Accounts Payable				
9. Miscellaneous Expense				
10. Office Equipment				
11. Rent Expense				
12. Fees Earned				
13. Cash				
14. Rental Revenue				
15. Utilities Expense				

EXERCISE 3-4

General Journal

Page 1

	Date	Account Title	P.R.	Debit	Credit	
1						1
2						2
3						3
4						4
5						5
6						6
7						7
8						8
9						9
10						10
11						11
12						12
13						13
14						14
15						15
16						16
17						17

EXERCISE 3-4 (continued)

ACCOUNT Cash   ACCOUNT NO. 111

DATE	ITEM	P.R.	DEBIT	CREDIT	BALANCE	
					DEBIT	CREDIT

ACCOUNT Supplies   ACCOUNT NO. 112

DATE	ITEM	P.R.	DEBIT	CREDIT	BALANCE	
					DEBIT	CREDIT

ACCOUNT Equipment   ACCOUNT NO. 115

DATE	ITEM	P.R.	DEBIT	CREDIT	BALANCE	
					DEBIT	CREDIT

ACCOUNT Accounts Payable   ACCOUNT NO. 211

DATE	ITEM	P.R.	DEBIT	CREDIT	BALANCE	
					DEBIT	CREDIT

EXERCISE 3-4 (continued)

ACCOUNT D. D. Payne   ACCOUNT NO. 311

DATE	ITEM	P.R.	DEBIT	CREDIT	BALANCE	
					DEBIT	CREDIT

EXERCISE 3-5

ACCOUNT TITLE	DEBIT	CREDIT

EXERCISE 3-6

General Journal

Page 1

	Date		Account Title	P.R.	Debit	Credit	
1							1
2							2
3							3
4							4
5							5
6							6
7							7
8							8
9							9
10							10
11							11
12							12
13							13

EXERCISE 3-7

	Trial Balance Will Balance	Trial Balance Will NOT Balance
1.		
2.		
3.		
4.		
5.		

This page intentionally left blank.

Case Problems

PROBLEM 3-1A OR 3-1B

General Journal   Page 1

	Date		Account Title	P.R.	Debit	Credit	
1							1
2							2
3							3
4							4
5							5
6							6
7							7
8							8
9							9
10							10
11							11
12							12
13							13
14							14
15							15
16							16
17							17
18							18
19							19
20							20
21							21
22							22
23							23
24							24
25							25
26							26
27							27
28							28
29							29
30							30
31							31
32							32

PROBLEM 3-1A OR 3-1B (continued)

General Journal

Page 2

	Date		Account Title	P.R.	Debit	Credit	
1							1
2							2
3							3
4							4
5							5
6							6
7							7
8							8
9							9
10							10
11							11
12							12
13							13
14							14
15							15
16							16
17							17
18							18
19							19
20							20
21							21
22							22
23							23
24							24
25							25
26							26
27							27
28							28
29							29
30							30
31							31
32							32
33							33

PROBLEM 3-2A OR 3-2B

General Journal

	Date		Account Title	P.R.	Debit	Credit	
1							1
2							2
3							3
4							4
5							5
6							6
7							7
8							8
9							9
10							10
11							11
12							12
13							13
14							14
15							15
16							16
17							17
18							18
19							19
20							20
21							21
22							22
23							23
24							24
25							25
26							26
27							27
28							28
29							29
30							30
31							31
32							32
33							33

PROBLEM 3-2A OR 3-2B (continued)

General Journal

Page 2

	Date		Account Title	P.R.	Debit	Credit	
1							1
2							2
3							3
4							4
5							5
6							6
7							7
8							8
9							9
10							10
11							11
12							12
13							13
14							14
15							15
16							16
17							17
18							18
19							19
20							20
21							21
22							22
23							23
24							24
25							25
26							26
27							27
28							28
29							29
30							30
31							31
32							32
33							33

PROBLEM 3-3A OR 3-3B

2.   **General Journal**   Page 1

	Date		Account Title	P.R.	Debit	Credit	
1							1
2							2
3							3
4							4
5							5
6							6
7							7
8							8
9							9
10							10
11							11
12							12
13							13
14							14
15							15
16							16
17							17
18							18
19							19
20							20
21							21
22							22
23							23
24							24
25							25
26							26
27							27
28							28
29							29
30							30
31							31
32							32
33							33
34							34
35							35
36							36

2.

General Journal

Page 2

	Date		Account Title	P.R.	Debit	Credit	
1							1
2							2
3							3
4							4
5							5
6							6
7							7
8							8
9							9
10							10
11							11
12							12
13							13
14							14
15							15
16							16
17							17
18							18
19							19
20							20
21							21
22							22
23							23
24							24
25							25
26							26
27							27
28							28
29							29
30							30
31							31
32							32
33							33
34							34
35							35
36							36

1., 3.

ACCOUNT Cash   ACCOUNT NO. 111

DATE		ITEM	P.R.	DEBIT	CREDIT	BALANCE	
						DEBIT	CREDIT

ACCOUNT Accounts Receivable   ACCOUNT NO. 112

DATE		ITEM	P.R.	DEBIT	CREDIT	BALANCE	
						DEBIT	CREDIT

ACCOUNT Office Supplies   ACCOUNT NO. 113

DATE		ITEM	P.R.	DEBIT	CREDIT	BALANCE	
						DEBIT	CREDIT

PROBLEM 3-3A OR 3-3B (continued)

ACCOUNT Office Equipment   ACCOUNT NO. 118

DATE	ITEM	P.R.	DEBIT	CREDIT	BALANCE DEBIT	BALANCE CREDIT

ACCOUNT Accounts Payable   ACCOUNT NO. 211

DATE	ITEM	P.R.	DEBIT	CREDIT	BALANCE DEBIT	BALANCE CREDIT

ACCOUNT _____, Capital   ACCOUNT NO. 311

DATE	ITEM	P.R.	DEBIT	CREDIT	BALANCE DEBIT	BALANCE CREDIT

ACCOUNT _____, Drawing   ACCOUNT NO. 312

DATE	ITEM	P.R.	DEBIT	CREDIT	BALANCE DEBIT	BALANCE CREDIT

PROBLEM 3-3A OR 3-3B (continued)

ACCOUNT Accounting Fees Earned   ACCOUNT NO. 411

DATE	ITEM	P.R.	DEBIT	CREDIT	BALANCE DEBIT	BALANCE CREDIT

ACCOUNT Rent Expense   ACCOUNT NO. 511

DATE	ITEM	P.R.	DEBIT	CREDIT	BALANCE DEBIT	BALANCE CREDIT

ACCOUNT Salaries Expense   ACCOUNT NO. 512

DATE	ITEM	P.R.	DEBIT	CREDIT	BALANCE DEBIT	BALANCE CREDIT

ACCOUNT Utilities Expense   ACCOUNT NO. 513

DATE	ITEM	P.R.	DEBIT	CREDIT	BALANCE DEBIT	BALANCE CREDIT

PROBLEM 3-3A OR 3-3B (continued)

ACCOUNT Telephone Expense   ACCOUNT NO. 514

DATE	ITEM	P.R.	DEBIT	CREDIT	BALANCE	
					DEBIT	CREDIT

ACCOUNT Repairs Expense   ACCOUNT NO. 515

DATE	ITEM	P.R.	DEBIT	CREDIT	BALANCE	
					DEBIT	CREDIT

ACCOUNT Miscellaneous Expense   ACCOUNT NO. 516

DATE	ITEM	P.R.	DEBIT	CREDIT	BALANCE	
					DEBIT	CREDIT

PROBLEM 3-3A OR 3-3B (continued)

4.

ACCOUNT TITLE	DEBIT	CREDIT

This page intentionally left blank.

PROBLEM 3-4A OR 3-4B

General Journal

Page 1

	Date		Account Title	P.R.	Debit	Credit	
1							1
2							2
3							3
4							4
5							5
6							6
7							7
8							8
9							9
10							10
11							11
12							12
13							13
14							14
15							15
16							16
17							17
18							18
19							19
20							20
21							21
22							22
23							23
24							24
25							25
26							26
27							27
28							28
29							29
30							30
31							31
32							32
33							33

This page intentionally left blank.

PROBLEM 3-5A OR 3-5B

2.

General Journal

	Date		Account Title	P.R.	Debit	Credit	
1							1
2							2
3							3
4							4
5							5
6							6
7							7
8							8
9							9
10							10
11							11
12							12
13							13
14							14
15							15
16							16
17							17
18							18
19							19
20							20
21							21
22							22
23							23
24							24
25							25
26							26
27							27
28							28
29							29
30							30
31							31
32							32
33							33
34							34
35							35
36							36

PROBLEM 3-5A OR 3-5B (continued)

General Journal

	Date		Account Title	P.R.	Debit	Credit	
1							1
2							2
3							3
4							4
5							5
6							6
7							7
8							8
9							9
10							10
11							11
12							12
13							13
14							14
15							15
16							16
17							17
18							18
19							19
20							20
21							21
22							22
23							23
24							24
25							25
26							26
27							27
28							28
29							29
30							30
31							31
32							32
33							33
34							34
35							35

PROBLEM 3-5A OR 3-5B (continued)

General Journal

	Date	Account Title	P.R.	Debit	Credit	
1						1
2						2
3						3
4						4
5						5
6						6
7						7
8						8
9						9
10						10
11						11
12						12
13						13

1., 3.

ACCOUNT Cash   ACCOUNT NO. 111

DATE	ITEM	P.R.	DEBIT	CREDIT	BALANCE	
					DEBIT	CREDIT

PROBLEM 3-5A OR 3-5B (continued)

ACCOUNT **Accounts Receivable**   ACCOUNT NO. 112

DATE		ITEM	P.R.	DEBIT	CREDIT	BALANCE	
						DEBIT	CREDIT

ACCOUNT **Office Supplies**   ACCOUNT NO. 113

DATE		ITEM	P.R.	DEBIT	CREDIT	BALANCE	
						DEBIT	CREDIT

ACCOUNT **Medical Supplies**   ACCOUNT NO. 114

DATE		ITEM	P.R.	DEBIT	CREDIT	BALANCE	
						DEBIT	CREDIT

ACCOUNT **Office Equipment**   ACCOUNT NO. 117

DATE		ITEM	P.R.	DEBIT	CREDIT	BALANCE	
						DEBIT	CREDIT

PROBLEM 3-5A OR 3-5B (continued)

ACCOUNT Medical Equipment   ACCOUNT NO. 118

DATE	ITEM	P.R.	DEBIT	CREDIT	BALANCE DEBIT	BALANCE CREDIT

ACCOUNT Accounts Payable   ACCOUNT NO. 211

DATE	ITEM	P.R.	DEBIT	CREDIT	BALANCE DEBIT	BALANCE CREDIT

ACCOUNT _____, Capital   ACCOUNT NO. 311

DATE	ITEM	P.R.	DEBIT	CREDIT	BALANCE DEBIT	BALANCE CREDIT

ACCOUNT _____, Drawing   ACCOUNT NO. 312

DATE	ITEM	P.R.	DEBIT	CREDIT	BALANCE DEBIT	BALANCE CREDIT

PROBLEM 3-5A OR 3-5B (continued)

ACCOUNT Medical Fees Earned   ACCOUNT NO. 411

DATE	ITEM	P.R.	DEBIT	CREDIT	BALANCE DEBIT	BALANCE CREDIT

ACCOUNT Salaries Expense   ACCOUNT NO. 511

DATE	ITEM	P.R.	DEBIT	CREDIT	BALANCE DEBIT	BALANCE CREDIT

ACCOUNT Rent Expense   ACCOUNT NO. 512

DATE	ITEM	P.R.	DEBIT	CREDIT	BALANCE DEBIT	BALANCE CREDIT

ACCOUNT Utilities Expense   ACCOUNT NO. 513

DATE	ITEM	P.R.	DEBIT	CREDIT	BALANCE DEBIT	BALANCE CREDIT

PROBLEM 3-5A OR 3-5B (continued)

ACCOUNT Laboratory Fees Expense   ACCOUNT NO. 514

DATE	ITEM	P.R.	DEBIT	CREDIT	BALANCE	
					DEBIT	CREDIT

ACCOUNT Miscellaneous Expense   ACCOUNT NO. 515

DATE	ITEM	P.R.	DEBIT	CREDIT	BALANCE	
					DEBIT	CREDIT

4.

ACCOUNT TITLE	DEBIT	CREDIT

Critical Thinking Problems

Challenge Problem

1.

Georgian Theater
Chart of Accounts

Assets	Owner's Equity
	Revenue
	Expenses
Liabilities	

Challenge Problem (continued)

3.   **General Journal**   Page 1

	Date		Account Title	P.R.	Debit	Credit	
1							1
2							2
3							3
4							4
5							5
6							6
7							7
8							8
9							9
10							10
11							11
12							12
13							13
14							14
15							15
16							16
17							17
18							18
19							19
20							20
21							21
22							22
23							23
24							24
25							25
26							26
27							27
28							28
29							29
30							30
31							31
32							32
33							33
34							34

Challenge Problem (continued)

General Journal

	Date		Account Title	P.R.	Debit	Credit	
1							1
2							2
3							3
4							4
5							5
6							6
7							7
8							8
9							9
10							10
11							11
12							12
13							13
14							14
15							15
16							16
17							17
18							18
19							19
20							20
21							21
22							22
23							23
24							24
25							25
26							26
27							27
28							28
29							29
30							30
31							31
32							32
33							33

Challenge Problem (continued)

General Journal

	Date		Account Title	P.R.	Debit	Credit	
1							1
2							2
3							3
4							4
5							5
6							6
7							7
8							8
9							9
10							10
11							11
12							12
13							13
14							14
15							15
16							16
17							17
18							18
19							19
20							20
21							21
22							22
23							23
24							24
25							25
26							26
27							27
28							28
29							29
30							30
31							31
32							32

Challenge Problem (continued)

General Journal

	Date		Account Title	P.R.	Debit	Credit	
1							1
2							2
3							3
4							4
5							5
6							6
7							7
8							8
9							9
10							10
11							11
12							12
13							13
14							14
15							15
16							16
17							17
18							18
19							19
20							20
21							21
22							22
23							23
24							24
25							25
26							26
27							27
28							28
29							29
30							30
31							31
32							32

Challenge Problem (continued)

2., 4.

ACCOUNT _____ ACCOUNT NO. _____

DATE	ITEM	P.R.	DEBIT	CREDIT	BALANCE	
					DEBIT	CREDIT

ACCOUNT _____ ACCOUNT NO. _____

DATE	ITEM	P.R.	DEBIT	CREDIT	BALANCE	
					DEBIT	CREDIT

Challenge Problem (continued)

ACCOUNT _____ ACCOUNT NO. _____

DATE		ITEM	P.R.	DEBIT	CREDIT	BALANCE	
						DEBIT	CREDIT

ACCOUNT _____ ACCOUNT NO. _____

DATE		ITEM	P.R.	DEBIT	CREDIT	BALANCE	
						DEBIT	CREDIT

ACCOUNT _____ ACCOUNT NO. _____

DATE		ITEM	P.R.	DEBIT	CREDIT	BALANCE	
						DEBIT	CREDIT

ACCOUNT _____ ACCOUNT NO. _____

DATE		ITEM	P.R.	DEBIT	CREDIT	BALANCE	
						DEBIT	CREDIT

Challenge Problem (continued)

ACCOUNT _____ ACCOUNT NO. _____

DATE	ITEM	P.R.	DEBIT	CREDIT	BALANCE	
					DEBIT	CREDIT

ACCOUNT _____ ACCOUNT NO. _____

DATE	ITEM	P.R.	DEBIT	CREDIT	BALANCE	
					DEBIT	CREDIT

ACCOUNT _____ ACCOUNT NO. _____

DATE	ITEM	P.R.	DEBIT	CREDIT	BALANCE	
					DEBIT	CREDIT

ACCOUNT _____ ACCOUNT NO. _____

DATE	ITEM	P.R.	DEBIT	CREDIT	BALANCE	
					DEBIT	CREDIT

Challenge Problem (continued)

ACCOUNT _____   ACCOUNT NO. _____

DATE	ITEM	P.R.	DEBIT	CREDIT	BALANCE	
					DEBIT	CREDIT

ACCOUNT _____   ACCOUNT NO. _____

DATE	ITEM	P.R.	DEBIT	CREDIT	BALANCE	
					DEBIT	CREDIT

ACCOUNT _____   ACCOUNT NO. _____

DATE	ITEM	P.R.	DEBIT	CREDIT	BALANCE	
					DEBIT	CREDIT

ACCOUNT _____   ACCOUNT NO. _____

DATE	ITEM	P.R.	DEBIT	CREDIT	BALANCE	
					DEBIT	CREDIT

Challenge Problem (continued)

ACCOUNT _____   ACCOUNT NO. _____

DATE	ITEM	P.R.	DEBIT	CREDIT	BALANCE	
					DEBIT	CREDIT

ACCOUNT _____   ACCOUNT NO. _____

DATE	ITEM	P.R.	DEBIT	CREDIT	BALANCE	
					DEBIT	CREDIT

ACCOUNT _____   ACCOUNT NO. _____

DATE	ITEM	P.R.	DEBIT	CREDIT	BALANCE	
					DEBIT	CREDIT

ACCOUNT _____   ACCOUNT NO. _____

DATE	ITEM	P.R.	DEBIT	CREDIT	BALANCE	
					DEBIT	CREDIT

Challenge Problem (continued)

ACCOUNT ___ **ACCOUNT NO.** ___

DATE	ITEM	P.R.	DEBIT	CREDIT	BALANCE	
					DEBIT	CREDIT

ACCOUNT ___ **ACCOUNT NO.** ___

DATE	ITEM	P.R.	DEBIT	CREDIT	BALANCE	
					DEBIT	CREDIT

ACCOUNT ___ **ACCOUNT NO.** ___

DATE	ITEM	P.R.	DEBIT	CREDIT	BALANCE	
					DEBIT	CREDIT

ACCOUNT ___ **ACCOUNT NO.** ___

DATE	ITEM	P.R.	DEBIT	CREDIT	BALANCE	
					DEBIT	CREDIT

Challenge Problem (continued)

ACCOUNT _____ ACCOUNT NO. _____

DATE	ITEM	P.R.	DEBIT	CREDIT	BALANCE	
					DEBIT	CREDIT

ACCOUNT _____ ACCOUNT NO. _____

DATE	ITEM	P.R.	DEBIT	CREDIT	BALANCE	
					DEBIT	CREDIT

Challenge Problem (continued)

5.

ACCOUNT TITLE	DEBIT	CREDIT

Challenge Problem (continued)

6.

Communications

_____

_____

_____

_____

_____

_____

_____

_____

_____

_____

_____

_____

_____

_____

_____

_____

_____

Team Internet Project

_____

_____

_____

_____

_____

_____

_____

_____

_____

_____

_____

_____

_____

_____

_____

_____

_____

Ethics

In The Real World

Practice Test Answers

True/False

1. T
2. F
3. T
4. T
5. F
6. T
7. T
8. F
9. T
10. F
11. T
12. T
13. T
14. F
15. F

Matching

1. o
2. g
3. d
4. l
5. p
6. c
7. b
8. m
9. f
10. i
11. n
12. j
13. h
14. k
15. e
16. a

Fill in the Blanks

1. post
2. objective evidence
3. general journal
4. Journalizing
5. Sue Smith, Capital
6. indented
7. Office Supplies, Cash
8. chronological
9. posting
10. asset

Multiple Choice

1. c
2. b
3. a
4. d
5. a
6. c
7. b
8. c
9. c
10. a
11. c
12. d
13. a
14. e
15. b

Writing/Short Answer

Answers will vary. Please discuss questions with your instructor.

The Accounting Cycle Continued: The Work Sheet, Financial Statements, and Adjusting Entries

Chapter Summary

STUDY PARTNER

Interactive Summary in English and Spanish

Chapter 3 presented the first four steps in the accounting cycle for a service business. Chapter 4 continued the study of the accounting cycle for a service business.

At the end of an accounting period, there are usually some accounts that are not up to date. This happens because changes in the nature of certain accounts occur as time passes, and it is usually not practical to attempt to keep up with the changes as they occur. For example, supplies (and other prepaid items) are consumed constantly. In most businesses, it would be an enormously time-consuming task for the accountant or bookkeeper to make an entry each time supply items are used, so no regular recording for supplies used is made during the accounting period. Instead, the accounting for supplies used is postponed until the end of the accounting period. The balance of the Supplies account is then adjusted to reflect the cost of supplies used during the period. An **adjusting entry** is an entry made at the end of an accounting period to show up-to-date or accurate amounts in certain accounts. Adjusting entries record **internal transactions** (transactions that involve no outside parties).

The portion of a prepaid asset that has been used no longer provides a future benefit to the business; therefore, it becomes an expense. The expense for supplies used is recognized by debiting the Supplies Expense account and crediting the Supplies account. Other adjustments typically needed by a service business include those for insurance expired, depreciation of long-term assets, and liability for unpaid salaries.

Insurance paid in advance is considered to be an asset because it has money value and will provide a service that will benefit the business in the future. Insurance paid in advance is debited to an asset account entitled the Prepaid Insurance account. The adjustment for insurance expired is determined by dividing the amount of the prepayment of the **premium**, a fee paid for insurance coverage that will benefit the business in the future, by the number of months prepaid. The resulting amount is then multiplied by the number of months in the accounting period that the policy was prepaid. The adjusting entry involves a debit to the Insurance Expense account and a credit to the Prepaid Insurance account.

With the exception of land, all long-term physical assets used by a business are said to depreciate. **Depreciation** is an allocation process in which the cost of a long-term asset is divided up over the periods the asset is used to produce revenue. The amount of depreciation can be calculated in various ways. This chapter uses the **straight-line method**, which is a method that yields the same amount of depreciation for each full period in which the asset is used. Depreciation is recorded by debiting a depreciation expense account and crediting an accumulated depreciation account. The accumulated depreciation account is an example of a contra account. In a **contra asset account**, the balance is opposite the asset to which it relates. Thus, accumulated depreciation accounts have credit balances that are opposite to the debit balances of asset accounts. The difference between the balance of the asset account and the balance of the accumulated depreciation account is the asset's **book value**.

Unpaid salaries occur when the accounting period ends on a date different from the end of the payroll period. Unpaid salaries have been earned by the employees and thus are an expense to the business. However, they have not yet been paid by the employer. The adjustment for unpaid salaries involves a debit to the Salaries Expense account and a credit to the Salaries Payable account.

Adjusting entries are based on the matching principle of accounting. The **matching principle** states that revenue earned during an accounting period should be offset by the expenses that were necessary to produce the revenue, and the difference should be reported as the net income or net loss of the period.

A **work sheet** is an informal working paper used by the accountant to organize data and lessen the possibility of overlooking an adjustment. The exact form of work sheet varies with the needs of the business. In this chapter, we worked with a 10-column work sheet in completing the accounting cycle for Walker and Associates.

Data for the preparation of the financial statements are taken directly from the financial statement columns of the work sheet. The income statement shows the revenues, expenses, and net income or net loss for the accounting period and is prepared from the Income Statement columns. The statement of owner's equity shows changes that have occurred in the owner's equity during the accounting period. It is prepared by adding the net income or subtracting the net loss and subtracting the owner's withdrawals from the beginning balance of the owner's capital. The resulting amount is the ending balance of the owner's capital. The balance sheet is a statement of assets, liabilities, and owner's equity as of the last day of the accounting period. Data for preparation of the balance sheet come from the Balance Sheet columns of the work sheet. In addition, the balance sheet needs an updated amount for the owner's capital. The statement of owner's equity supplies this figure.

After financial statements are prepared, the next step in the accounting cycle is to journalize adjusting entries. After the adjusting entries are journalized and posted, the ledger will be up to date and will agree with the amounts reported on the financial statements.

True/False

Please circle the correct answer.

T   F   **1.** The fifth step in the accounting cycle is to determine needed adjustments.

T   F   **2.** Adjustments are needed to correct any mistakes made during the accounting period.

T   F   **3.** Adjusting entries are needed at the end of an accounting period to bring certain accounts up to date.

T   F   **4.** Adjusting entries record internal transactions.

T   F   **5.** Depreciation is an allocation process in which the cost of an asset is spread over its useful life.

T   F   **6.** Depreciation is very exact.

T   F   **7.** When depreciation is recorded on equipment used by a company, the Equipment account is credited.

T   F   **8.** An accumulated depreciation account is an example of a contra account.

T   F   **9.** Depreciation is recorded on all assets that will last for more than one year.

T   F   **10.** When the end of the accounting period differs from the last day of the pay period, unpaid salaries must be recorded.

T   F   **11.** If expenses are greater than revenues, the difference is reported as net income.

T   F   **12.** Unrecorded expenses result in an understatement of net income.

T   F   **13.** A work sheet is often referred to as the accountant's scratch pad.

T   F   **14.** When a work sheet is used, there is no need to prepare financial statements.

T   F   **15.** When a work sheet is used, everything necessary for preparation of the financial statements is placed on one page.

T   F   **16.** After the financial statements are prepared, the adjustments must be journalized and posted.

T   F   **17.** Journalizing adjusting entries is unnecessary when a work sheet is used.

T   F   **18.** There is usually no rush to prepare financial statements at the end of an accounting period.

T   F   **19.** The work sheet is not a formal financial statement.

T   F   **20.** A 10-column work sheet has a special set of columns for statement of owner's equity items.

Matching

Please match each of the following terms with its definition.

a. adjusting entry   f. journalizing
b. Accumulated Depreciation   g. matching principle
c. contra asset   h. Prepaid Insurance
d. depreciation   i. straight-line method
e. internal transactions   j. work sheet

_____   1. A depreciation method that records the same amount of depreciation for every full period that the asset is used.

_____   2. An entry made at the end of an accounting period to show up-to-date or accurate amounts in certain accounts.

_____   3. An account whose balance is opposite to the balance of the asset account to which it relates.

_____   4. An informal working paper used by the accountant to organize data and lessen the possibility of overlooking an adjustment.

_____   5. The process of recording transactions in the journal.

_____   6. An allocation process in which the cost of an asset is divided up over the periods the asset is used in the production of revenue.

_____   7. The account used to record insurance that is paid in advance.

_____   8. The contra asset account that summarizes the depreciation taken on an asset during its useful life.

_____   9. The principle that states that revenue earned during an accounting period should be offset by the expenses that were necessary to produce the revenue.

_____   10. Transactions, recorded by adjusting entries, that occur within a company and do not affect parties outside the company.

Fill in the Blanks

Please complete each sentence with the correct word or words.

1. The sixth step in the accounting cycle is to prepare a(n) _____.

2. _____ are prepared from the completed work sheet.

3. When insurance is paid in advance for a period of time, the _____ account is debited and the _____ account is credited.

4. At the end of the accounting period, insurance that has expired must be removed from the asset account by debiting _____ and crediting _____.

5. Adjusting entries record _____ transactions.

6. Depreciation is a way of _____ the cost of equipment and other long-term assets over the period of time they will be used in the production of revenue.

7. The amount of depreciation is a(n) _____.

8. One common method of depreciation is the _____ method.

9. Depreciation is recorded by debiting a depreciation expense account and crediting a(n) _____ account.

10. Recording depreciation in a separate account allows the original _____ of the asset to be shown in the asset account.

11. Generally accepted accounting principles do not allow depreciation to be taken on the asset _____.

12. When an adjustment is made to record unpaid salaries at the end of the accounting period, the _____ account is debited and the _____ account is credited.

13. Adjusting entries are _____ caused by errors; they are a(n) _____ part of the accounting cycle.

14. The _____ states that revenue earned during an accounting period should be offset by the expenses that were necessary to produce the revenue.

15. Without adjusting entries, some _____ would be unrecorded and some _____ would be overvalued.

16. The first pair of money columns on the work sheet is for the _____.

17. After the trial balance is entered on the work sheet, the _____ are recorded.

18. The Income Statement columns of a work sheet contain the balances of the _____ and _____ accounts.

19. The _____ or _____ for the accounting period is the figure needed to balance the Income Statement and Balance Sheet columns.

20. After the financial statements are prepared, the adjustments must be _____ and _____.

Multiple Choice

Please circle the correct answer.

1. Adjusting entries are necessary at the end of the accounting period because
   a. errors have been made that need to be corrected.
   b. certain internal transactions have not been recorded.
   c. certain external transactions have not been recorded.
   d. All of the above

2. If the Supplies account has a balance of $200 and a count of supplies shows $50 on hand, the adjusting entry needed to record supplies used would be
   a. a debit to Supplies and a credit to Supplies Expense for $50.
   b. a debit to Supplies Expense and a credit to Supplies for $200.
   c. a debit to Supplies Expense and a credit to Supplies for $150.
   d. a debit to Supplies and a credit to Supplies Expense for $150.

3. If a company has a printer that costs $600 and the printer is expected to last five years, what is the depreciation per month using the straight-line method?
   a. $120
   b. $600
   c. $10
   d. None of the above

4. When recording depreciation for the period, which account is credited?
   a. Accumulated depreciation account
   b. Depreciation expense account
   c. Asset account
   d. None of the above

5. Examples of assets that are depreciated are
   a. trucks, automobiles, and office supplies.
   b. buildings, furniture, and prepaid insurance.
   c. cash registers, computers, and printers.
   d. accounts receivable and accounts payable.

6. Which asset cannot be depreciated according to GAAP?
   a. Trucks
   b. Computers
   c. Carpeting
   d. Land

7. If adjusting entries are not made, which of the following problems will result?
   a. Certain assets will be overvalued.
   b. Certain expenses will be understated.
   c. Net income will be overstated.
   d. All of the above will result.

8. The Balance Sheet columns of the work sheet contain which of the following accounts?
   a. Assets, liabilities, and owner's equity
   b. Revenues and expenses
   c. Assets, revenues, and expenses
   d. Assets, liabilities, and expenses

9. Which account balances are used in preparing the financial statements?
   a. Balances from the original trial balance on the work sheet
   b. Amounts from the adjustment columns
   c. Balances determined by taking the original balances in the trial balance columns and adding or subtracting any adjustments
   d. Balances from the ledger accounts

10. The eighth step in the accounting cycle is to
    a. prepare the work sheet.
    b. enter adjustments on the work sheet.
    c. prepare financial statements.
    d. journalize and post the adjusting entries.

Part V Writing/Short Answer

1. **Reflect** Make a list, in words or simple phrases, of the most important and meaningful points in this chapter.

2. **Question** Think about the most confusing points or the material you do not understand in this chapter. Write down two or three questions that remain unanswered.

3. **Connect** Explain, in one or two sentences, the connection between the main points of this chapter and the major goals of the entire course.

4. **Summarize** Review this chapter's Joining the Pieces visual summary, and explain the concept(s) illustrated in a few sentences.

This page intentionally left blank.

Skills Review

Quick Practice

QUICK PRACTICE 4-1

(a) _____

(b) _____

(c) _____

(d) _____

QUICK PRACTICE 4-2

General Journal   Page 1

	Date		Account Title	P.R.	Debit	Credit	
1							1
2							2
3							3
4							4
5							5

QUICK PRACTICE 4-3

General Journal   Page 1

	Date		Account Title	P.R.	Debit	Credit	
1							1
2							2
3							3
4							4
5							5

QUICK PRACTICE 4-4

General Journal

Page 1

	Date		Account Title	P.R.	Debit	Credit	
1							1
2							2
3							3
4							4
5							5

QUICK PRACTICE 4-5

General Journal

Page 1

	Date		Account Title	P.R.	Debit	Credit	
1							1
2							2
3							3
4							4
5							5

QUICK PRACTICE 4-6

(Balance Sheet)
Supplies

TB

Adj. _____

Bal. _____

(Income Statement)
Supplies Expense

Adj. _____

QUICK PRACTICE 4-7

(Balance Sheet)
Prepaid Insurance

Bal.

Adj. _____

New Bal. _____

(Income Statement)
Insurance Expense

Adj. _____

QUICK PRACTICE 4-8

QUICK PRACTICE 4-9

QUICK PRACTICE 4-10

Work Sheet

Adjusted Trial Balance	Income Statement		Balance Sheet	
Account Title	**Debit**	**Credit**	**Debit**	**Credit**
Cash				
Accounts Receivable				
Office Supplies				
Prepaid Insurance				
Office Equipment				
Accumulated Depreciation—Office Equipment				
Accounts Payable				
Salaries Payable				
Shunda Ware, Capital				
Shunda Ware, Drawing				
Service Revenue				
Rent Expense				
Salaries Expense				
Depreciation Expense—Office Equipment				
Office Supplies Expense				
Insurance Expense				

	Work Sheet				
		Income Statement		**Balance Sheet**	
Account Title		**Debit**	**Credit**	**Debit**	**Credit**
Net Income					

	Work Sheet				
		Income Statement		**Balance Sheet**	
Account Title		**Debit**	**Credit**	**Debit**	**Credit**
Net Loss					

Exercises

(a)

(b)

(c)

(d)

(e)

EXERCISE 4-2

Account Title	Trial Balance		Adjustments	
	Dr.	Cr.	Dr.	Cr.

Adjusted Trial Balance		Income Statement		Balance Sheet	
Dr.	Cr.	Dr.	Cr.	Dr.	Cr.

EXERCISE 4-3

	Date		Account Title	P.R.	Debit	Credit	
1							1
2							2
3							3
4							4
5							5
6							6
7							7
8							8
9							9
10							10
11							11
12							12
13							13

EXERCISE 4-4

General Journal   Page 1

	Date		Account Title	P.R.	Debit	Credit	
1							1
2							2
3							3
4							4
5							5
6							6
7							7
8							8
9							9
10							10
11							11
12							12
13							13
14							14
15							15
16							16

EXERCISE 4-5

General Journal

	Date		Account Title	P.R.	Debit	Credit	
1							1
2							2
3							3
4							4
5							5
6							6
7							7
8							8
9							9
10							10
11							11
12							12
13							13
14							14
15							15
16							16

EXERCISE 4-6

1. _____

2. _____

3. _____

4. _____

5. _____

EXERCISE 4-7

1.

2.

EXERCISE 4-7 (continued)

3.

This page intentionally left blank.

Case Problems

PROBLEM 4-1A OR 4-1B

General Journal

Page 1

	Date		Account Title	P.R.	Debit	Credit	
1							1
2							2
3							3
4							4
5							5
6							6
7							7
8							8
9							9
10							10
11							11
12							12
13							13
14							14
15							15
16							16
17							17

This page intentionally left blank.

This page intentionally left blank.

PROBLEM 4-2A OR 4-2B

Account Title	Trial Balance		Adjustments	
	Dr.	Cr.	Dr.	Cr.

Adjusted Trial Balance		Income Statement		Balance Sheet	
Dr.	Cr.	Dr.	Cr.	Dr.	Cr.

This page intentionally left blank.

PROBLEM 4-3A OR 4-3B

1.

2.

3.

PROBLEM 4-4A OR 4-4B

1.

2.

3.

This page intentionally left blank.

1.

Account Title	Trial Balance		Adjustments	
	Dr.	Cr.	Dr.	Cr.

	Adjusted Trial Balance		Income Statement		Balance Sheet	
	Dr.	Cr.	Dr.	Cr.	Dr.	Cr.

2.

3.

4.

PROBLEM 4-5A OR 4-5B (continued)

5.   **General Journal**   Page 1

	Date		Account Title	P.R.	Debit	Credit	
1							1
2							2
3							3
4							4
5							5
6							6
7							7
8							8
9							9
10							10
11							11
12							12
13							13
14							14
15							15
16							16
17							17
18							18
19							19
20							20
21							21
22							22
23							23
24							24
25							25
26							26
27							27
28							28
29							29
30							30
31							31
32							32

Critical Thinking Problems

Challenge Problem

2.   **General Journal**   Page 17

	Date		Account Title	P.R.	Debit	Credit	
1							1
2							2
3							3
4							4
5							5
6							6
7							7
8							8
9							9
10							10
11							11
12							12
13							13
14							14
15							15
16							16
17							17
18							18
19							19
20							20
21							21
22							22
23							23
24							24
25							25
26							26
27							27
28							28
29							29
30							30
31							31
32							32
33							33

Challenge Problem (continued)

	Date	Account Title	P.R.	Debit	Credit	
1						1
2						2
3						3
4						4
5						5
6						6
7						7
8						8
9						9
10						10
11						11
12						12
13						13
14						14
15						15
16						16
17						17
18						18
19						19
20						20
21						21
22						22
23						23
24						24
25						25
26						26
27						27
28						28
29						29
30						30
31						31
32						32
33						33

Challenge Problem (continued)

	Date		Account Title	P.R.	Debit	Credit	
1							1
2							2
3							3
4							4
5							5
6							6
7							7
8							8
9							9
10							10
11							11
12							12
13							13
14							14
15							15
16							16
17							17
18							18
19							19
20							20
21							21
22							22
23							23
24							24
25							25
26							26
27							27
28							28
29							29
30							30
31							31
32							32
33							33

Challenge Problem (continued)

	Date		Account Title	P.R.	Debit	Credit	
1							1
2							2
3							3
4							4
5							5
6							6
7							7
8							8
9							9
10							10
11							11
12							12
13							13
14							14
15							15
16							16
17							17
18							18
19							19
20							20
21							21
22							22
23							23
24							24
25							25
26							26
27							27
28							28
29							29
30							30
31							31
32							32
33							33

This page intentionally left blank.

Challenge Problem (continued)

4., 5.

Account Title	Trial Balance		Adjustments	
	Dr.	Cr.	Dr.	Cr.

	Adjusted Trial Balance		Income Statement		Balance Sheet	
	Dr.	Cr.	Dr.	Cr.	Dr.	Cr.

Challenge Problem (continued)

1., 3., 9.

ACCOUNT _____ ACCOUNT NO. _____

DATE		ITEM	P.R.	DEBIT	CREDIT	BALANCE	
						DEBIT	CREDIT

ACCOUNT _____ ACCOUNT NO. _____

DATE		ITEM	P.R.	DEBIT	CREDIT	BALANCE	
						DEBIT	CREDIT

Challenge Problem (continued)

ACCOUNT _____   ACCOUNT NO. _____

DATE		ITEM	P.R.	DEBIT	CREDIT	BALANCE	
						DEBIT	CREDIT

ACCOUNT _____   ACCOUNT NO. _____

DATE		ITEM	P.R.	DEBIT	CREDIT	BALANCE	
						DEBIT	CREDIT

ACCOUNT _____   ACCOUNT NO. _____

DATE		ITEM	P.R.	DEBIT	CREDIT	BALANCE	
						DEBIT	CREDIT

ACCOUNT _____   ACCOUNT NO. _____

DATE		ITEM	P.R.	DEBIT	CREDIT	BALANCE	
						DEBIT	CREDIT

Challenge Problem (continued)

ACCOUNT _____ **ACCOUNT NO.** _____

DATE		ITEM	P.R.	DEBIT	CREDIT	BALANCE	
						DEBIT	CREDIT

ACCOUNT _____ **ACCOUNT NO.** _____

DATE		ITEM	P.R.	DEBIT	CREDIT	BALANCE	
						DEBIT	CREDIT

ACCOUNT _____ **ACCOUNT NO.** _____

DATE		ITEM	P.R.	DEBIT	CREDIT	BALANCE	
						DEBIT	CREDIT

ACCOUNT _____ **ACCOUNT NO.** _____

DATE		ITEM	P.R.	DEBIT	CREDIT	BALANCE	
						DEBIT	CREDIT

Challenge Problem (continued)

ACCOUNT _____   ACCOUNT NO. _____

DATE		ITEM	P.R.	DEBIT	CREDIT	BALANCE	
						DEBIT	CREDIT

ACCOUNT _____   ACCOUNT NO. _____

DATE		ITEM	P.R.	DEBIT	CREDIT	BALANCE	
						DEBIT	CREDIT

ACCOUNT _____   ACCOUNT NO. _____

DATE		ITEM	P.R.	DEBIT	CREDIT	BALANCE	
						DEBIT	CREDIT

ACCOUNT _____   ACCOUNT NO. _____

DATE		ITEM	P.R.	DEBIT	CREDIT	BALANCE	
						DEBIT	CREDIT

Challenge Problem (continued)

ACCOUNT   ACCOUNT NO.

DATE	ITEM	P.R.	DEBIT	CREDIT	BALANCE	
					DEBIT	CREDIT

ACCOUNT   ACCOUNT NO.

DATE	ITEM	P.R.	DEBIT	CREDIT	BALANCE	
					DEBIT	CREDIT

ACCOUNT   ACCOUNT NO.

DATE	ITEM	P.R.	DEBIT	CREDIT	BALANCE	
					DEBIT	CREDIT

Challenge Problem (continued)

ACCOUNT _____ ACCOUNT NO. _____

DATE		ITEM	P.R.	DEBIT	CREDIT	BALANCE	
						DEBIT	CREDIT

ACCOUNT _____ ACCOUNT NO. _____

DATE		ITEM	P.R.	DEBIT	CREDIT	BALANCE	
						DEBIT	CREDIT

ACCOUNT _____ ACCOUNT NO. _____

DATE		ITEM	P.R.	DEBIT	CREDIT	BALANCE	
						DEBIT	CREDIT

ACCOUNT _____ ACCOUNT NO. _____

DATE		ITEM	P.R.	DEBIT	CREDIT	BALANCE	
						DEBIT	CREDIT

Challenge Problem (continued)

ACCOUNT _____ ACCOUNT NO. _____

DATE		ITEM	P.R.	DEBIT	CREDIT	BALANCE	
						DEBIT	CREDIT

ACCOUNT _____ ACCOUNT NO. _____

DATE		ITEM	P.R.	DEBIT	CREDIT	BALANCE	
						DEBIT	CREDIT

ACCOUNT _____ ACCOUNT NO. _____

DATE		ITEM	P.R.	DEBIT	CREDIT	BALANCE	
						DEBIT	CREDIT

ACCOUNT _____ ACCOUNT NO. _____

DATE		ITEM	P.R.	DEBIT	CREDIT	BALANCE	
						DEBIT	CREDIT

Challenge Problem (continued)

ACCOUNT _____ ACCOUNT NO. _____

DATE	ITEM	P.R.	DEBIT	CREDIT	BALANCE	
					DEBIT	CREDIT

ACCOUNT _____ ACCOUNT NO. _____

DATE	ITEM	P.R.	DEBIT	CREDIT	BALANCE	
					DEBIT	CREDIT

Challenge Problem (continued)

6.

7.

Challenge Problem (continued)

8.

This page intentionally left blank.

Communications

_____
_____
_____
_____
_____
_____
_____
_____
_____
_____
_____
_____
_____
_____
_____
_____
_____
_____

Team Internet Project

_____
_____
_____
_____
_____
_____
_____
_____
_____
_____
_____
_____
_____
_____
_____
_____
_____
_____

Ethics

_____
_____
_____
_____
_____
_____
_____
_____
_____
_____
_____
_____
_____
_____
_____
_____
_____

In The Real World

_____
_____
_____
_____
_____
_____
_____
_____
_____
_____
_____
_____
_____
_____
_____

Practice Test Answers

True/False

1. T
2. F
3. T
4. T
5. T
6. F
7. F
8. T
9. F
10. T
11. F
12. F
13. T
14. F
15. T
16. T
17. F
18. F
19. T
20. F

Matching

1. i
2. a
3. c
4. j
5. f
6. d
7. h
8. b
9. g
10. e

Fill in the Blanks

1. work sheet
2. Financial statements
3. Prepaid Insurance, Cash
4. Insurance Expense, Prepaid Insurance
5. internal
6. allocating (dividing)
7. estimate
8. straight-line
9. accumulated depreciation
10. cost
11. land
12. Salaries Expense, Salaries Payable
13. not, planned
14. matching principle
15. expenses, assets
16. trial balance
17. adjustments
18. revenue, expense
19. net income, net loss
20. journalized, posted

Multiple Choice

1. b
2. c
3. c
4. a
5. c
6. d
7. d
8. a
9. c
10. d

Writing/Short Answer

Answers will vary. Please discuss questions with your instructor.

Completing the Accounting Cycle for a Service Business: Closing Entries and the Post-Closing Trial Balance

Chapter Summary

Interactive Summary in English and Spanish

Closing entries are entries made at the end of an accounting period to transfer the balances of temporary accounts to the owner's capital account. The **temporary accounts** are revenues, expenses, and drawing. Revenue and expense accounts are closed to a clearing account entitled Income Summary. The **Income Summary account** is a **clearing account** to which revenue and expense accounts are closed and then is closed to the owner's capital account. Thus, the Income Summary account is used only at the end of the accounting period and is only opened and closed during the closing process. The owner's drawing account, not being part of the net income calculation, is closed directly to the owner's capital account. All of these entries are part of the **closing process**, or the process of transferring the balances of temporary accounts to the owner's capital account.

A temporary account is closed by making an entry that will balance out the account. Since revenue accounts have credit balances, a revenue account is closed by making an equal debit entry in the account and a credit entry in the Income Summary account. Expense accounts, having debit balances, are closed by crediting each expense account for its balance and making a compound debit to Income Summary. The balance of Income Summary, representing the net income or net loss, is then transferred to the owner's capital account. The owner's drawing account, with a debit balance, is closed by making an equal credit entry in the account and a debit entry in the owner's capital account.

After closing entries are posted, the balances of the **permanent accounts** (assets, contra-assets, liabilities, and owner's capital) will be up to date. The balances of the temporary accounts will be reduced to zero and will be ready for entries in the next accounting period. To ensure that the ledger is still in balance after closing entries are posted, a **post-closing trial balance** is taken.

Only the balances of the permanent accounts will appear on the post-closing trial balance.

The 10 steps in the accounting cycle for a service business can be summarized as follows:

1. Analyze transactions from source documents.
2. Record transactions in a journal.
3. Post entries to the ledger.
4. Prepare a trial balance of the ledger.
5. Determine needed adjustments.
6. Prepare a work sheet.
7. Prepare financial statements.
8. Journalize and post adjusting entries.
9. Journalize and post closing entries.
10. Prepare a post-closing trial balance.

A **fiscal period** is the span of time covering the accounting cycle. A **fiscal year** is a fiscal period covering 12 months. The fiscal year does not necessarily coincide with the calendar year. Many businesses have adopted a fiscal year that parallels their **natural business year**—that is, they end their fiscal year at the lowest point of activity in their operating cycle.

Adjusting entries are based on the *matching principle* of accounting, which states that revenue for a period should be offset by the expenses necessary to generate that revenue. To apply the matching principle, most accounting systems operate on the accrual basis. The **accrual basis of accounting** requires that revenue be recorded when it is earned, no matter when cash is received, and expenses be recorded when they are incurred, no matter when cash is paid out. Revenue is considered to be earned when services have been satisfactorily performed or when goods have been properly delivered, and a legal claim to the revenue results. Expenses are recorded when a legal obligation to pay for goods or services used in operating the business is incurred or when the cost of assets consumed in the business is recognized.

Another basis of accounting is referred to as the cash basis. Under the **cash basis of accounting**, revenue is recorded only when cash is received, and expenses are recorded only when cash is paid. The cash basis may not result in a proper matching of revenue and expenses, because under this method, revenue and expense transactions are recorded only when cash changes hands.

The modified cash basis, a combination of the cash basis and the accrual basis, is used by many professional and service businesses today. Under the **modified cash basis of accounting**, revenue and expenses are recorded only when cash is received and paid. However, adjustments are made for depreciation, expired insurance, and supplies used (if large amounts of supplies are purchased).

True/False

Please circle the correct answer.

T F 1. Revenue and expense accounts and the owner's drawing account are called permanent accounts.

T F 2. When the accounting period is over, the balances of all temporary accounts are reduced to zero.

T F 3. At the end of the accounting period, the balances of the revenue and expense accounts are transferred to Income Summary and then the net income or net loss is transferred to the owner's capital account.

T F 4. The entries necessary to close the temporary accounts are called adjusting entries.

T F 5. The first step in the closing process is to close the balance of each expense account to the Income Summary account.

T F 6. The owner's drawing account is closed to Income Summary.

T F 7. The Income Summary account is used as a clearing account.

T F 8. The Income Summary account is closed to the owner's capital account.

T F 9. The balance in the Income Summary account before it is closed represents the revenue of the company minus expenses and withdrawals.

T F 10. An account with a debit balance is closed by crediting the account for the amount of its balance.

T F 11. A revenue account is closed by debiting the account and crediting Income Summary.

T F 12. Information needed for the closing process can be found on the work sheet.

T F 13. Temporary accounts are closed before the adjusting process.

T F 14. The balance in the Income Summary account before it is closed will be the net income or net loss for the period.

T F 15. The owner's drawing account is closed directly to the owner's capital account.

T F 16. Closing entries are not journalized or posted.

T F 17. The purpose of the post-closing trial balance is to assure that the ledger is in balance to begin the new accounting period.

T F 18. A fiscal year is always the same as the calendar year.

T F 19. A fiscal year ending at the lowest point of business activity is called a natural business year.

T F 20. The adjusting and closing processes must be done on the last day of the fiscal period.

Matching

Please match each of the following terms with its definition.

a. cash basis of accounting
b. calendar year
c. closing entries
d. closing process
e. fiscal period

f. Income Summary account
g. natural business year
h. permanent accounts
i. post-closing trial balance
j. temporary accounts

_____ 1. Assets, liabilities, and the owner's capital account.

_____ 2. Entries made at the end of an accounting period to transfer the balances of the temporary accounts to Income Summary and transfer the net income or net loss to the owner's capital account.

_____ 3. Revenue, expense, and drawing accounts.

_____ 4. A trial balance that includes only the balances of the permanent accounts.

_____ 5. A fiscal year that ends at the lowest point of business activity.

_____ 6. The span of time covering the accounting cycle.

_____ 7. The year that begins January 1 and ends December 31.

_____ 8. A clearing account used to summarize the balances of revenue and expense accounts.

_____ 9. The process of transferring the balances of the temporary accounts to Income Summary and transferring the net income or net loss to the owner's capital account.

_____ 10. The basis of accounting in which revenues and expenses are recorded only when cash is received or paid.

Fill in the Blanks

Please complete each sentence with the correct word or words.

1. The ninth step in the accounting cycle is to journalize and post the _____.

2. Revenue and expense accounts and the owner's drawing account are called _____ accounts.

3. The process of transferring the balances of the temporary accounts to Income Summary and transferring the net income or net loss to the owner's capital account is called the _____ process.

4. One purpose of the closing process is to reduce the balances of the temporary accounts to _____.

5. The first step in the closing process is to transfer the balance of each revenue account to the _____ account.

6. The second step in the closing process is to transfer the balance of each _____ account to the _____ account.

7. The Income Summary account is closed to the owner's _____ account.

8. The owner's drawing account is closed to the _____ account.

9. The balance in the Income Summary account before it is closed represents the _____ or _____ for the period.

10. The temporary accounts are closed _____ the adjusting process.

11. A revenue account is closed by _____ the account for the amount of its balance.

12. An expense account is closed by _____ the account for the amount of its balance.

13. Information needed for the closing entries is taken from the _____.

14. After the closing entries are posted, all _____ accounts will have zero balances.

15. A(n) _____ is prepared to assure that the ledger is in balance to begin the new accounting period.

16. A(n) _____ trial balance will contain only the balances of the _____ accounts.

17. The _____ accounts are assets, contra-assets, liabilities, and the owner's capital account.

18. A fiscal period 12 months in length is called a(n) _____.

19. When a fiscal year ends at the lowest point in business activity, it is called a(n) _____.

20. In accrual basis accounting, revenue is recorded when _____, no matter when cash is received; and _____ are recorded when incurred, no matter when cash is paid.

Multiple Choice

Please circle the correct answer.

1. Revenue and expense accounts and the owner's drawing account are called
   a. permanent accounts.
   b. real accounts.
   c. temporary accounts.
   d. balance sheet accounts.

2. The third step in the closing process is to
   a. close the balance of each revenue account to Income Summary.
   b. close the balance of Income Summary to the owner's capital account.
   c. close the balance of each expense account to Income Summary.
   d. close the balance of the owner's drawing account to the owner's capital account.

3. Information for the closing process is taken from the
   a. work sheet.
   b. source documents.
   c. journal.
   d. trial balance.

4. The balance in the Income Summary account before it is closed is equal to the
   a. total assets of the firm.
   b. total liabilities of the firm.
   c. owner's equity of the firm.
   d. net income or net loss for the period.

5. The balance in the owner's drawing account is closed to the
   a. Cash account.
   b. Income Summary account.
   c. owner's capital account.
   d. The owner's drawing account is not closed.

6. The post-closing trial balance contains the balances of the following accounts:
   a. assets, liabilities, and owner's capital.
   b. revenues and expenses.
   c. assets, contra-assets, liabilities, and revenues.
   d. revenues, expenses, and owner's drawing.

7. A fiscal period is
   a. a month.
   b. a year.
   c. the period of time covering the accounting cycle.
   d. None of the above

8. The steps necessary to complete the accounting cycle are performed
   a. as of the last day of the accounting period.
   b. during the last month of the accounting period.
   c. on the last day of the accounting period.
   d. None of the above

9. Of the 10 steps in the accounting cycle, most are performed only at the end or when financial statements are needed. These are
   a. steps 1 through 4.
   b. steps 3 through 10.
   c. steps 5 through 10.
   d. steps 8 through 10.

10. The accounting basis in which revenue and expenses are recognized only when cash is received or paid out is the
    a. matching basis.
    b. accrual basis.
    c. cash basis.
    d. cost basis.

Writing/Short Answer

1. **Reflect** Make a list, in words or simple phrases, of the most important and meaningful points in this chapter.

2. **Question** Think about the most confusing points or the material you do not understand in this chapter. Write down two or three questions that remain unanswered.

3. **Connect** Explain, in one or two sentences, the connection between the main points of this chapter and the major goals of the entire course.

4. **Summarize** Review this chapter's Joining the Pieces visual summary, and explain the concept(s) illustrated in a few sentences.

Skills Review

Quick Practice

QUICK PRACTICE 5-1

1. _____
2. _____
3. _____
4. _____

QUICK PRACTICE 5-2

2.   **General Journal**   Page 1

	Date		Account Title	P.R.	Debit	Credit	
1							1
2							2
3							3
4							4
5							5
6							6
7							7
8							8
9							9
10							10
11							11
12							12
13							13
14							14
15							15
16							16
17							17
18							18

QUICK PRACTICE 5-3

General Journal

Page 1

	Date		Account Title	P.R.	Debit	Credit	
1							1
2							2
3							3
4							4
5							5
6							6
7							7
8							8
9							9
10							10
11							11
12							12
13							13
14							14
15							15
16							16
17							17
18							18

QUICK PRACTICE 5-4

General Journal

Page 1

	Date		Account Title	P.R.	Debit	Credit	
1							1
2							2
3							3
4							4

1. _____

2. _____

3. _____

QUICK PRACTICE 5-5

General Journal

Page 1

	Date		Account Title	P.R.	Debit	Credit	
1							1
2							2
3							3
4							4
5							5
6							6
7							7
8							8
9							9
10							10
11							11
12							12
13							13
14							14
15							15
16							16
17							17
18							18

QUICK PRACTICE 5-6

General Journal

	Date		Account Title	P.R.	Debit	Credit	
1							1
2							2
3							3
4							4
5							5
6							6
7							7
8							8
9							9
10							10
11							11
12							12
13							13
14							14
15							15
16							16
17							17
18							18

QUICK PRACTICE 5-7

		Appear On Post-Closing Trial Balance?	
Account Title		**Yes**	**No**
1.	Accounts Payable		
2.	Accounts Receivable		
3.	Building		
4.	Cash		
5.	Delivery Truck		
6.	Equipment		
7.	Pam Knight, Capital		
8.	Pam Knight, Drawing		
9.	Mortgage Note Payable		
10.	Rent Expense		
11.	Repairs Expense		
12.	Revenue from Services		
13.	Supplies		
14.	Utilities Expense		

QUICK PRACTICE 5-8

QUICK PRACTICE 5-9

Exercises

EXERCISE 5-1

Account Title	Permanent	Temporary	Closed?	Reported On Balance Sheet	Reported On Income Statement
Cash					
Salaries Payable					
Accumulated Depreciation					
Fees Earned					
Accounts Receivable					
Supplies Expense					
Owner, Capital					
Accounts Payable					
Rent Expense					
Supplies					
Equipment					

EXERCISE 5-2

General Journal

Page 1

	Date	Account Title	P.R.	Debit	Credit	
1						1
2						2
3						3
4						4
5						5
6						6
7						7
8						8
9						9
10						10
11						11
12						12
13						13
14						14
15						15
16						16
17						17
18						18

EXERCISE 5-3

General Journal

Page 1

	Date		Account Title	P.R.	Debit	Credit	
1							1
2							2
3							3
4							4
5							5
6							6
7							7
8							8
9							9
10							10
11							11
12							12
13							13
14							14
15							15
16							16
17							17
18							18
19							19
20							20

EXERCISE 5-4

1.

General Journal

Page 1

	Date		Account Title	P.R.	Debit	Credit	
1							1
2							2
3							3
4							4

2. _____

3. _____

4. _____

EXERCISE 5-5

	Date		Account Title	P.R.	Debit	Credit	
1							1
2							2
3							3
4							4
5							5
6							6
7							7
8							8
9							9
10							10
11							11
12							12
13							13
14							14
15							15
16							16
17							17
18							18
19							19
20							20
21							21
22							22
23							23
24							24
25							25
26							26
27							27
28							28
29							29
30							30
31							31
32							32

EXERCISE 5-6

General Journal

	Date	Account Title	P.R.	Debit	Credit	
1						1
2						2
3						3
4						4
5						5
6						6
7						7
8						8
9						9
10						10
11						11
12						12
13						13
14						14
15						15
16						16
17						17
18						18
19						19
20						20
21						21
22						22
23						23
24						24
25						25
26						26
27						27
28						28
29						29
30						30
31						31
32						32

EXERCISE 5-7

Accounts That Will Appear
on a Post-Closing Trial Balance

_____

_____

_____

_____

_____

_____

_____

_____

_____

EXERCISE 5-8

Proper Sequence of Steps
in the Accounting Cycle

_____

_____

_____

_____

_____

_____

_____

_____

_____

This page intentionally left blank.

Case Problems

PROBLEM 5-1A OR 5-1B

General Journal

	Date		Account Title	P.R.	Debit	Credit	
1							1
2							2
3							3
4							4
5							5
6							6
7							7
8							8
9							9
10							10
11							11
12							12
13							13
14							14
15							15
16							16
17							17
18							18
19							19
20							20
21							21
22							22
23							23
24							24
25							25
26							26
27							27
28							28
29							29
30							30
31							31
32							32

This page intentionally left blank.

PROBLEM 5-2A OR 5-2B

1.
General Journal

Page 1

	Date		Account Title	P.R.	Debit	Credit	
1							1
2							2
3							3
4							4
5							5
6							6
7							7
8							8
9							9
10							10
11							11
12							12
13							13
14							14
15							15
16							16
17							17
18							18
19							19
20							20
21							21
22							22

2. _____

_____

_____

_____

This page intentionally left blank.

This page intentionally left blank.

1.

Account Title	Trial Balance				Adjustments			
	Dr.		Cr.		Dr.		Cr.	

Adjusted Trial Balance		Income Statement		Balance Sheet	
Dr.	Cr.	Dr.	Cr.	Dr.	Cr.

PROBLEM 5-3A OR 5-3B (continued)

2.   **General Journal**   Page 1

	Date		Account Title	P.R.	Debit	Credit	
1							1
2							2
3							3
4							4
5							5
6							6
7							7
8							8
9							9
10							10
11							11
12							12
13							13
14							14
15							15
16							16
17							17
18							18
19							19
20							20
21							21
22							22
23							23
24							24
25							25
26							26
27							27
28							28
29							29
30							30
31							31
32							32
33							33

PROBLEM 5-3A OR 5-3B (continued)

General Journal

Page 1

	Date		Account Title	P.R.	Debit	Credit	
1							1
2							2
3							3
4							4
5							5
6							6
7							7
8							8
9							9
10							10
11							11
12							12
13							13
14							14
15							15
16							16
17							17
18							18
19							19
20							20
21							21
22							22
23							23
24							24
25							25
26							26
27							27
28							28
29							29
30							30
31							31
32							32
33							33

PROBLEM 5-4A

<table>
<thead>
<tr><th rowspan="3">Account Title</th><th colspan="5" rowspan="2">Trial Balance
Debit</th><th colspan="5" rowspan="2">Credit</th><th colspan="6" rowspan="2">Adjustments
Debit</th><th colspan="6" rowspan="2">Credit</th></tr>
<tr></tr>
<tr></tr>
</thead>
</table>

Comprehensive Management Services

Work Sheet

For Year Ended December 31, 20X2

Account Title	Trial Balance Debit	Credit	Adjustments Debit	Credit
Cash	9 0 0 0 00			
Office Supplies	1 7 0 0 00			(a) 1 4 0 0 00
Prepaid Insurance	1 2 0 0 00			(b) 5 0 0 00
Office Equipment	20 0 0 0 00			
Accum. Depr.—Office Equipment		5 0 0 0 00		(c) 2 0 0 0 00
Accounts Payable		2 2 0 0 00		
Salaries Payable		—		(d) 3 0 0 00
J.B. Smith, Capital		19 8 5 0 00		
J.B. Smith, Drawing	32 0 0 0 00			
Fees Earned		74 0 0 0 00		
Salaries Expense	29 0 0 0 00		(d) 3 0 0 00	
Rent Expense	3 9 0 0 00			
Advertising Expense	2 7 0 0 00			
Telephone Expense	1 1 0 0 00			
Office Supplies Expense	—		(a) 1 4 0 0 00	
Insurance Expense	—		(b) 5 0 0 00	
Depr. Expense—Office Equipment	—		(c) 2 0 0 0 00	
Miscellaneous Expense	4 5 0 00			
	101 0 5 0 00	101 0 5 0 00	4 2 0 0 00	4 2 0 0 00
Net Income				

226   PART I   Accounting for the Service Business

PROBLEM 5-4A (continued)

Adjusted Trial Balance Debit	Adjusted Trial Balance Credit	Income Statement Debit	Income Statement Credit	Balance Sheet Debit	Balance Sheet Credit
9 0 0 0 00				9 0 0 0 00	
3 0 0 00				3 0 0 00	
7 0 0 00				7 0 0 00	
20 0 0 0 00				20 0 0 0 00	
	7 0 0 0 00				7 0 0 0 00
	2 2 0 0 00				2 2 0 0 00
	3 0 0 00				3 0 0 00
	19 8 5 0 00				19 8 5 0 00
32 0 0 0 00				32 0 0 0 00	
	74 0 0 0 00		74 0 0 0 00		
29 3 0 0 00		29 3 0 0 00			
3 9 0 0 00		3 9 0 0 00			
2 7 0 0 00		2 7 0 0 00			
1 1 0 0 00		1 1 0 0 00			
1 4 0 0 00		1 4 0 0 00			
5 0 0 00		5 0 0 00			
2 0 0 0 00		2 0 0 0 00			
4 5 0 00		4 5 0 00			
103 3 5 0 00	103 3 5 0 00	41 3 5 0 00	74 0 0 0 00	62 0 0 0 00	29 3 5 0 00
		32 6 5 0 00			32 6 5 0 00
		74 0 0 0 00	74 0 0 0 00	62 0 0 0 00	62 0 0 0 00

PROBLEM 5-4B

DataPlus Bookkeeping Service
Work Sheet
For Year Ended December 31, 20X2

Account Title	Trial Balance Debit	Trial Balance Credit	Adjustments Debit	Adjustments Credit
Cash	12 0 0 0 00			
Office Supplies	2 1 0 0 00			(a) 1 8 0 0 00
Prepaid Insurance	3 6 0 0 00			(b) 2 0 0 0 00
Office Equipment	25 0 0 0 00			
Accum. Depr.—Office Equipment		8 0 0 0 00		(c) 4 0 0 0 00
Accounts Payable		2 7 0 0 00		
Salaries Payable		—		(d) 5 0 0 00
Mary Lamb, Capital		27 7 0 0 00		
Mary Lamb, Drawing	38 0 0 0 00			
Fees Earned		93 0 0 0 00		
Salaries Expense	41 0 0 0 00		(d) 5 0 0 00	
Rent Expense	4 2 0 0 00			
Advertising Expense	3 3 0 0 00			
Telephone Expense	1 5 0 0 00			
Office Supplies Expense	—		(a) 1 8 0 0 00	
Insurance Expense	—		(b) 2 0 0 0 00	
Depr. Expense—Office Equipment	—		(c) 4 0 0 0 00	
Miscellaneous Expense	7 0 0 00			
	131 4 0 0 00	131 4 0 0 00	8 3 0 0 00	8 3 0 0 00
Net Income				

	Adjusted Trial Balance		Income Statement		Balance Sheet	
	Debit	Credit	Debit	Credit	Debit	Credit
	12 0 0 0 00				12 0 0 0 00	
	3 0 0 00				3 0 0 00	
	1 6 0 0 00				1 6 0 0 00	
	25 0 0 0 00				25 0 0 0 00	
		12 0 0 0 00				12 0 0 0 00
		2 7 0 0 00				2 7 0 0 00
		5 0 0 00				5 0 0 00
		27 7 0 0 00				27 7 0 0 00
	38 0 0 0 00				38 0 0 0 00	
		93 0 0 0 00		93 0 0 0 00		
	41 5 0 0 00		41 5 0 0 00			
	4 2 0 0 00		4 2 0 0 00			
	3 3 0 0 00		3 3 0 0 00			
	1 5 0 0 00		1 5 0 0 00			
	1 8 0 0 00		1 8 0 0 00			
	2 0 0 0 00		2 0 0 0 00			
	4 0 0 0 00		4 0 0 0 00			
	7 0 0 00		7 0 0 00			
	135 9 0 0 00	135 9 0 0 00	59 0 0 0 00	93 0 0 0 00	76 9 0 0 00	42 9 0 0 00
			34 0 0 0 00			34 0 0 0 00
			93 0 0 0 00	93 0 0 0 00	76 9 0 0 00	76 9 0 0 00

2., 3.   **General Journal**   Page 10

	Date		Account Title	P.R.	Debit	Credit	
1							1
2							2
3							3
4							4
5							5
6							6
7							7
8							8
9							9
10							10
11							11
12							12
13							13
14							14
15							15
16							16
17							17
18							18
19							19
20							20
21							21
22							22
23							23
24							24
25							25
26							26
27							27
28							28
29							29
30							30
31							31
32							32
33							33

PROBLEM 5-4A OR 5-4B (continued)

1., 2., 3.

ACCOUNT Cash   ACCOUNT NO. 111

DATE	ITEM	P.R.	DEBIT	CREDIT	BALANCE DEBIT	BALANCE CREDIT

ACCOUNT Office Supplies   ACCOUNT NO. 112

DATE	ITEM	P.R.	DEBIT	CREDIT	BALANCE DEBIT	BALANCE CREDIT

ACCOUNT Prepaid Insurance   ACCOUNT NO. 115

DATE	ITEM	P.R.	DEBIT	CREDIT	BALANCE DEBIT	BALANCE CREDIT

ACCOUNT Office Equipment   ACCOUNT NO. 116

DATE	ITEM	P.R.	DEBIT	CREDIT	BALANCE DEBIT	BALANCE CREDIT

ACCOUNT Accumulated Depreciation—Office Equipment   ACCOUNT NO. 116.1

DATE	ITEM	P.R.	DEBIT	CREDIT	BALANCE DEBIT	BALANCE CREDIT

ACCOUNT **Accounts Payable**   ACCOUNT NO. **211**

DATE	ITEM	P.R.	DEBIT	CREDIT	BALANCE DEBIT	BALANCE CREDIT

ACCOUNT **Salaries Payable**   ACCOUNT NO. **212**

DATE	ITEM	P.R.	DEBIT	CREDIT	BALANCE DEBIT	BALANCE CREDIT

ACCOUNT _____, **Capital**   ACCOUNT NO. **311**

DATE	ITEM	P.R.	DEBIT	CREDIT	BALANCE DEBIT	BALANCE CREDIT

ACCOUNT _____, **Drawing**   ACCOUNT NO. **312**

DATE	ITEM	P.R.	DEBIT	CREDIT	BALANCE DEBIT	BALANCE CREDIT

ACCOUNT **Income Summary**   ACCOUNT NO. **313**

DATE	ITEM	P.R.	DEBIT	CREDIT	BALANCE DEBIT	BALANCE CREDIT

PROBLEM 5-4A OR 5-4B (continued)

ACCOUNT Fees Earned   ACCOUNT NO. 411

DATE		ITEM	P.R.	DEBIT	CREDIT	BALANCE	
						DEBIT	CREDIT

ACCOUNT Salaries Expense   ACCOUNT NO. 511

DATE		ITEM	P.R.	DEBIT	CREDIT	BALANCE	
						DEBIT	CREDIT

ACCOUNT Rent Expense   ACCOUNT NO. 512

DATE		ITEM	P.R.	DEBIT	CREDIT	BALANCE	
						DEBIT	CREDIT

ACCOUNT Advertising Expense   ACCOUNT NO. 513

DATE		ITEM	P.R.	DEBIT	CREDIT	BALANCE	
						DEBIT	CREDIT

ACCOUNT Telephone Expense   ACCOUNT NO. 514

DATE		ITEM	P.R.	DEBIT	CREDIT	BALANCE	
						DEBIT	CREDIT

ACCOUNT Office Supplies Expense   ACCOUNT NO. 515

DATE	ITEM	P.R.	DEBIT	CREDIT	BALANCE	
					DEBIT	CREDIT

ACCOUNT Insurance Expense   ACCOUNT NO. 516

DATE	ITEM	P.R.	DEBIT	CREDIT	BALANCE	
					DEBIT	CREDIT

ACCOUNT Depreciation Expense—Office Equipment   ACCOUNT NO. 517

DATE	ITEM	P.R.	DEBIT	CREDIT	BALANCE	
					DEBIT	CREDIT

ACCOUNT Miscellaneous Expense   ACCOUNT NO. 518

DATE	ITEM	P.R.	DEBIT	CREDIT	BALANCE	
					DEBIT	CREDIT

4.

ACCOUNT TITLE	DEBIT	CREDIT

This page intentionally left blank.

This page intentionally left blank.

PROBLEM 5-5A OR 5-5B

1.

Account Title	Trial Balance		Adjustments	
	Dr.	Cr.	Dr.	Cr.

	Adjusted Trial Balance		Income Statement		Balance Sheet	
	Dr.	Cr.	Dr.	Cr.	Dr.	Cr.

2.

3.

PROBLEM 5-5A OR 5-5B (continued)

4.

5. **General Journal** Page 1

	Date		Account Title	P.R.	Debit	Credit	
1							1
2							2
3							3
4							4
5							5
6							6
7							7
8							8
9							9
10							10
11							11
12							12
13							13
14							14
15							15
16							16
17							17
18							18
19							19
20							20
21							21
22							22
23							23
24							24
25							25
26							26
27							27
28							28
29							29
30							30
31							31
32							32

6.   **General Journal**   Page 2

	Date		Account Title	P.R.	Debit	Credit	
1							1
2							2
3							3
4							4
5							5
6							6
7							7
8							8
9							9
10							10
11							11
12							12
13							13
14							14
15							15
16							16
17							17
18							18
19							19
20							20
21							21
22							22
23							23
24							24
25							25
26							26
27							27
28							28
29							29
30							30
31							31
32							32

This page intentionally left blank.

Critical Thinking Problems

Challenge Problem

1.

General Journal Page 1

	Date		Account Title	P.R.	Debit	Credit	
1							1
2							2
3							3
4							4
5							5
6							6
7							7
8							8
9							9
10							10

2.

3. _____

_____

_____

_____

_____

This page intentionally left blank.

Communications

_____

_____

_____

_____

_____

_____

_____

_____

_____

_____

_____

_____

_____

_____

_____

_____

Team Internet Project

_____

_____

_____

_____

_____

_____

_____

_____

_____

_____

_____

_____

_____

_____

_____

_____

Ethics

_____

_____

_____

_____

_____

_____

_____

_____

_____

_____

_____

_____

_____

_____

_____

In the Real World

_____

_____

_____

_____

_____

_____

_____

_____

_____

_____

_____

_____

_____

_____

_____

Practice Test Answers

True/False

1. F
2. T
3. T
4. F
5. F
6. F
7. T
8. T
9. F
10. T
11. T
12. T
13. F
14. T
15. T
16. F
17. T
18. F
19. T
20. F

Matching

1. h
2. c
3. j
4. i
5. g
6. e
7. b
8. f
9. d
10. a

Fill in the Blanks

1. closing entries
2. temporary
3. closing

4. zero
5. Income Summary
6. expense, Income Summary
7. capital
8. owner's capital
9. net income, net loss
10. after
11. debiting
12. crediting
13. work sheet
14. temporary
15. post-closing trial balance
16. post-closing, permanent
17. permanent
18. fiscal year
19. natural business year
20. earned, expenses

Multiple Choice

1. c
2. b
3. a
4. d
5. c
6. a
7. c
8. a
9. c
10. c

Writing/Short Answer

Answers will vary. Please discuss questions with your instructor.

Jim Arnold's Photography Studio

2.   **General Journal**   Page 1

	Date		Account Title	P.R.	Debit	Credit	
1							1
2							2
3							3
4							4
5							5
6							6
7							7
8							8
9							9
10							10
11							11
12							12
13							13
14							14
15							15
16							16
17							17
18							18
19							19
20							20
21							21
22							22
23							23
24							24
25							25
26							26
27							27
28							28
29							29
30							30
31							31
32							32

	Date		Account Title	P.R.	Debit	Credit	
1							1
2							2
3							3
4							4
5							5
6							6
7							7
8							8
9							9
10							10
11							11
12							12
13							13
14							14
15							15
16							16
17							17
18							18
19							19
20							20
21							21
22							22
23							23
24							24
25							25
26							26
27							27
28							28
29							29
30							30
31							31
32							32
33							33

	Date		Account Title	P.R.	Debit	Credit	
1							1
2							2
3							3
4							4
5							5
6							6
7							7
8							8
9							9
10							10
11							11
12							12
13							13
14							14
15							15
16							16
17							17
18							18
19							19
20							20
21							21
22							22
23							23
24							24
25							25
26							26
27							27
28							28
29							29
30							30
31							31
32							32

	Date		Account Title	P.R.	Debit		Credit		
1									1
2									2
3									3
4									4
5									5
6									6
7									7
8									8
9									9
10									10
11									11
12									12
13									13
14									14
15									15
16									16
17									17
18									18
19									19
20									20
21									21
22									22
23									23
24									24
25									25
26									26
27									27
28									28
29									29
30									30
31									31
32									32

General Journal

	Date		Account Title	P.R.	Debit		Credit		
1									1
2									2
3									3
4									4
5									5
6									6
7									7
8									8
9									9
10									10
11									11
12									12
13									13
14									14
15									15
16									16
17									17
18									18
19									19
20									20
21									21
22									22
23									23
24									24
25									25
26									26
27									27
28									28
29									29
30									30
31									31
32									32

	Date		Account Title	P.R.	Debit	Credit	
1							1
2							2
3							3
4							4
5							5
6							6
7							7
8							8
9							9
10							10
11							11
12							12
13							13
14							14
15							15
16							16
17							17
18							18
19							19
20							20
21							21
22							22
23							23
24							24
25							25
26							26
27							27
28							28
29							29
30							30
31							31
32							32

	Date		Account Title	P.R.	Debit	Credit	
1							1
2							2
3							3
4							4
5							5
6							6
7							7
8							8
9							9
10							10
11							11
12							12
13							13
14							14
15							15
16							16
17							17
18							18
19							19
20							20
21							21
22							22
23							23
24							24
25							25
26							26
27							27
28							28
29							29
30							30
31							31
32							32

1., 3., 11.

ACCOUNT **Cash**   ACCOUNT NO. 111

DATE		ITEM	P.R.	DEBIT	CREDIT	BALANCE	
						DEBIT	CREDIT

ACCOUNT **Accounts Receivable**   ACCOUNT NO. 112

DATE		ITEM	P.R.	DEBIT	CREDIT	BALANCE	
						DEBIT	CREDIT

ACCOUNT **Office Supplies**   ACCOUNT NO. 113

DATE		ITEM	P.R.	DEBIT	CREDIT	BALANCE	
						DEBIT	CREDIT

ACCOUNT **Photography Supplies**   ACCOUNT NO. 114

DATE		ITEM	P.R.	DEBIT	CREDIT	BALANCE	
						DEBIT	CREDIT

ACCOUNT **Prepaid Insurance**   ACCOUNT NO. 115

DATE		ITEM	P.R.	DEBIT	CREDIT	BALANCE	
						DEBIT	CREDIT

ACCOUNT **Office Equipment**　　　　　　　　　　　　　　　　　　ACCOUNT NO. 121

DATE		ITEM	P.R.	DEBIT	CREDIT	BALANCE	
						DEBIT	CREDIT

ACCOUNT **Accumulated Depreciation—Office Equipment**　　　　　ACCOUNT NO. 121.1

DATE		ITEM	P.R.	DEBIT	CREDIT	BALANCE	
						DEBIT	CREDIT

ACCOUNT **Photography Equipment**　　　　　　　　　　　　　　　ACCOUNT NO. 122

DATE		ITEM	P.R.	DEBIT	CREDIT	BALANCE	
						DEBIT	CREDIT

ACCOUNT **Accumulated Depreciation—Photography Equipment**　　ACCOUNT NO. 122.1

DATE		ITEM	P.R.	DEBIT	CREDIT	BALANCE	
						DEBIT	CREDIT

ACCOUNT **Furniture and Fixtures**　　　　　　　　　　　　　　　ACCOUNT NO. 123

DATE		ITEM	P.R.	DEBIT	CREDIT	BALANCE	
						DEBIT	CREDIT

ACCOUNT **Accumulated Depreciation—Furniture and Fixtures**   ACCOUNT NO. **123.1**

DATE	ITEM	P.R.	DEBIT	CREDIT	BALANCE DEBIT	BALANCE CREDIT

ACCOUNT **Accounts Payable**   ACCOUNT NO. **211**

DATE	ITEM	P.R.	DEBIT	CREDIT	BALANCE DEBIT	BALANCE CREDIT

ACCOUNT **Notes Payable**   ACCOUNT NO. **212**

DATE	ITEM	P.R.	DEBIT	CREDIT	BALANCE DEBIT	BALANCE CREDIT

ACCOUNT **Salaries Payable**   ACCOUNT NO. **213**

DATE	ITEM	P.R.	DEBIT	CREDIT	BALANCE DEBIT	BALANCE CREDIT

ACCOUNT Jim Arnold, Capital   ACCOUNT NO. 311

DATE		ITEM	P.R.	DEBIT	CREDIT	BALANCE	
						DEBIT	CREDIT

ACCOUNT Jim Arnold, Drawing   ACCOUNT NO. 312

DATE		ITEM	P.R.	DEBIT	CREDIT	BALANCE	
						DEBIT	CREDIT

ACCOUNT Income Summary   ACCOUNT NO. 313

DATE		ITEM	P.R.	DEBIT	CREDIT	BALANCE	
						DEBIT	CREDIT

ACCOUNT Photography Revenue   ACCOUNT NO. 411

DATE		ITEM	P.R.	DEBIT	CREDIT	BALANCE	
						DEBIT	CREDIT

ACCOUNT Vending Machine Revenue   ACCOUNT NO. 412

DATE	ITEM	P.R.	DEBIT	CREDIT	BALANCE DEBIT	CREDIT

ACCOUNT Salaries Expense   ACCOUNT NO. 511

DATE	ITEM	P.R.	DEBIT	CREDIT	BALANCE DEBIT	CREDIT

ACCOUNT Advertising Expense   ACCOUNT NO. 512

DATE	ITEM	P.R.	DEBIT	CREDIT	BALANCE DEBIT	CREDIT

ACCOUNT Rent Expense   ACCOUNT NO. 513

DATE	ITEM	P.R.	DEBIT	CREDIT	BALANCE DEBIT	CREDIT

ACCOUNT Repairs Expense   ACCOUNT NO. 514

| DATE | | ITEM | P.R. | DEBIT | CREDIT | BALANCE | |
						DEBIT	CREDIT

ACCOUNT Insurance Expense   ACCOUNT NO. 515

| DATE | | ITEM | P.R. | DEBIT | CREDIT | BALANCE | |
						DEBIT	CREDIT

ACCOUNT Office Supplies Expense   ACCOUNT NO. 516

| DATE | | ITEM | P.R. | DEBIT | CREDIT | BALANCE | |
						DEBIT	CREDIT

ACCOUNT Photography Supplies Expense   ACCOUNT NO. 517

| DATE | | ITEM | P.R. | DEBIT | CREDIT | BALANCE | |
						DEBIT	CREDIT

ACCOUNT Depreciation Expense—Office Equipment   ACCOUNT NO. 518

DATE	ITEM	P.R.	DEBIT	CREDIT	BALANCE DEBIT	BALANCE CREDIT

ACCOUNT Depreciation Expense—Photography Equipment   ACCOUNT NO. 519

DATE	ITEM	P.R.	DEBIT	CREDIT	BALANCE DEBIT	BALANCE CREDIT

ACCOUNT Depreciation Expense—Furniture and Fixtures   ACCOUNT NO. 520

DATE	ITEM	P.R.	DEBIT	CREDIT	BALANCE DEBIT	BALANCE CREDIT

ACCOUNT Utilities Expense   ACCOUNT NO. 521

DATE	ITEM	P.R.	DEBIT	CREDIT	BALANCE DEBIT	BALANCE CREDIT

ACCOUNT Miscellaneous Expense   ACCOUNT NO. 522

DATE	ITEM	P.R.	DEBIT	CREDIT	BALANCE	
					DEBIT	CREDIT

This page intentionally left blank.

4., 5.

	Arnold's Photos							
	Work Sheet							
	For Month Ended July 31, 20X1							
Account Title	Trial Balance		Adjustments	
	Dr.	Cr.	Dr.	Cr.

4., 5.

Adjusted Trial Balance		Income Statement		Balance Sheet	
Dr.	Cr.	Dr.	Cr.	Dr.	Cr.

6.

Arnold's Photos Income Statement For Month Ended July 31, 20X1														

7.

Fred's Photos Statement of Owner's Equity For Month Ended July 31, 20X1														

8.

Arnold's Photos													
Balance Sheet													
July 31, 20X1													

12.

Arnold's Photos					
Post-Closing Trial Balance					
July 31, 20X1					
ACCOUNT TITLE	DEBIT		CREDIT	

Internal Control and Accounting for Cash

Chapter Summary  Interactive Summary in English and Spanish

Several highly publicized business scandals in the early 2000s shook the public's confidence in the financial statements of American companies. To address the problem, Congress passed the Sarbanes-Oxley Act of 2002 (SOX). To ensure that the act is enforced, the **Public Company Accounting Oversight Board (PCAOB)** was created. Among other things, SOX requires public companies to maintain a strong and effective system of internal control.

Internal control refers to the methods and procedures a business uses to internally protect its assets. The objectives of internal control are as follows:

- *Safeguard assets.* First and foremost, a company must have procedures in place to protect its assets from theft, loss, improper use, and unauthorized use. Most companies use a variety of safeguards, ranging from sophisticated electronic surveillance systems to requiring employees to wear name badges so that unauthorized personnel can be quickly identified.

- *Ensure the accuracy and reliability of accounting records.* Good financial records are essential to the success of any organization; without good records, you cannot accurately measure revenue, track and control expenses, protect assets, and determine the overall success of your business.

- *Promote operational efficiency.* Inefficiency hurts a business in many ways:

  - Untrained, poorly trained, and unmotivated employees can make mistakes that take time and money to correct.

  - Excessive employee breaks and other waste of company time, such as surfing the Web and conducting personal business, are estimated to cost businesses more than the combined loss from all crimes.

  - A company's assets should meet the needs and objectives of its operations. Purchasing assets that are not needed, or whose benefits don't justify their cost, hurts a company's operating efficiency. Likewise, not having sufficient assets to get the job done also hurts efficiency. Imagine having a large grocery store with only two cash registers. The long wait during peak hours would cause many customers to shop elsewhere.

- *Ensure compliance with laws and regulations.* Businesses must comply with all applicable laws and regulations. Examples include filing proper tax forms, meeting safety regulations, and complying with various laws.

Cash includes currency (paper money), coins, checks made payable to the business, money orders, and amounts on deposit in banks and other financial institutions. Basically, if it can be deposited in a bank account, we classify it as cash. Cash is an asset that is particularly vulnerable to theft, loss, and misuse. Therefore, special controls are necessary to protect and control cash. Some common steps used to protect and control cash include the following:

- Limiting those who actually handle cash to a few properly designated persons.
- Separating the duties of those who physically handle cash (cashiers and clerks) from those who account for cash (bookkeepers and accountants).
- Physically protecting cash by keeping it in a secure place and making daily bank deposits.
- Documents such as cash register tapes and summaries of checks received in the mail should be maintained to show total cash receipts. Checks should be prenumbered so that it is easy to see what checks have been written and when.
- There should be independent verification of those involved in handling and accounting for cash. Supervisors should count cash and review cash register summaries prepared by cashiers. The company treasurer should compare total cash receipts with daily bank deposits.
- Only a small amount of cash (referred to as petty cash) should be kept on hand for making minor expenditures. All other payments should be made by check.

The use of a bank account offers physical and internal control of cash. However, it is not always practical or possible to write checks for small expenditures. Thus, it is common for businesses to establish an office fund—known as the **petty cash fund**—for making small expenditures. The amount of cash in the petty cash fund varies with the individual business. It can be established for any amount considered necessary. Furthermore, the fund can be increased or decreased at any time.

The petty cash fund is established by debiting the **Petty Cash account** and crediting the Cash account. Often, one person—the **petty cashier**—is responsible for the maintenance of the fund. When a payment is made from the fund, a petty cash voucher is prepared; the **petty cash voucher** shows the amount of the payment, the purpose, and the account to be debited. Records of petty cash are kept in an **auxiliary record**, called the **petty cash payments record**.

The petty cash fund is replenished periodically, usually at the end of the month. A check is written for the amount paid out of the fund, and when this amount is placed in the fund, the fund is brought back up to the balance that it had at the beginning of the month. The entry to **replenish the petty cash fund** involves a debit to each expense listed in the petty cash payments record and a credit to Cash.

Many businesses will keep a **change fund** for their cash registers. The **Change Fund account** is debited for the amount of the fund. Businesses that have many cash transactions often have a small **cash shortage**, less than the amount indicated by cash sales, or a **cash overage**, more than the amount indicated by cash sales. If the source of the shortage or overage cannot be determined, the **Cash Short and Over account** can be used to bring the accounting records into agreement with the actual amount of cash on hand. The Cash Short and Over account is debited for the amount of a shortage and credited for the amount of an overage. Thus, the account will show either a net shortage (debit balance) or a net overage (credit balance). A net shortage is reported on the income statement as miscellaneous expense; a net overage is reported on the income statement as miscellaneous income.

A bank is a financial institution that offers a variety of services to its customers. A primary service offered by banks is the bank checking account. A **bank checking account** is an amount of cash on deposit with a bank that the bank must pay at the order of the depositor. The **depositor** is the person (or business) under whose name the checking account is maintained.

A deposit slip should be prepared when a deposit is made in a checking account. A **deposit slip** summarizes the amount deposited and is the depositor's record of the deposit. A **check** is used to pay money from a checking account. A check is recorded in a bound book of checks called a **checkbook** by filling in the **check stub**. Each check has an **American Bankers Association (ABA) transit number** that identifies the bank and allows efficient processing of the check.

Checks must be endorsed before they can be deposited or cashed. There are three common forms of **endorsement**. A **blank endorsement** is simply a signature on the back of the check. A check with a blank endorsement can be cashed by anyone who has possession of it. A **full endorsement** specifies the party to whom the check is being transferred. A **restrictive endorsement** specifies the purpose for which money from a check is to be used.

There are three parties to a check: (1) the **drawer** is the person (or business) who writes the check, (2) the **drawee** is the bank on which the check is written, and (3) the **payee** is the person (or business) to whom the check is written. When a checking account is opened, a **signature card** must be signed by each person who will be writing checks on the account. The bank uses the signature card as an aid in spotting possible forgeries.

An increasingly popular way for businesses to handle cash transactions is by **electronic funds transfer (EFT)**, which is a movement of cash by electronic communication. An electronic funds transfer is less costly than conventional means of handling cash because cash is moved electronically through computers and networks, thus eliminating the need to write and mail checks and process customer receipts face to face.

At regular intervals—usually once a month—a bank sends each of its checking account customers a bank statement. A **bank statement** is a copy of the bank's record of the checking account transactions and usually includes canceled checks. A **canceled check** is a check that has been paid by the bank out of the depositor's account. The bank statement should be compared with the depositor's checkbook. Due to several normal factors, the bank statement balance seldom agrees with the checkbook balance. The lack of agreement may be due to (1) **outstanding checks**, or checks that were not listed on the statement because they did not reach the bank's accounting department in time for processing; (2), **deposits in transit**, which are deposits that appear in the checkbook but do not appear on the statement; (3) a **NSF (Not Sufficient Funds) check**, or check drawn against an account in which there were not sufficient funds to cover the check; and/or (4) a **service charge**, which is a maintenance fee charged by the bank that is deducted directly from the depositor's account. To bring the cash balance of the bank statement into agreement with the checkbook balance, a **bank reconciliation** is prepared by the depositor, which accounts for the mentioned factors.

True/False

Please circle the correct answer.

T F 1. The internal control policies of a business depend on factors such as the size of the company, the nature of its operations, the number of employees, and how cash is received.

T F 2. Cash includes currency, coins, checks made payable to the business, money orders, traveler's checks, and cashier's checks.

T F 3. Bookkeepers and accountants should be assigned to handle cash because they record the cash transactions.

T F 4. Cash should be deposited in the bank daily.

T F 5. All cash payments, except for petty cash, should be made by check.

T F 6. Checks should be prenumbered so that it is easy to spot a check that is unrecorded.

T F 7. A petty cash fund is used as a convenient way to pay small expenses.

T F 8. A petty cash payments record is an example of an auxiliary record.

T F 9. To replenish a petty cash fund, it is necessary to debit Petty Cash and credit Cash for the amount that is needed to bring the fund back up to its original total.

T F 10. Cash Short and Over is debited whenever there is a cash overage and credited whenever there is a cash shortage.

T F 11. The balance in Cash Short and Over is reported on the income statement as miscellaneous income or miscellaneous expense.

T F 12. When a payment is made by check, the check stub should always be filled out first.

T F 13. A bank statement is the bank's way of informing the depositor of the transactions that have been recorded in the depositor's account during the period.

T F 14. The bank statement will always have the same ending balance as the balance shown in the depositor's checkbook and the Cash account unless there is a mistake.

T F 15. Outstanding checks are checks that have been written by the business but that have not yet been paid by the bank.

T F 16. A bank reconciliation is necessary to arrive at the true cash balance.

T F 17. *All* adjustments to the checkbook balance need to be recorded in the journal and posted.

T F 18. In order to deposit a check in the bank, the depositor must use a restrictive endorsement.

Matching

Please match each of the following terms with its definition.

a. bank charge
b. bank reconciliation
c. bank statement
d. blank endorsement
e. cash
f. Cash Short and Over account
g. deposit in transit
h. depositor
i. drawee
j. drawer

k. full endorsement
l. internal control
m. NSF check charge
n. outstanding check
o. payee
p. petty cash fund
q. restrictive endorsement
r. Sarbanes-Oxley Act of 2002
s. signature card
t. petty cash voucher

_____ 1. An endorsement that specifies the purpose for which the money from a check is to be used.

_____ 2. A report, usually sent out monthly by the bank, that shows the bank's record of the checking account transactions.

_____ 3. A check that was written and is recorded in the checkbook but does not appear on the bank statement.

_____ 4. Making the bank statement balance agree with the checkbook balance.

_____ 5. A small amount of cash kept in the office for making small payments for items such as postage and office supplies.

_____ 6. The methods used within a company to protect its assets.

_____ 7. An account used to bring the accounting records into agreement with the actual amount of cash on hand when that amount is less or more than it should be.

_____ 8. A record prepared when opening a checking account that lists personal information about the depositor and the signatures of all persons who are authorized to sign checks.

_____ 9. The person or business who writes a check.

_____ 10. The endorsement that uses the phrase "pay to the order of" so that the check can only be cashed by that person or business.

_____ 11. The person or business to whom a check is made payable.

_____ 12. Currency, coins, checks, money orders, bank drafts, etc.

_____ 13. Requires an effective system of internal control.

_____ 14. A form prepared to support a payment from the petty cash fund.

_____ 15. A deposit made and appearing in the checkbook but not appearing on the bank statement.

_____ 16. A charge made by the bank when a check that was deposited is returned because of insufficient funds.

_____ 17. A charge or fee that is subtracted by the bank directly from the depositor's account and appears on the bank statement; also referred to as a service charge.

_____ 18. An endorsement that consists only of a signature on the back of a check and allows anyone who possesses the check to cash it.

_____ 19. The person or business in whose name a checking account is opened.

_____ 20. The bank on which a check is drawn.

Fill in the Blanks

Please complete each sentence with the correct word or words.

1. A system designed to internally protect a company's assets is called _____.

2. The _____ Act was passed by Congress in 2002 to help restore the public's confidence in the financial statements of companies.

3. An amount of cash kept on hand for making small expenditures is called _____.

4. When a petty cash fund is established, the _____ is debited.

5. A(n) _____ is prepared when payment is made from the petty cash fund. It shows the purpose and amount of the payment and the account to be debited.

6. When the petty cash fund is low, it is necessary to _____ it.

7. When the petty cash fund is replenished, the _____ account is credited.

8. A petty cash record is an example of a(n) _____ record.

9. The _____ fund is an amount of cash kept on hand to make change for cash customers.

10. Cash shortages are recorded with a(n) _____ to the Cash Short and Over account; cash overages are recorded with a(n) _____.

11. A bank reconciliation is prepared to bring the ending balance shown on the bank statement into agreement with the balance shown in the _____.

12. On a bank reconciliation, deposits in transit should be _____ to the _____ balance.

13. On a bank reconciliation, outstanding checks should be _____ from the _____ balance.

14. On a bank reconciliation, bank services charges should be _____ from the _____ balance.

15. On a bank reconciliation, adjustments to the _____ balance will normally need journal entries to update the Cash account.

Multiple Choice

Please circle the correct answer.

1. A system designed to internally protect a company's assets is called
   a. operating efficiency.
   b. internal control.
   c. legal control.
   d. asset safeguarding.

2. Which of the following items are included in cash?
   a. Coins and currency
   b. Checks
   c. Money on deposit in a bank account
   d. All of the above

3. Steps to control and protect cash include which of the following?
   a. Making bank deposits daily
   b. Assigning the handling of cash to the bookkeeper or accountant
   c. Keeping enough cash on hand so that all bills can be paid with cash
   d. None of the above

4. When a petty cash fund is established,
   a. the Cash account is debited and the Petty Cash account is credited.
   b. various expense accounts are debited and the Cash account is credited.
   c. the Petty Cash account is debited and the Cash account is credited.
   d. no entry is needed because there is a transfer of cash from one account to another.

5. When the petty cash fund is replenished,
   a. the Petty Cash account is debited and the Cash account is credited.
   b. various expense accounts are debited and the Cash account is credited.
   c. the Cash account is debited and various expense accounts are credited.
   d. the Petty Cash account is debited and various expense accounts are credited.

6. When the amount in the petty cash fund is increased,
   a. the Cash account is debited and the Petty Cash account is credited.
   b. various expense accounts are debited and the Cash account is credited.
   c. the Petty Cash account is debited and the Cash account is credited.
   d. no entry is needed as the fund has already been established.

7. When a change fund is established,
   a. the Cash account is debited and the Petty Cash account is credited.
   b. an expense account is debited and the Cash account is credited.
   c. the Change Fund account is debited and the Cash account is credited.
   d. the Cash account is debited and the Change Fund account is credited.

8. On a bank reconciliation, outstanding checks are
   a. deducted from the checkbook balance.
   b. added to the bank statement balance.
   c. added to the checkbook balance.
   d. deducted from the bank statement balance.

9. On a bank reconciliation, bank service charges are
   a. deducted from the checkbook balance.
   b. added to the bank statement balance.
   c. added to the checkbook balance.
   d. deducted from the bank statement balance.

10. On a bank reconciliation, deposits in transit are
    a. deducted from the checkbook balance.
    b. added to the bank statement balance.
    c. added to the checkbook balance.
    d. deducted from the bank statement balance.

11. On a bank reconciliation, collections made by the bank are
    a. deducted from the checkbook balance.
    b. added to the bank statement balance.
    c. added to the checkbook balance.
    d. deducted from the bank statement balance.

12. On a bank reconciliation, a NSF (Not Sufficient Funds) check is
    a. deducted from the checkbook balance.
    b. added to the bank statement balance.
    c. added to the checkbook balance.
    d. deducted from the bank statement balance.

Writing/Short Answer

1. **Reflect** Make a list, in words or simple phrases, of the most important and meaningful points in this chapter.

2. **Question** Think about the most confusing points or the material you do not understand in this chapter. Write down two or three questions that remain unanswered.

3. **Connect** Explain, in one or two sentences, the connection between the main points of this chapter and the major goals of the entire course.

4. **Summarize** Review this chapter's Joining the Pieces visual summary, and explain the concept(s) illustrated in a few sentences.

This page intentionally left blank.

Skills Review

Quick Practice

QUICK PRACTICE 6-1

General Journal Page 1

	Date		Account Title	P.R.	Debit	Credit	
1							1
2							2
3							3
4							4
5							5
6							6
7							7
8							8
9							9
10							10
11							11
12							12
13							13
14							14

QUICK PRACTICE 6-2

General Journal Page 1

	Date		Account Title	P.R.	Debit	Credit	
1							1
2							2
3							3
4							4
5							5
6							6
7							7

QUICK PRACTICE 6-3

General Journal

Page 1

	Date		Account Title	P.R.	Debit	Credit	
1							1
2							2
3							3
4							4
5							5
6							6
7							7
8							8
9							9
10							10
11							11
12							12
13							13
14							14

QUICK PRACTICE 6-4

General Journal

Page 5

	Date		Account Title	P.R.	Debit	Credit	
1							1
2							2
3							3
4							4
5							5
6							6
7							7
8							8
9							9
10							10
11							11
12							12
13							13
14							14
15							15
16							16
17							17
18							18

QUICK PRACTICE 6-5

ACCOUNT Cash Short and Over   ACCOUNT NO. 530

DATE		ITEM	P.R.	DEBIT	CREDIT	BALANCE	
						DEBIT	CREDIT

QUICK PRACTICE 6-6

QUICK PRACTICE 6-7

QUICK PRACTICE 6-8

General Journal   Page 1

	Date	Account Title	P.R.	Debit	Credit	
1						1
2						2
3						3
4						4
5						5
6						6
7						7
8						8

Exercises

EXERCISE 6-1

		Classified as Cash	
		Yes	**No**
(a)	Checks made payable to the business		
(b)	Money orders		
(c)	Postage stamps		
(d)	Savings bonds due to mature in 10 years		
(e)	Currency		
(f)	Cashier's check		
(g)	Coin		
(h)	Traveler's check		
(i)	Petty cash		
(j)	Change fund		
(k)	Amount on deposit in a bank checking account		

EXERCISE 6-2

General Journal   Page 1

	Date	Account Title	P.R.	Debit	Credit	
1						1
2						2
3						3
4						4
5						5
6						6
7						7
8						8
9						9
10						10

EXERCISE 6-3

General Journal

Page 1

	Date		Account Title	P.R.	Debit	Credit	
1							1
2							2
3							3
4							4
5							5
6							6
7							7
8							8
9							9
10							10

EXERCISE 6-4

General Journal

Page 1

	Date		Account Title	P.R.	Debit	Credit	
1							1
2							2
3							3
4							4
5							5
6							6
7							7
8							8
9							9
10							10
11							11
12							12
13							13
14							14
15							15
16							16
17							17
18							18

EXERCISE 6-5

General Journal

Page 1

	Date		Account Title	P.R.	Debit	Credit	
1							1
2							2
3							3
4							4
5							5
6							6
7							7
8							8
9							9
10							10

EXERCISE 6-6

General Journal

Page 1

	Date		Account Title	P.R.	Debit	Credit	
1							1
2							2
3							3
4							4
5							5
6							6
7							7
8							8
9							9
10							10
11							11
12							12
13							13
14							14
15							15
16							16
17							17
18							18

EXERCISE 6-7

1. _____
2. _____
3. _____
4. _____
5. _____
6. _____

EXERCISE 6-8

_____							
_____							
_____							

EXERCISE 6-9

EXERCISE 6-10

General Journal

Page 1

	Date	Account Title	P.R.	Debit	Credit	
1						1
2						2
3						3
4						4
5						5
6						6
7						7
8						8
9						9
10						10

This page intentionally left blank.

Case Problems

a. _____

b. _____

c. _____

d. _____

e. _____

f. _____

g. _____

h. _____

This page intentionally left blank.

PROBLEM 6-2A OR 6-2B

1. <div align="center">**General Journal**</div> Page 1

	Date		Account Title	P.R.	Debit	Credit	
1							1
2							2
3							3
4							4
5							5
6							6
7							7
8							8
9							9
10							10
11							11
12							12
13							13
14							14
15							15
16							16
17							17
18							18
19							19
20							20
21							21
22							22
23							23
24							24
25							25
26							26
27							27
28							28
29							29
30							30
31							31
32							32

This page intentionally left blank.

PROBLEM 6-3A OR 6-3B

1., 4.   **General Journal**   Page 1

	Date	Account Title	P.R.	Debit	Credit	
1						1
2						2
3						3
4						4
5						5
6						6
7						7
8						8
9						9
10						10
11						11
12						12

2., 3.

Petty Cash Payments for Month of _____, 20X___

Page 1

Day	Description	Vou. No.	Total Amount	Distribution of Charges				
				Office Supp. Exp.	Misc. Exp.	Postage Exp.	Other Accounts	Amount

PROBLEM 6-4A OR 6-4B

1.

2.   **General Journal**   Page 1

	Date		Account Title	P.R.	Debit	Credit	
1							1
2							2
3							3
4							4
5							5
6							6
7							7
8							8
9							9
10							10

Critical Thinking Problems

Challenge Problem

1.

Challenge Problem (continued)

2.

                                                    General Journal   Page 1

	Date		Account Title	P.R.	Debit	Credit	
1							1
2							2
3							3
4							4
5							5
6							6
7							7
8							8
9							9
10							10
11							11
12							12
13							13
14							14

Communications

_____
_____
_____
_____
_____
_____
_____
_____
_____
_____
_____
_____
_____
_____
_____
_____
_____

Team Internet Project

_____
_____
_____
_____
_____
_____
_____
_____
_____
_____
_____
_____
_____
_____
_____

Ethics

_____

_____

_____

_____

_____

_____

_____

_____

_____

_____

_____

_____

_____

_____

_____

_____

In the Real World

_____

_____

_____

_____

_____

_____

_____

_____

_____

_____

_____

_____

_____

_____

_____

Practice Test Answers

True/False

1. T
2. T
3. F
4. T
5. T
6. T
7. T
8. T
9. F
10. F
11. T
12. T
13. T
14. F
15. T
16. T
17. F
18. F

Matching

1. q
2. c
3. n
4. b
5. p
6. l
7. f
8. s
9. j
10. k
11. o
12. e
13. r
14. t
15. g
16. m
17. a
18. d
19. h
20. i

Fill in the Blanks

1. internal control
2. Sarbanes-Oxley
3. petty cash
4. Petty Cash account
5. petty cash voucher
6. replenish
7. Cash
8. auxiliary
9. change
10. debit, credit
11. checkbook
12. added, bank statement
13. deducted, bank statement
14. deducted, checkbook
15. checkbook

Multiple Choice

1. b
2. d
3. a
4. c
5. b
6. c
7. c
8. d
9. a
10. b
11. c
12. a

Writing/Short Answer

Answers will vary. Please discuss questions with your instructor.

The Combined Journal

Summary  Interactive Summary in English and Spanish

All transactions that involve increases and decreases in cash can be recorded in a two-column general journal. However, the use of a two-column journal is very time-consuming when the volume of transactions is large. Therefore, businesses look for a more efficient way to record business transactions. The **combined journal**—also referred to as a combination journal—is a multicolumn journal that is designed to save journalizing and posting time. The combined journal has several special columns for recording transactions that occur often and two general columns for recording transactions that occur less often. Because it is not necessary to write account titles when recording transactions in special columns, the combined journal saves journalizing time. Special columns are posted by totals, not item by item, thereby saving posting time.

Column totals are checked each month to make sure that the debits and credits are equal. One way to check the equality of debits and credits is the zero proof test, which is done with a calculator by entering debit amounts using the plus key, and entering credit amounts using the minus key. Passing the **zero proof test** means that equal columns have a zero difference.

The combined journal is mainly used by small businesses whose accounting system is not computerized or is only partially computerized.

True/False

Please circle the correct answer.

T   F   1. The combined journal is designed to save both journalizing and posting time.

T   F   2. When a combined journal is used, entries should also be recorded in the general journal.

T   F   3. The use of a combined journal makes it easier and faster to journalize and post.

T   F   4. It is not necessary for debits to equal credits when using a combined journal.

T   F   5. Special columns in a combined journal are posted by totals.

T   F   6. The combined journal is used mainly by small businesses that do not have a computerized accounting system.

Matching

Please match each of the following terms with its definition.

a. combination journal
b. combined journal
c. general columns
d. posted individually

e. posted monthly
f. special columns
g. zero proof test

_____   1. A multicolumn journal used by small businesses to save journalizing and posting time.

_____   2. A test performed by adding all debit balances and subtracting all credit balances—debits equal credits when the total is zero.

_____   3. Columns in a combined journal for recording transactions that occur often.

_____   4. Another name for the combined journal.

_____   5. Totals of special columns.

_____   6. Two columns for recording transactions that occur less often.

_____   7. Entries in the general columns.

Fill in the Blanks

Please complete each sentence with the correct word or words.

1. The _____ journal is a multicolumn journal used to save journalizing and posting time.

2. A combined journal is also called a(n) _____ journal.

3. Posting of special columns of a combined journal is done by _____.

4. The _____ columns of a combined journal are used to record transactions that occur less often.

5. The combined journal is used mainly by _____.

Multiple Choice

Please circle the correct answer.

1. The combined journal is used by small businesses
   a. as a second journal in which to record transactions before posting.
   b. to save journalizing and posting time.
   c. instead of a ledger.
   d. because there is no need to post when the combined journal is used.

2. The combined journal is used mostly by
   a. businesses with several bookkeepers.
   b. businesses with highly computerized accounting systems.
   c. small businesses without computerized accounting systems.
   d. small businesses with computerized accounting systems.

3. The combined journal has special columns for
   a. every account in the ledger.
   b. accounts that are used infrequently.
   c. accounts such as the Cash account that are used often.
   d. only the Cash account.

4. The equality of debits and credits in the combined journal can be found by
   a. preparing a trial balance.
   b. adding the totals of all debit columns and comparing them with the totals of all credit columns.
   c. posting and determining the account balances.
   d. None of the above. Debits do not equal credits when a combined journal is used.

5. Posting is done from the combined journal by
   a. posting the totals of the special columns and posting items from the general columns individually.
   b. posting each item individually.
   c. posting only the items in the general columns.
   d. None of the above. It is not necessary to post from the combined journal.

6. The general columns of a combined journal are for recording
   a. transactions that occur frequently.
   b. cash transactions.
   c. major purchases of assets on credit.
   d. transactions that occur less frequently.

7. The zero proof test is
   a. another name for the combined journal.
   b. certifying that there are zero errors in the ledger.
   c. a test performed using the plus and minus keys on a calculator to prove that there is a zero difference between total debits and total credits.
   d. another name for the trial balance.

This page intentionally left blank.

Skills Review

Exercises

EXERCISE A-1

	Posted by Total	Posted Individually
(a) Cash Debit column		
(b) Cash Credit column		
(c) General Debit column		
(d) General Credit column		
(e) Accounts Payable Debit column		
(f) Accounts Payable Credit column		
(g) Fees Earned Credit column		
(h) Salaries Expense Debit column		

EXERCISE A-2

ACCOUNT Cash   ACCOUNT NO. 111

DATE	ITEM	P.R.	DEBIT	CREDIT	BALANCE DEBIT	BALANCE CREDIT

EXERCISE A-3

This page intentionally left blank.

This page intentionally left blank.

Case Problems

PROBLEM A-1

1., 2.

Combined Journal for Month of July, 20X2

Cash		Ck. No.	Day	Description	P.R.	General	
Debit	Credit					Debit	Credit

Accounts Payable		Fees Earned	Salaries Expense
Debit	Credit	Credit	Debit

This page intentionally left blank.

This page intentionally left blank.

PROBLEM A-2

1., 2.   **Combined Journal for Month of July, 20X2**

Cash Debit	Cash Credit	Ck. No.	Day	Description	P.R.	General Debit	General Credit

Accounts Payable				Fees Earned		Salaries Expense	
Debit		Credit		Credit		Debit	

This page intentionally left blank.

This page intentionally left blank.

PROBLEM A-3

2., 3.   **Combined Journal for Month of June, 20X1**

Cash		Ck. No.	Day	Description	P.R.	General	
Debit	Credit					Debit	Credit

Accounts Payable		Fees Earned Credit	Salaries Expense Debit
Debit	Credit		

PROBLEM A-3 (continued)

1., 3.

ACCOUNT Cash   ACCOUNT NO. 111

DATE	ITEM	P.R.	DEBIT	CREDIT	BALANCE	
					DEBIT	CREDIT

ACCOUNT Office Supplies   ACCOUNT NO. 114

DATE	ITEM	P.R.	DEBIT	CREDIT	BALANCE	
					DEBIT	CREDIT

ACCOUNT Advertising Supplies   ACCOUNT NO. 115

DATE	ITEM	P.R.	DEBIT	CREDIT	BALANCE	
					DEBIT	CREDIT

ACCOUNT Office Equipment   ACCOUNT NO. 125

DATE	ITEM	P.R.	DEBIT	CREDIT	BALANCE	
					DEBIT	CREDIT

ACCOUNT Accounts Payable   ACCOUNT NO. 211

DATE	ITEM	P.R.	DEBIT	CREDIT	BALANCE	
					DEBIT	CREDIT

PROBLEM A-3 (continued)

ACCOUNT Notes Payable   ACCOUNT NO. 215

DATE	ITEM	P.R.	DEBIT	CREDIT	BALANCE DEBIT	CREDIT

ACCOUNT Melinda Platt, Capital   ACCOUNT NO. 311

DATE	ITEM	P.R.	DEBIT	CREDIT	BALANCE DEBIT	CREDIT

ACCOUNT Melinda Platt, Drawing   ACCOUNT NO. 312

DATE	ITEM	P.R.	DEBIT	CREDIT	BALANCE DEBIT	CREDIT

ACCOUNT Fees Earned   ACCOUNT NO. 411

DATE	ITEM	P.R.	DEBIT	CREDIT	BALANCE DEBIT	CREDIT

ACCOUNT Rent Expense   ACCOUNT NO. 511

DATE	ITEM	P.R.	DEBIT	CREDIT	BALANCE DEBIT	CREDIT

PROBLEM A-3 (continued)

ACCOUNT **Salaries Expense**   ACCOUNT NO. 512

DATE		ITEM	P.R.	DEBIT	CREDIT	BALANCE	
						DEBIT	CREDIT

ACCOUNT **Repairs Expense**   ACCOUNT NO. 513

DATE		ITEM	P.R.	DEBIT	CREDIT	BALANCE	
						DEBIT	CREDIT

ACCOUNT **Utilities**   ACCOUNT NO. 514

DATE		ITEM	P.R.	DEBIT	CREDIT	BALANCE	
						DEBIT	CREDIT

ACCOUNT **Miscellaneous Expense**   ACCOUNT NO. 518

DATE		ITEM	P.R.	DEBIT	CREDIT	BALANCE	
						DEBIT	CREDIT

PROBLEM A-3 (continued)

4.

ACCOUNT TITLE	DEBIT	CREDIT

This page intentionally left blank.

This page intentionally left blank.

1., 2.   **Combined Journal for Month of July, 20X2**

Cash		Ck. No.	Day	Description	P.R.	General	
Debit	Credit					Debit	Credit

Accounts Payable		Fees Earned	Salaries Expense
Debit	Credit	Credit	Debit

1., 3.

ACCOUNT Cash   ACCOUNT NO. 111

DATE	ITEM	P.R.	DEBIT	CREDIT	BALANCE	
					DEBIT	CREDIT

ACCOUNT Office Supplies   ACCOUNT NO. 114

DATE	ITEM	P.R.	DEBIT	CREDIT	BALANCE	
					DEBIT	CREDIT

ACCOUNT Advertising Supplies   ACCOUNT NO. 115

DATE	ITEM	P.R.	DEBIT	CREDIT	BALANCE	
					DEBIT	CREDIT

ACCOUNT Office Equipment   ACCOUNT NO. 125

DATE	ITEM	P.R.	DEBIT	CREDIT	BALANCE	
					DEBIT	CREDIT

ACCOUNT Accounts Payables   ACCOUNT NO. 211

DATE	ITEM	P.R.	DEBIT	CREDIT	BALANCE	
					DEBIT	CREDIT

PROBLEM A-4 (continued)

ACCOUNT Notes Payable   ACCOUNT NO. 215

DATE	ITEM	P.R.	DEBIT	CREDIT	BALANCE DEBIT	BALANCE CREDIT

ACCOUNT Holly Hutchins, Capital   ACCOUNT NO. 311

DATE	ITEM	P.R.	DEBIT	CREDIT	BALANCE DEBIT	BALANCE CREDIT

ACCOUNT Holly Hutchins, Drawing   ACCOUNT NO. 312

DATE	ITEM	P.R.	DEBIT	CREDIT	BALANCE DEBIT	BALANCE CREDIT

ACCOUNT Fees Earned   ACCOUNT NO. 411

DATE	ITEM	P.R.	DEBIT	CREDIT	BALANCE DEBIT	BALANCE CREDIT

ACCOUNT Rent Expense   ACCOUNT NO. 511

DATE	ITEM	P.R.	DEBIT	CREDIT	BALANCE DEBIT	BALANCE CREDIT

PROBLEM A-4 (continued)

ACCOUNT Salaries Expense   ACCOUNT NO. 512

DATE		ITEM	P.R.	DEBIT	CREDIT	BALANCE	
						DEBIT	CREDIT

ACCOUNT Repairs Expense   ACCOUNT NO. 513

DATE		ITEM	P.R.	DEBIT	CREDIT	BALANCE	
						DEBIT	CREDIT

ACCOUNT Utilities Expense   ACCOUNT NO. 514

DATE		ITEM	P.R.	DEBIT	CREDIT	BALANCE	
						DEBIT	CREDIT

ACCOUNT Miscellaneous Expense   ACCOUNT NO. 518

DATE		ITEM	P.R.	DEBIT	CREDIT	BALANCE	
						DEBIT	CREDIT

PROBLEM A-4 (continued)

4.

This page intentionally left blank.

Practice Test Answers

True/False

1. T
2. F
3. T
4. F
5. T
6. T

Matching

1. b
2. g
3. f
4. a
5. e
6. c
7. d

Fill in the Blanks

1. combined
2. combination
3. totals
4. general
5. small businesses

Multiple Choice

1. b
2. c
3. c
4. b
5. a
6. d
7. c

B

The Voucher System

Summary Interactive Summary in English and Spanish

In Chapter 6, we learned that cash control is part of a company's overall system of internal control. To help control cash, some companies use the **voucher system**, which is a set of steps and procedures for authorizing, recording, and making cash payments. With a voucher system, no purchase of a good or service and no payment of a liability may happen without authorization.

No cash payment can be made without a properly prepared **voucher**, which is a form authorizing a purchase or a payment. Even routine payments such as rent and utilities cannot be made without an approved voucher. The amount of a voucher is credited to the **Vouchers Payable account**. The account debited will be either an asset account, an expense account, or a liability account. If a voucher is to be paid immediately, it is passed on for payment authorization. If payment will not be made until a future date, the voucher is kept in an **unpaid vouchers file**. For example, an $800 voucher prepared to authorize the payment of rent is recorded by debiting the Rent Expense account and crediting the Vouchers Payable account. The voucher is then passed on for payment authorization. When paid, the amount of the payment is debited to the Vouchers Payable account and credited to the Cash account, and the voucher is filed in a **paid vouchers file**.

True/False

Please circle the correct answer.

T F 1. The voucher system is designed to control cash payments.

T F 2. A voucher is a form used to authorize cash payments.

T F 3. Vouchers are not prepared for routine payments such as rent and utilities.

T F 4. The payment of an account payable would not require a voucher since the amount due is already in a liability account.

T F 5. Vouchers are recorded by debiting an asset, expense, or liability account and crediting the Vouchers Payable account.

Matching

Please match each of the following terms with its definition.

a. paid vouchers file   c. voucher   e. Vouchers Payable account
b. unpaid vouchers file   d. voucher system

_____ 1. A form authorizing a purchase or a payment.

_____ 2. A method of accounting for cash payments in which all payments are approved when a transaction occurs rather than when payment is actually made.

_____ 3. Credited when a voucher is prepared.

_____ 4. Where vouchers that will be paid at a future date are kept.

_____ 5. A file of vouchers that have been paid.

Fill in The Blanks

Please complete each sentence with the correct word or words.

1. A(n) _____ is a form authorizing a purchase or a payment.

2. The _____ account is credited when a voucher is prepared.

3. The _____ is a set of steps and procedures for authorizing, recording, and making cash payments.

4. Vouchers that will be paid at a future date are kept in a(n) _____ file.

5. The _____ account is credited when a voucher is paid.

6. The _____ account is debited when a voucher is paid.

Multiple Choice

Please circle the correct answer.

1. The voucher system
   a. is another name for internal control.
   b. is used only by small businesses.
   c. is designed to control cash payments.
   d. takes the place of the checking account.

2. The voucher is
   a. a form of check.
   b. prepared when correcting mistakes.
   c. a form authorizing a purchase or payment.
   d. prepared when cash registers are checked.

3. What account is credited when a voucher is prepared?
   a. Accounts Payable
   b. Vouchers Payable
   c. Cash
   d. Vouchers Expense

4. What account is debited when a voucher is paid?
   a. Accounts Payable
   b. Vouchers Payable
   c. Cash
   d. Vouchers Expense

5. What account is credited when a voucher is paid?
   a. Cash
   b. Vouchers Payable
   c. Accounts Payable
   d. Depends on the purpose of the payment

This page intentionally left blank.

342   PART II | Accounting for Cash and the Merchandising Business

Skills Review

Exercises

EXERCISE B-1

	Date		Account Title	P.R.	Debit	Credit	
1							1
2							2
3							3
4							4
5							5
6							6
7							7
8							8
9							9

EXERCISE B-2

	Date		Account Title	P.R.	Debit	Credit	
1							1
2							2
3							3
4							4

	Date		Account Title	P.R.	Debit	Credit	
1							1
2							2
3							3
4							4

Case Problems

PROBLEM B-1

General Journal

Page 1

	Date		Account Title	P.R.	Debit	Credit	
1							1
2							2
3							3
4							4
5							5
6							6
7							7
8							8
9							9
10							10
11							11
12							12
13							13
14							14
15							15
16							16
17							17
18							18
19							19
20							20
21							21
22							22
23							23
24							24
25							25
26							26
27							27
28							28
29							29
30							30
31							31
32							32
33							33
34							34

PROBLEM B-1 (continued)

General Journal

	Date		Account Title	P.R.	Debit	Credit	
1							1
2							2
3							3
4							4
5							5
6							6
7							7
8							8
9							9
10							10
11							11
12							12
13							13
14							14
15							15
16							16
17							17

This page intentionally left blank.

PROBLEM B-2

	Date	Account Title	P.R.	Debit	Credit	
1						1
2						2
3						3
4						4
5						5
6						6
7						7
8						8
9						9
10						10
11						11
12						12
13						13
14						14
15						15
16						16
17						17
18						18
19						19
20						20
21						21
22						22
23						23
24						24
25						25
26						26
27						27
28						28
29						29
30						30
31						31
32						32
33						33
34						34
35						35

PROBLEM B-2 (continued)

General Journal

	Date		Account Title	P.R.	Debit	Credit	
1							1
2							2
3							3
4							4
5							5
6							6
7							7
8							8
9							9
10							10
11							11
12							12
13							13
14							14
15							15
16							16
17							17
18							18
19							19
20							20
21							21
22							22
23							23
24							24
25							25
26							26
27							27
28							28
29							29
30							30
31							31
32							32
33							33
34							34
35							35

Practice Test Answers

True/False

1. T
2. T
3. F
4. F
5. T

Matching

1. c
2. d
3. e
4. b
5. a

Fill in the Blanks

1. voucher
2. Vouchers Payable
3. voucher system
4. unpaid vouchers
5. Cash
6. Vouchers Payable

Multiple Choice

1. c
2. c
3. b
4. b
5. a

Accounting for a Merchandising Business

Purchases and Cash Payments

Chapter Summary  Interactive Summary in English and Spanish

A **merchandising business** is a business that buys and resells goods. Goods held for sale to customers are called **merchandise**, also referred to as merchandise inventory and stock in trade.

Merchandising activity occurs at both the retail level and the wholesale level. At the retail level, merchandisers sell directly to the consuming public. At the wholesale level, merchandise is purchased in bulk from a manufacturer or other **wholesaler** and is sold primarily to a **retail business**.

The purchase of merchandise requires specific procedures and forms for proper control. In a small merchandising business, purchasing is usually done by the store manager or the owner. In a large merchandising business, purchasing begins with the preparation of a **purchase requisition** by a department in the organization. The purchasing department, on receipt of a properly prepared requisition, prepares a **purchase order**, which is sent to a supplier. When the ordered goods are received, a **receiving report** is prepared to verify that all the goods arrived and were accepted.

An **invoice** is a form prepared by the seller to describe the goods and the terms of the sale. A copy of the invoice is sent to the purchaser. Thus, the same document is both a **sales invoice** and a **purchase invoice**. It is the source document for recording the sale on the books of the seller and the purchase on the books of the buyer.

Sellers often offer buyers discounts on goods purchased. The **trade discount** and **cash discount** are two types of discounts. A trade discount is a reduction from the **list price** of goods, such as offering goods at $600 less a 10% discount. This practice allows sellers to vary the price of the merchandise without having to print new catalogs. Trade discounts are not recorded on the books of the seller or the buyer.

Cash discounts include the sales discount and purchases discount. A **sales discount** is a discount offered by the seller to encourage prompt payment from a buyer. The most common form of cash discount is 2/10,n/30 (two ten, net thirty), which means that if a buyer makes payment for a credit purchase within 10 days from the date of the invoice, a 2% discount can be taken. The buyer records the amount of the **purchases discount** on merchandise in the **Purchases Discounts account**.

The cost of merchandise purchased is debited to a temporary owner's equity account entitled Purchases. The **Purchases account** is a **cost account** used only for recording the cost of merchandise purchased for resale to customers. It is one of several cost accounts.

All purchases can be recorded in the general journal. When the volume of purchases is large, however, it is more efficient to use a **purchases journal**. A purchases journal is a **special journal** that is designed to meet the needs of the business using it. In this chapter, we worked with a purchases journal that was designed to record only credit purchases of merchandise. It has one money column, entitled Purchases Debit, Accounts Payable Credit.

The Accounts Payable account is a liability account that shows amounts owed to the creditors of a business. However, the Accounts Payable account does not show information regarding the balances owed to individual creditors. Therefore, it is a common practice to set up accounts for creditors in a separate ledger. A separate ledger containing only one type of account is called a **subsidiary ledger**. A subsidiary ledger containing only creditors' accounts is called an **accounts payable ledger**.

Accounts in the accounts payable ledger are arranged in alphabetical order to make it easier to add new accounts and remove old accounts. Accounts in the **general ledger**, or main ledger, are numbered in the standard way.

The balances of creditors' accounts, when fully posted, should equal the balance of the Accounts Payable account. Thus, the Accounts Payable account is said to *control* or summarize the accounts payable ledger. A **controlling account** is an account in the general ledger that summarizes the balances of accounts in a related subsidiary ledger.

There are two types of postings from the purchases journal: (1) posting of individual credits to creditors' accounts on a daily basis and (2) monthly posting of the total of the money column as a debit to Purchases and as a credit to Accounts Payable.

In merchandising businesses, **Purchases returns and allowances** often occur. A return of merchandise results when a buyer sends back part, or all, of a purchase to the seller. An allowance results when the buyer keeps the goods purchased but asks for a price reduction due to some factor, such as damage to the goods while in shipment. Source documents for returns and allowances are the **debit memorandum**, prepared by the buyer, and the **credit memorandum**, prepared by the seller.

The buyer records returns and allowances involving merchandise in a contra purchases account entitled Purchases Returns and Allowances. Since the **Purchases Returns and Allowances account** is contra to the Purchases account, it will have a credit balance that is opposite to the debit balance of the Purchases account.

Cash payments can be recorded in the general journal. However, a more efficient use of journalizing and posting time is to record them in another special journal, the **cash payments journal**. The cash payments journal is used to record all types of cash payments.

Because the cash payments journal is designed to record decreases in the Cash account, a Cash Credit column must be used. The number of other special columns and their titles are determined by the needs of the business. Posting the cash payments journal follows the same procedures as those for posting the purchases journal: There is daily posting to the accounts payable ledger and monthly posting to the general ledger.

The posting accuracy of a subsidiary ledger is proved by preparing a schedule. A **schedule of accounts payable** is a listing of the balances of the creditors' accounts. The total of this schedule should agree with the balance of the Accounts Payable controlling account in the general ledger.

Purchases carry freight terms. The **Freight In account** is used to record the freight costs on incoming merchandise. FOB destination and FOB shipping point are common freight terms. **FOB (free on board) destination** means that the seller is responsible for all freight costs while the goods are in transit. **FOB (free on board) shipping point** means that the buyer is responsible for all freight costs while the goods are in transit.

True/False

Please circle the correct answer.

T   F   1. A merchandising business buys merchandise for resale to its customers.

T   F   2. Office desks are merchandise inventory to a dealer in office furniture but are equipment to a business that is using them in the office.

T   F   3. A purchase requisition is a form sent to a supplier by the business making the purchase.

T   F   4. An invoice is a bill.

T   F   5. A trade discount is given by a seller of merchandise to encourage prompt payment of the invoice.

T   F   6. Trade discounts are not recorded in the accounting records by either the buyer or the seller.

T   F   7. The Purchases account is a temporary owner's equity account.

T   F   8. All purchases made by a company for any purpose are debited to the Purchases account.

T   F   9. Cost accounts are used only to determine the cost of merchandise sold to customers.

T   F   10. The source document used to record a purchase in the accounting records is usually the purchase order.

T   F   11. The purchases journal is used to record only purchases of merchandise for cash.

T   F   12. A separate ledger containing only one type of account is called a subsidiary ledger.

T   F   13. Management usually does not wish to maintain a separate account for purchases returns and allowances.

T   F   14. Items from special journals are usually posted to the subsidiary ledger daily and to the general ledger at the end of the month.

T   F   15. The schedule of accounts payable is prepared to see if the subsidiary ledger is in balance with the controlling account in the general ledger.

Matching

Please match each of the following terms with its definition.

a. cash discount
b. cash payments journal
c. controlling account
d. cost account
e. debit memorandum
f. FOB destination
g. FOB shipping point
h. Freight In
i. invoice
j. merchandise

k. Purchases account
l. Purchases Discounts account
m. purchases journal
n. purchase order
o. purchase requisition
p. Purchases Returns and Allowances account
q. receiving report
r. schedule of accounts payable
s. subsidiary ledger
t. trade discount

_____ 1. Goods held for sale to customers.

_____ 2. A percentage reduction in the list price of merchandise.

_____ 3. A form prepared by the purchasing department describing the goods ordered to the seller.

_____ 4. A business document that shows the names and addresses of the buyer and the seller, the date and terms of the sale, a description of the goods purchased, and the mode of transportation to ship the goods. It is a bill.

_____ 5. A form indicating what goods were received and in what quantity.

_____ 6. A discount offered to encourage prompt payment from buyers.

_____ 7. A written request for certain goods.

_____ 8. An account that is presented on the income statement and that is used to determine the cost of goods sold.

_____ 9. A ledger that contains only one type of account.

_____ 10. An account in the general ledger that summarizes accounts in the related subsidiary ledger.

_____ 11. A contra account that is used to record returns of merchandise and allowances received on merchandise.

_____ 12. A special journal used only to record credit purchases of merchandise.

_____ 13. A form issued by a buyer to the seller when merchandise is being returned.

_____ 14. The temporary owner's equity account used to record the cost of all merchandise purchased for resale to customers.

_____ 15. The shipping term that means the buyer is responsible for all freight costs while the goods are in transit.

_____ 16. The account used to record the shipping charges on incoming merchandise.

_____ 17. A listing of accounts and balances from the accounts payable ledger.

_____ 18. A special journal that is used to record only cash payments.

_____ 19. A contra account that a buyer uses to record discounts received for prompt payment of invoices.

_____ 20. The shipping term that means the seller is responsible for all freight costs until the goods reach the buyer.

Fill in the Blanks

Please complete each sentence with the correct word or words.

1. A(n) _____ is a business that sells directly to consumers, such as drugstores, grocery stores, and department stores; a(n) _____ is a business that buys in bulk from manufacturers.

2. Managers identify goods needed and request them by preparing a(n) _____.

3. When goods arrive, they are counted and checked against the purchase order and a(n) _____ is prepared.

4. To permit price changes without the necessity of printing new catalogs, many businesses offer a(n) _____.

5. When goods are purchased below list price, the buyer always records the purchase at actual _____.

6. A(n) _____ is given to encourage prompt payment of invoices.

7. The Purchases account is used to record purchases of _____.

8. If supplies are purchased for use in a firm's office, the account debited would be the _____ account.

9. The balances of all the accounts in the accounts payable ledger should equal the balance of the _____ account in the general ledger.

10. In the purchases journal, individual credits should be posted to the _____ accounts in the _____ ledger on a daily basis; the total of the money column should be posted as a(n) _____ to Purchases and a(n) _____ to Accounts Payable at the end of the month.

11. Purchases Returns and Allowances is a(n) _____ account to Purchases.

12. When a buyer returns merchandise to the seller, the buyer issues a(n) _____.

13. The seller will usually respond to a debit memorandum with a(n) _____.

14. When the seller must pay all shipping costs, the term used is _____.

15. _____ means that the buyer must pay all shipping costs.

Multiple Choice

Please circle the correct answer.

1. Which of the following would be considered merchandise?
   a. Company delivery truck
   b. Desks and fax machines in the office
   c. Items on the shelves in the store that are for sale to customers
   d. Supplies in the supply room

2. Which of the following is a step in the purchasing process?
   a. Preparing a purchase order
   b. Preparing a receiving report
   c. Recording an invoice in the journal
   d. All of the above

3. ABC Company purchases merchandise for $500, terms 2/10,n/30. The date of the invoice is May 1. Payment is made on May 9. What is the amount of the check prepared by the company?
   a. $500
   b. $490
   c. $400
   d. None of the above

4. When a company purchases merchandise on account,
   a. Purchases is debited and Accounts Payable is credited.
   b. Merchandise Inventory is debited and Accounts Payable is credited.
   c. Accounts Payable is debited and Purchases is credited.
   d. None of the above

5. On June 25, 20X9, Wendell Company purchased merchandise costing $8,000 at a 20% trade discount and credit terms of 2/10,n/30. If the invoice is paid by July 5, 20X9, the amount of payment will be
   a. $8,000.
   b. $6,400.
   c. $6,272.
   d. $1,600.

6. BGD Mens Clothing purchased a new electronic cash register. The cash register is recorded by debiting
   a. Purchases.
   b. Store Equipment.
   c. Store Supplies.
   d. Stock in Trade.

7. The purchases journal is designed to record
   a. purchases of merchandise for cash.
   b. purchases of merchandise for cash or on account.
   c. purchases of merchandise on account.
   d. purchases of any items for cash or on account.

8. Subsidiary ledgers and special journals are used in order to
   a. make it possible to divide the work between several persons in the accounting department.
   b. simplify the trial balance and balance sheet.
   c. streamline recording and posting of common transactions.
   d. All of the above

9. Which of the following best describes the difference between costs and expenses?
   a. Costs are associated with merchandise and cost of goods sold, while expenses are the costs of operating the company.
   b. Costs are the prices of the items purchased by the company, while expenses are bills that are paid for services.
   c. Costs are just another term for expenses.
   d. None of the above

10. Two contra accounts to Purchases are
    a. Freight In and Purchases Discounts.
    b. Purchases Discounts and Purchases Returns and Allowances.
    c. Purchases Returns and Allowances and Freight In.
    d. None of the above

Writing/Short Answer

1. **Reflect** Make a list, in words or simple phrases, of the most important and meaningful points in this chapter.

2. **Question** Think about the most confusing points or the material you do not understand in this chapter. Write down two or three questions that remain unanswered.

3. **Connect** Explain, in one or two sentences, the connection between the main points of this chapter and the major goals of the entire course.

4. **Summarize** Review this chapter's Joining the Pieces visual summary, and explain the concept(s) illustrated in a few sentences.

Skills Review

Quick Practice

QUICK PRACTICE 7-1

1. _____
2. _____
3. _____
4. _____

QUICK PRACTICE 7-2

(a) _____

(b) _____

(c) _____

(d) _____

QUICK PRACTICE 7-3

(a) _____

(b) _____

(c) _____

(d) _____

QUICK PRACTICE 7-4

1. _____

2. _____

QUICK PRACTICE 7-5

General Journal Page 1

	Date		Account Title	P.R.	Debit	Credit	
1							1
2							2
3							3
4							4
5							5
6							6

QUICK PRACTICE 7-6

General Journal

Page 1

	Date		Account Title	P.R.	Debit	Credit	
1							1
2							2
3							3
4							4
5							5
6							6
7							7
8							8
9							9
10							10
11							11
12							12
13							13
14							14
15							15
16							16
17							17
18							18

QUICK PRACTICE 7-7

General Journal

Page 1

	Date		Account Title	P.R.	Debit	Credit	
1							1
2							2
3							3
4							4
5							5
6							6

Purchases Journal

Page 4

	Date	Invoice No.	Account Credited	P.R.	Purchases Dr. Accts. Pay. Cr.	
1						1
2						2
3						3
4						4

QUICK PRACTICE 7-8

Page 1

	Date		Account Title	P.R.	Debit	Credit	
1							1
2							2
3							3
4							4
5							5
6							6
7							7
8							8
9							9
10							10
11							11
12							12
13							13
14							14
15							15
16							16
17							17
18							18
19							19
20							20
21							21
22							22
23							23
24							24
25							25
26							26
27							27
28							28
29							29
30							30
31							31
32							32

QUICK PRACTICE 7-9

General Journal Page 1

	Date		Account Title	P.R.	Debit	Credit	
1							1
2							2
3							3
4							4
5							5
6							6
7							7
8							8
9							9
10							10
11							11
12							12
13							13
14							14
15							15
16							16
17							17
18							18
19							19
20							20
21							21
22							22
23							23

QUICK PRACTICE 7-10

Cash Payments Journal Page 1

Date	Ck. No.	Account Debited	P.R.	General Dr.	Accounts Payable Dr.	Purchases Discounts Cr.	Cash Cr.

QUICK PRACTICE 7-11

General Journal   Page 1

	Date	Account Title	P.R.	Debit	Credit	
1						1
2						2
3						3
4						4
5						5
6						6
7						7
8						8
9						9
10						10
11						11
12						12
13						13
14						14
15						15

QUICK PRACTICE 7-12

	Purchases Journal	General Journal	Cash Payments Journal
(a) Purchased store supplies on account			
(b) Purchased merchandise on account			
(c) Purchased merchandise for cash			
(d) Purchased store equipment on account			
(e) Returned store supplies purchased on account			
(f) Returned merchandise purchased for cash			
(g) Returned merchandise purchased on account			

Exercises

EXERCISE 7-1

(a) _____   (d) _____

(b) _____   (e) _____

(c) _____

EXERCISE 7-2

(a) _____   (d) _____

(b) _____   (e) _____

(c) _____

EXERCISE 7-3

General Journal   Page 1

	Date		Account Title	P.R.	Debit	Credit	
1							1
2							2
3							3
4							4
5							5
6							6
7							7
8							8
9							9
10							10
11							11
12							12
13							13
14							14
15							15
16							16
17							17
18							18
19							19
20							20
21							21
22							22
23							23
24							24
25							25
26							26
27							27
28							28
29							29

EXERCISE 7-4

General Journal

Page 1

	Date		Account Title	P.R.	Debit	Credit	
1							1
2							2
3							3
4							4
5							5
6							6
7							7
8							8
9							9
10							10
11							11
12							12
13							13
14							14
15							15
16							16
17							17
18							18

Purchases Journal

Page 1

	Date	Invoice No.	Account Credited	P.R.	Purchases Dr. Accts. Pay. Cr.	
1						1
2						2
3						3
4						4
5						5
6						6
7						7
8						8
9						9
10						10
11						11
12						12

EXERCISE 7-5

Page 1

	Date		Account Title	P.R.	Debit	Credit	
1							1
2							2
3							3
4							4
5							5
6							6
7							7
8							8
9							9
10							10
11							11
12							12
13							13
14							14
15							15
16							16
17							17
18							18
19							19
20							20
21							21
22							22
23							23
24							24
25							25
26							26
27							27
28							28
29							29
30							30
31							31
32							32
33							33
34							34

EXERCISE 7-5 (continued)

General Journal

Page 2

	Date		Account Title	P.R.	Debit	Credit	
1							1
2							2
3							3
4							4
5							5
6							6

EXERCISE 7-6

General Journal

Page 1

	Date		Account Title	P.R.	Debit	Credit	
1							1
2							2
3							3
4							4
5							5
6							6
7							7
8							8
9							9
10							10
11							11
12							12
13							13
14							14
15							15
16							16
17							17
18							18
19							19
20							20
21							21

EXERCISE 7-6 (continued)

General Journal

Page 2

	Date		Account Title	P.R.	Debit	Credit	
1							1
2							2
3							3
4							4
5							5
6							6
7							7
8							8
9							9
10							10
11							11
12							12
13							13

EXERCISE 7-7

Cash Payments Journal

Page 1

Date	Ck. No.	Account Debited	P.R.	General Dr.	Accounts Payable Dr.	Purchases Discounts Cr.	Cash Cr.

EXERCISE 7-8

General Journal   Page 1

	Date		Account Title	P.R.	Debit	Credit	
1							1
2							2
3							3
4							4
5							5
6							6
7							7
8							8

EXERCISE 7-9

General Journal   Page 1

	Date		Account Title	P.R.	Debit	Credit	
1							1
2							2
3							3
4							4
5							5
6							6
7							7
8							8
9							9
10							10
11							11
12							12
13							13
14							14
15							15

This page intentionally left blank.

Case Problems

PROBLEM 7-1A OR 7-1B

General Journal

Page 1

	Date		Account Title	P.R.	Debit	Credit	
1							1
2							2
3							3
4							4
5							5
6							6
7							7
8							8
9							9
10							10
11							11
12							12
13							13
14							14
15							15
16							16
17							17
18							18
19							19
20							20
21							21
22							22
23							23
24							24
25							25
26							26
27							27
28							28
29							29
30							30
31							31
32							32

PROBLEM 7-1A OR 7-1B (continued)

* FOR 7-1B ONLY

General Journal

Page 2

	Date	Account Title	P.R.	Debit	Credit	
1						1
2						2
3						3
4						4
5						5
6						6
7						7

Purchases Journal

Page 1

	Date	Invoice No.	Account Credited	P.R.	Purchases Dr. Accts. Pay. Cr.	
1						1
2						2
3						3
4						4
5						5
6						6

PROBLEM 7-2A OR 7-2B

3., 4.

General Journal

Page 1

	Date		Account Title	P.R.	Debit	Credit	
1							1
2							2
3							3
4							4
5							5
6							6
7							7
8							8
9							9
10							10
11							11
12							12
13							13
14							14
15							15
16							16
17							17
18							18
19							19
20							20
21							21
22							22
23							23
24							24

General Journal

Page 2

	Date	Account Title	P.R.	Debit	Credit	
1						1
2						2
3						3
4						4
5						5
6						6
7						7
8						8
9						9
10						10
11						11

Purchases Journal

Page 1

	Date	Invoice No.	Account Credited	P.R.	Purchases Dr. Accts. Pay. Cr.	
1						1
2						2
3						3
4						4
5						5
6						6
7						7
8						8
9						9
10						10

1., 4.

General Ledger

ACCOUNT Store Supplies   ACCOUNT NO. 113

DATE	ITEM	P.R.	DEBIT	CREDIT	BALANCE	
					DEBIT	CREDIT

PROBLEM 7-2A OR 7-2B (continued)

ACCOUNT Office Supplies   ACCOUNT NO. 114

DATE		ITEM	P.R.	DEBIT	CREDIT	BALANCE	
						DEBIT	CREDIT

ACCOUNT Office Equipment   ACCOUNT NO. 121

DATE		ITEM	P.R.	DEBIT	CREDIT	BALANCE	
						DEBIT	CREDIT

ACCOUNT Accounts Payable   ACCOUNT NO. 211

DATE		ITEM	P.R.	DEBIT	CREDIT	BALANCE	
						DEBIT	CREDIT

ACCOUNT Purchases   ACCOUNT NO. 511

DATE		ITEM	P.R.	DEBIT	CREDIT	BALANCE	
						DEBIT	CREDIT

ACCOUNT Purchases Returns and Allowances   ACCOUNT NO. 511.1

DATE	ITEM	P.R.	DEBIT	CREDIT	BALANCE DEBIT	BALANCE CREDIT

2., 3.

Accounts Payable Ledger

NAME

ADDRESS

Date	Item	P.R.	Debit	Credit	Balance

NAME

ADDRESS

Date	Item	P.R.	Debit	Credit	Balance

NAME

ADDRESS

Date	Item	P.R.	Debit	Credit	Balance

PROBLEM 7-2A OR 7-2B (continued)

NAME

ADDRESS

Date		Item	P.R.	Debit	Credit	Balance

NAME

ADDRESS

Date		Item	P.R.	Debit	Credit	Balance

NAME

ADDRESS

Date		Item	P.R.	Debit	Credit	Balance

5.

6. The balance of the Accounts Payable controlling account: _____

PROBLEM 7-3A OR 7-3B

3., 4.

General Journal Page 1

	Date	Account Title	P.R.	Debit	Credit	
1						1
2						2
3						3
4						4
5						5
6						6
7						7
8						8
9						9
10						10
11						11

Purchases Journal Page 1

Date	Account Credited	Inv No.	Post. Ref.	Accounts Payable Credit	Freight In Debit	Purchases Debit

1., 4.   **General Ledger**

ACCOUNT Office Equipment   ACCOUNT NO. 118

DATE	ITEM	P.R.	DEBIT	CREDIT	BALANCE DEBIT	BALANCE CREDIT

ACCOUNT Store Equipment   ACCOUNT NO. 119

DATE	ITEM	P.R.	DEBIT	CREDIT	BALANCE DEBIT	BALANCE CREDIT

ACCOUNT Accounts Payable   ACCOUNT NO. 211

DATE	ITEM	P.R.	DEBIT	CREDIT	BALANCE DEBIT	BALANCE CREDIT

ACCOUNT Purchases   ACCOUNT NO. 511

DATE	ITEM	P.R.	DEBIT	CREDIT	BALANCE DEBIT	BALANCE CREDIT

PROBLEM 7-3A OR 7-3B (continued)

ACCOUNT Freight In   ACCOUNT NO. 512

DATE		ITEM	P.R.	DEBIT	CREDIT	BALANCE	
						DEBIT	CREDIT

2., 3.   **Accounts Payable Ledger**

NAME

ADDRESS

Date		Item	P.R.	Debit	Credit	Balance	

NAME

ADDRESS

Date		Item	P.R.	Debit	Credit	Balance	

NAME

ADDRESS

Date		Item	P.R.	Debit	Credit	Balance	

PROBLEM 7-3A OR 7-3B (continued)

NAME

ADDRESS

Date		Item	P.R.	Debit	Credit	Balance

NAME

ADDRESS

Date		Item	P.R.	Debit	Credit	Balance

NAME

ADDRESS

Date		Item	P.R.	Debit	Credit	Balance

* FOR 7-3B ONLY

NAME

ADDRESS

Date		Item	P.R.	Debit	Credit	Balance

5.

The balance of the Accounts Payable controlling account: _____

This page intentionally left blank.

PROBLEM 7-4A OR 7-4B

3., 4.   **General Journal**   Page 1

	Date	Account Title	P.R.	Debit	Credit	
1						1
2						2
3						3
4						4
5						5
6						6
7						7
8						8
9						9
10						10
11						11

Purchases Journal   Page 1

	Date	Invoice No.	Account Credited	P.R.	Purchases Dr. Accts. Pay. Cr.	
1						1
2						2
3						3
4						4
5						5
6						6

Cash Payments Journal

Date	Ck. No.	Account Debited	P.R.	General Dr.	Accounts Payable Dr.	Purchases Discounts Cr.	Cash Cr.

1., 4.

General Ledger

ACCOUNT Cash

ACCOUNT NO. 111

DATE	ITEM	P.R.	DEBIT	CREDIT	BALANCE DEBIT	BALANCE CREDIT

ACCOUNT Office Supplies

ACCOUNT NO. 112

DATE	ITEM	P.R.	DEBIT	CREDIT	BALANCE DEBIT	BALANCE CREDIT

PROBLEM 7-4A OR 7-4B (continued)

ACCOUNT Prepaid Insurance   ACCOUNT NO. 113

DATE	ITEM	P.R.	DEBIT	CREDIT	BALANCE DEBIT	BALANCE CREDIT

ACCOUNT Store Equipment   ACCOUNT NO. 116

DATE	ITEM	P.R.	DEBIT	CREDIT	BALANCE DEBIT	BALANCE CREDIT

ACCOUNT Accounts Payable   ACCOUNT NO. 211

DATE	ITEM	P.R.	DEBIT	CREDIT	BALANCE DEBIT	BALANCE CREDIT

ACCOUNT _____, Drawing   ACCOUNT NO. 312

DATE	ITEM	P.R.	DEBIT	CREDIT	BALANCE DEBIT	BALANCE CREDIT

PROBLEM 7-4A OR 7-4B (continued)

ACCOUNT Purchases   ACCOUNT NO. 511

DATE	ITEM	P.R.	DEBIT	CREDIT	BALANCE DEBIT	BALANCE CREDIT

ACCOUNT Purchases Discounts   ACCOUNT NO. 511.2

DATE	ITEM	P.R.	DEBIT	CREDIT	BALANCE DEBIT	BALANCE CREDIT

ACCOUNT Freight In   ACCOUNT NO. 512

DATE	ITEM	P.R.	DEBIT	CREDIT	BALANCE DEBIT	BALANCE CREDIT

ACCOUNT Salaries Expense   ACCOUNT NO. 612

DATE	ITEM	P.R.	DEBIT	CREDIT	BALANCE DEBIT	BALANCE CREDIT

ACCOUNT Rent Expense   ACCOUNT NO. 613

DATE		ITEM	P.R.	DEBIT	CREDIT	BALANCE	
						DEBIT	CREDIT

2., 3.   **Accounts Payable Ledger**

NAME

ADDRESS

Date		Item	P.R.	Debit	Credit	Balance

NAME

ADDRESS

Date		Item	P.R.	Debit	Credit	Balance

NAME

ADDRESS

Date		Item	P.R.	Debit	Credit	Balance

NAME

ADDRESS

	Date	Item	P.R.	Debit	Credit	Balance

5.

6. The balance of the Accounts Payable controlling account: _____

PROBLEM 7-5A OR 7-5B

3., 4.   **General Journal**   Page 1

	Date	Account Title	P.R.	Debit	Credit	
1						1
2						2
3						3
4						4
5						5
6						6
7						7
8						8
9						9
10						10
11						11
12						12
13						13
14						14
15						15
16						16
17						17
18						18
19						19
20						20
21						21

Purchases Journal   Page 1

	Date	Invoice No.	Account Credited	P.R.	Purchases Dr. Accts. Pay. Cr.	
1						1
2						2
3						3
4						4
5						5

Cash Payments Journal

Page 1

Date	Ck. No.	Account Debited	P.R.	General Dr.	Accounts Payable Dr.	Purchases Discounts Cr.	Cash Cr.

2., 4.

General Ledger

ACCOUNT Cash

ACCOUNT NO. 111

DATE	ITEM	P.R.	DEBIT	CREDIT	BALANCE DEBIT	BALANCE CREDIT

ACCOUNT Office Supplies

ACCOUNT NO. 115

DATE	ITEM	P.R.	DEBIT	CREDIT	BALANCE DEBIT	BALANCE CREDIT

PROBLEM 7-5A OR 7-5B (continued)

ACCOUNT Store Supplies

ACCOUNT NO. 116

DATE	ITEM	P.R.	DEBIT	CREDIT	BALANCE DEBIT	BALANCE CREDIT

ACCOUNT Prepaid Insurance

ACCOUNT NO. 117

DATE	ITEM	P.R.	DEBIT	CREDIT	BALANCE DEBIT	BALANCE CREDIT

ACCOUNT Office Equipment

ACCOUNT NO. 121

DATE	ITEM	P.R.	DEBIT	CREDIT	BALANCE DEBIT	BALANCE CREDIT

ACCOUNT Store Equipment

ACCOUNT NO. 122

DATE	ITEM	P.R.	DEBIT	CREDIT	BALANCE DEBIT	BALANCE CREDIT

ACCOUNT Accounts Payable

ACCOUNT NO. 211

DATE		ITEM	P.R.	DEBIT	CREDIT	BALANCE	
						DEBIT	CREDIT

ACCOUNT Purchases

ACCOUNT NO. 511

DATE		ITEM	P.R.	DEBIT	CREDIT	BALANCE	
						DEBIT	CREDIT

ACCOUNT Purchases Returns and Allowances

ACCOUNT NO. 511.1

DATE		ITEM	P.R.	DEBIT	CREDIT	BALANCE	
						DEBIT	CREDIT

ACCOUNT Purchases Discounts

ACCOUNT NO. 511.2

DATE		ITEM	P.R.	DEBIT	CREDIT	BALANCE	
						DEBIT	CREDIT

PROBLEM 7-5A OR 7-5B (continued)

ACCOUNT Freight In   ACCOUNT NO. 512

DATE	ITEM	P.R.	DEBIT	CREDIT	BALANCE	
					DEBIT	CREDIT

ACCOUNT Rent Expense   ACCOUNT NO. 613

DATE	ITEM	P.R.	DEBIT	CREDIT	BALANCE	
					DEBIT	CREDIT

1., 3.   **Accounts Payable Ledger**

NAME   Best Diamond Co.

ADDRESS

Date	Item	P.R.	Debit	Credit	Balance

NAME   Carter's Supplies

ADDRESS

Date	Item	P.R.	Debit	Credit	Balance

NAME   Modern Equipment Co.

ADDRESS

Date	Item	P.R.	Debit	Credit	Balance

NAME   Nash Jewelers

ADDRESS

Date	Item	P.R.	Debit	Credit	Balance

NAME   Wilson's Gems

ADDRESS

Date	Item	P.R.	Debit	Credit	Balance

PROBLEM 7-5A OR 7-5B (continued)

5.

Diamond Jewelers Schedule of Accounts Payable July 31, 20X1													

The balance of the Accounts Payable controlling account: _____

This page intentionally left blank.

Critical Thinking Problems

Challenge Problem

General Journal

	Date		Account Title	P.R.	Debit	Credit	
1							1
2							2
3							3
4							4
5							5
6							6
7							7
8							8
9							9
10							10
11							11
12							12
13							13
14							14
15							15
16							16
17							17
18							18
19							19
20							20
21							21
22							22
23							23
24							24
25							25
26							26
27							27
28							28
29							29
30							30
31							31
32							32

Chapter 7 | Accounting for a Merchandising Business **399**

Challenge Problem (continued)

General Journal

	Date		Account Title	P.R.	Debit	Credit	
1							1
2							2
3							3
4							4
5							5
6							6
7							7
8							8
9							9
10							10
11							11
12							12
13							13
14							14
15							15
16							16
17							17
18							18
19							19
20							20
21							21
22							22
23							23
24							24
25							25
26							26
27							27
28							28
29							29
30							30
31							31
32							32

Communications

_____

Team Internet Project

_____

Ethics

_____

_____

_____

_____

_____

_____

_____

_____

_____

_____

_____

_____

_____

_____

_____

_____

In the Real World

_____

_____

_____

_____

_____

_____

_____

_____

_____

_____

_____

_____

_____

Practice Test Answers

True/False

1. T
2. T
3. F
4. T
5. F
6. T
7. T
8. F
9. T
10. F
11. F
12. T
13. F
14. T
15. T

Matching

1. j
2. t
3. n
4. i
5. q
6. a
7. o
8. d
9. s
10. c
11. p
12. m
13. e
14. k
15. g
16. h
17. r
18. b
19. l
20. f

Fill in the Blanks

1. retailer, wholesaler
2. purchase requisition
3. receiving report
4. trade discount
5. cost
6. cash discount
7. merchandise
8. Office Supplies
9. Accounts Payable
10. creditors', accounts payable, debit, credit
11. contra
12. debit memorandum
13. credit memorandum
14. FOB (free on board) destination
15. FOB (free on board) shipping point

Multiple Choice

1. c
2. d
3. b
4. a
5. c
6. b
7. c
8. d
9. a
10. b

Writing/Short Answer

Answers will vary. Please discuss questions with your instructor.

Accounting for a Merchandising Business

Sales and Cash Receipts

Chapter Summary  Interactive Sutmmary in English and Spanish

Sales of merchandise are made for cash and on credit, with the latter being more common in many businesses. Sales on credit are initiated when a purchase order is received from a customer or when one of a firm's salespersons prepares a sales order. A **sales order** is a document prepared when an order is received from a customer. A sales invoice is prepared by the billing department and sent to the buyer. Some sales are made on a **revolving charge plan**, allowing customers to pay a percentage of their account plus finance charges on a monthly basis.

Cash sales are written up on a **sales ticket**, which serves as a source document for later journal entries. A variation of the sales ticket is the **cash register tape**.

Sales of merchandise are recorded in a revenue account entitled Sales. The **Sales account**—like all revenue accounts—is a temporary owner's equity account that is closed to the Income Summary account at the end of the period.

Cash sales are recorded by debiting the Cash account and crediting the Sales account. Credit sales are recorded by debiting an asset account entitled Accounts Receivable and crediting the Sales account. The **Accounts Receivable account** shows the amount due from credit customers.

Accounts for customers are often set up in a subsidiary ledger called the accounts receivable ledger. The accounts receivable ledger is summarized (controlled) by the Accounts Receivable account in the general ledger. Thus, the **accounts receivable ledger** shows the amounts owed by individual credit customers, whereas the Accounts Receivable controlling account shows the aggregate amount owed by all credit customers.

When the volume of credit sales is large, many businesses use a **sales journal**, a special journal used only to record sales of merchandise, which saves journalizing and posting time. The sales journal introduced in this chapter has one money column, entitled Accounts Receivable Debit and

Sales Credit. One money column is sufficient, because all credit sales of merchandise involve a debit to the Accounts Receivable account and a credit to the Sales account unless sales tax is involved.

Each entry in the sales journal requires an individual posting to the account of the credit customer who made the purchase. To keep the accounts receivable ledger up to date, posting is usually done on a daily basis. At the end of the month, the money column of the sales journal is totaled, and the total is posted twice: to the debit side of the Accounts Receivable account and to the credit side of the Sales account.

In Chapter 7, merchandise returns and allowances were referred to as purchases returns and allowances by the buyer. In this chapter, sellers refer to merchandise returns and allowances as sales returns and allowances. The amount of sales returns and allowances is recorded on the debit side of a contra revenue account entitled **Sales Returns and Allowances**. Sellers usually issue a credit memorandum to customers to indicate that credit has been granted for a return or an allowance.

Every sale has a **credit period** and **credit terms**. When the seller grants a cash discount (such as the 2% discount available under credit terms of 2/10,n/30), it is referred to as a sales discount and is recorded as a debit to a contra revenue account entitled **Sales Discounts**. Certain sales have terms of C.O.D. (cash on delivery).

A **cash receipts journal** is a special journal used to record all cash receipts, regardless of the source. Source documents for entries in the cash receipts journal include checks, cash register tapes, and sales tickets.

Since the cash receipts journal is designed to record increases in the Cash account, a Cash Debit column must be included. The number of other special columns and their titles are determined by the accounts most often affected by the firm's cash receipts. The cash receipts journal also contains a General Credit column for recording credits to accounts for which no special column is provided.

The cash receipts journal is posted to the accounts receivable ledger daily. Two types of postings are made from the cash receipts journal to the general ledger: (1) individual amounts from the General Credit column and (2) special column totals. Individual amounts are posted from the General Credit column on a daily, weekly, or monthly basis. Special column totals are posted at the end of the month.

A **schedule of accounts receivable** is prepared periodically—usually at the end of the month—to check the posting accuracy of the accounts receivable ledger. The total of the schedule must agree with the balance of the Accounts Receivable controlling account in the general ledger.

A **sales tax** is a tax on the retail price of goods sold. Most state governments (and some local governments) charge a sales tax that ranges from 3% to 8% and higher. Sales taxes are recorded by crediting the **Sales Tax Payable account**.

Credit card sales have become a popular means for merchants to offer the convenience of credit to their customers. Yet, at the same time, certain types of credit card sales allow merchants to avoid the risks of traditional credit sales such as slow payments from customers and uncollectible accounts. There are three common types of credit cards: (1) those issued by banks (referred to as bank cards), such as VISA and MasterCard; (2) those issued by card systems (referred to as nonbank cards), such as American Express and Diners Club; and (3) those issued by private companies, such as Macy's, Exxon, and some airlines. Bank credit card sales are accounted for as cash sales since the receipts can be deposited in the bank and the firm's checking account is credited for the total of the receipts less a bank fee (discount). Nonbank credit card sales are recorded as sales on account since the receipts must be accumulated and sent to the system for payment. The **Accounts Receivable—Credit Cards account** is debited to record these sales. The **Credit Card Expense account** is debited for the fees (discounts) that a firm pays to banks and card systems when submitting receipts for sales made with their credit cards. Credit card sales made with a company's own card—such as a Macy's card—are recorded as regular sales on account since the company that issued the card does its own billing and collection.

This page intentionally left blank.

True/False

Please circle the correct answer.

T F 1. There should always be a definite understanding between the buyer and the seller concerning the terms of payment for merchandise.

T F 2. FOB shipping point means that the seller pays the freight.

T F 3. Just as with a purchase, the invoice serves as the source document for recording a sale.

T F 4. The revenue account used to record sales of merchandise is called Sales.

T F 5. The sales journal is used to record all sales of merchandise.

T F 6. The Accounts Receivable account in the general ledger is the controlling account for the accounts receivable ledger.

T F 7. It is customary to post to the accounts receivable subsidiary ledger on a daily basis and to the controlling account in the general ledger at the end of the month.

T F 8. Sales Returns and Allowances is a contra account to Sales.

T F 9. A sales discount is offered to customers as a way of changing the price of merchandise without issuing a new catalog.

T F 10. A cash receipts journal is a special journal used to record all receipts of cash.

T F 11. A schedule of accounts receivable is prepared to assure the accuracy of posting to the controlling account in the general ledger.

T F 12. Sales tax usually must be paid to the state tax authority by the end of the month in which it was collected.

T F 13. Bank credit card sales are treated as cash sales.

T F 14. Other credit card sales are treated as cash sales.

T F 15. The accounts receivable subsidiary ledger is used to keep individual records of all customers' accounts.

Matching

Please match each of the following terms with its definition.

a. accounts receivable ledger
b. cash receipts journal
c. cash register tape
d. Credit Card Expense
e. credit memorandum
f. credit period
g. credit terms
h. Sales account

i. Sales Discounts
j. sales journal
k. sales order
l. Sales Returns and Allowances
m. sales tax
n. sales ticket
o. schedule of accounts receivable

_____ 1. The terms set by a company for allowing its customers a certain amount of time in which to make payment.

_____ 2. A form prepared by a salesperson on receipt of a purchase order or when making a credit sale.

_____ 3. A subsidiary ledger containing only accounts of credit customers.

_____ 4. A contra revenue account that is used to record returns of merchandise accepted from customers and allowances granted to customers.

_____ 5. A form sent to customers showing the amount of credit granted for a return of merchandise.

_____ 6. A revenue account used only to record sales of merchandise.

_____ 7. The time allowed customers to make payment.

_____ 8. A form prepared by a salesperson when a cash sale is made.

_____ 9. A special journal used only to record credit sales of merchandise.

_____ 10. An account used to record the discounts a firm must pay on credit card sales when submitting receipts for these sales to banks and card systems.

_____ 11. A listing of the balances in the accounts receivable ledger.

_____ 12. A contra revenue account used to record cash discounts granted to credit customers for prompt payment.

_____ 13. A special journal used to record all receipts of cash.

_____ 14. A tax on the retail price of goods sold that is collected and paid to the government by the seller.

_____ 15. A variation of the sales ticket produced by the cash register and used as a source document for recording cash sales.

Fill in the Blanks

Please complete each sentence with the correct word or words.

1. Terms of _____ mean that no credit is allowed by the seller.

2. _____ means cash on delivery.

3. The revenue account used to record the sale of merchandise is called _____.

4. The sales journal is a special journal used only to record _____ sales of _____.

5. Posting from the sales journal is similar to posting from the _____ journal.

6. If a business has many credit customers, individual accounts for these customers are kept in a(n) _____ ledger called the _____ ledger.

7. Accounts in the _____ ledger are arranged _____, just as in the accounts payable ledger.

8. Sales Returns and Allowances is an example of a(n) _____ account.

9. Sales, Sales Returns and Allowances, and Sales Discounts are all _____ accounts that are closed at the end of the period.

10. A cash receipts journal is used to record all _____ of _____.

11. A cash receipts journal must have a column to record _____ to Cash.

12. Posting of the cash receipts journal is done by posting individual accounts receivable amounts to the _____ ledger daily; individual amounts from the general column to the _____ ledger accounts daily, weekly, or monthly; and column totals to the general ledger accounts _____.

13. Agreement between the Accounts Receivable controlling account and the accounts receivable ledger is checked by preparing a(n) _____ of accounts receivable.

14. A tax on the retail sale of goods is called a(n) _____.

15. A bank credit card sale is treated as a(n) _____ sale.

Multiple Choice

Please circle the correct answer.

1. The source document used to record a credit sale is the
   a. purchase order.
   b. sales order.
   c. invoice.
   d. shipping document.

2. The Sales account is a
   a. revenue account.
   b. cost account.
   c. permanent account.
   d. balance sheet account.

3. The sales journal is used to record
   a. sales of merchandise for cash.
   b. sales of merchandise on credit.
   c. sales of anything on credit.
   d. sales of anything for cash.

4. The accounts receivable ledger contains
   a. an account for each creditor.
   b. an account for each credit customer.
   c. an account for each customer whether cash or credit.
   d. None of the above

5. It is important to post to the accounts receivable ledger daily because
   a. customers may call to ask how much they owe.
   b. the credit manager may want to see how much a customer owes before granting additional credit.
   c. the bookkeeper may need to send out statements.
   d. All of the above

6. It is usually acceptable to post to the general ledger accounts
   a. monthly.
   b. weekly.
   c. daily.
   d. annually.

7. A record of sales returns and allowances is maintained in a separate account because
   a. management needs information about customer dissatisfaction.
   b. it is improper to record returns and allowances as a direct reduction of sales.
   c. it is traditionally done that way.
   d. None of the above

8. A sales discount is given to customers
   a. because the seller does not want to print a new catalog to show new prices.
   b. to encourage prompt payment of invoices.
   c. to reward special customers who buy often.
   d. to encourage customers to pay cash for their purchases.

9. A cash receipts journal is a special journal used to record
   a. all cash transactions.
   b. all receipts of cash from sales of merchandise.
   c. all receipts of cash from any source.
   d. only payments received on accounts receivable.

10. Posting from the cash receipts journal is similar to posting from the
    a. sales journal.
    b. purchases journal.
    c. general journal.
    d. cash payments journal.

11. A schedule of accounts receivable is a listing of all
    a. creditor accounts and their balances.
    b. accounts in the general ledger and their balances.
    c. credit customer accounts and their balances.
    d. sales made on account.

12. Sales tax is a tax on
    a. wholesale sales of merchandise.
    b. retail sales of merchandise.
    c. any sales of merchandise.
    d. any sales.

13. Types of credit cards include
    a. bank credit cards.
    b. credit cards issued by card systems.
    c. credit cards issued by private companies such as oil companies and department stores.
    d. All of the above

14. The type of credit card sale that is handled as a cash transaction is a sale made with a(n)
    a. American Express card.
    b. oil company credit card.
    c. bank credit card.
    d. Diners Club card.

15. One of the benefits of credit card sales is
    a. the merchant does not have to worry about uncollectible accounts.
    b. the merchant does not have to pay any fees.
    c. the merchant always gets the money on the day the sales receipts are deposited.
    d. None of the above

Writing/Short Answer

1. **Reflect** Make a list, in words or simple phrases, of the most important and meaningful points in this chapter.

2. **Question** Think about the most confusing points or the material you do not understand in this chapter. Write down two or three questions that remain unanswered.

3. **Connect** Explain, in one or two sentences, the connection between the main points of this chapter and the major goals of the entire course.

4. **Summarize** Review this chapter's Joining the Pieces visual summary, and explain the concept(s) illustrated in a few sentences.

This page intentionally left blank.

Skills Review

Quick Practice

QUICK PRACTICE 8-1

(a) _____

(b) _____

(c) _____

(d) _____

(e) _____

(f) _____

QUICK PRACTICE 8-2

General Journal

Page 1

	Date	Account Title	P.R.	Debit	Credit	
1						1
2						2
3						3
4						4
5						5
6						6
7						7
8						8
9						9
10						10
11						11
12						12
13						13
14						14
15						15
16						16

Sales Journal

	Date	Invoice No.	Customer's Name	P.R.	Accts. Rec. Dr. Sales Cr.	
1						1
2						2
3						3
4						4
5						5
6						6

General Ledger

ACCOUNT Accounts Receivable   ACCOUNT NO. 112

DATE	ITEM	P.R.	DEBIT	CREDIT	BALANCE DEBIT	BALANCE CREDIT

ACCOUNT Sales   ACCOUNT NO. 411

DATE	ITEM	P.R.	DEBIT	CREDIT	BALANCE DEBIT	BALANCE CREDIT

QUICK PRACTICE 8-3 (continued)

Accounts Receivable Ledger

NAME Samuel duPlessis Outlet

ADDRESS

Date		Item	P.R.	Debit	Credit	Balance

NAME Redeker Furnishing

ADDRESS

Date		Item	P.R.	Debit	Credit	Balance

NAME Shelton Industries

ADDRESS

Date		Item	P.R.	Debit	Credit	Balance

General Journal

Page 1

	Date		Account Title	P.R.	Debit	Credit	
1							1
2							2
3							3
4							4
5							5
6							6
7							7
8							8
9							9
10							10
11							11
12							12
13							13
14							14
15							15
16							16
17							17
18							18
19							19
20							20
21							21
22							22
23							23
24							24
25							25
26							26
27							27
28							28
29							29
30							30

QUICK PRACTICE 8-5

General Journal

Page 1

	Date		Account Title	P.R.	Debit	Credit	
1							1
2							2
3							3
4							4
5							5
6							6
7							7
8							8
9							9
10							10
11							11
12							12
13							13
14							14
15							15
16							16
17							17
18							18
19							19
20							20
21							21
22							22
23							23
24							24
25							25
26							26
27							27
28							28
29							29
30							30
31							31
32							32

Cash Receipts Journal

Date	Account Credited	P.R.	General Cr.	Sales Cr.	Accounts Receivable Cr.	Sales Discounts Dr.	Cash Dr.

Proof: _____

_____

QUICK PRACTICE 8-7

<table>
<tr><th colspan="2" style="text-align:center">General Journal</th><th style="text-align:right">Page 1</th></tr>
</table>

	Date		Account Title	P.R.	Debit	Credit	
1							1
2							2
3							3
4							4
5							5
6							6
7							7
8							8
9							9
10							10
11							11
12							12
13							13
14							14
15							15
16							16
17							17
18							18
19							19
20							20
21							21
22							22
23							23
24							24
25							25
26							26
27							27
28							28
29							29
30							30
31							31
32							32

QUICK PRACTICE 8-8

General Journal

Page 1

	Date	Account Title	P.R.	Debit	Credit	
1						1
2						2
3						3
4						4
5						5
6						6
7						7
8						8
9						9
10						10
11						11
12						12
13						13
14						14
15						15
16						16
17						17
18						18

QUICK PRACTICE 8-9

(a) _____

General Journal

Page 1

	Date	Account Title	P.R.	Debit	Credit	
1						1
2						2
3						3
4						4
5						5
6						6
7						7
8						8
9						9
10						10

QUICK PRACTICE 8-10

Sales Journal   Page 1

Date	Inv. No.	Customer's Name	P.R.	Accounts Receivable Dr.	Sales Cr.	Sales Tax Payable Cr.

QUICK PRACTICE 8-11

General Journal   Page 1

	Date	Account Title	P.R.	Debit	Credit	
1						1
2						2
3						3
4						4
5						5
6						6
7						7
8						8
9						9
10						10
11						11
12						12
13						13
14						14

(a) _____

(b) _____

QUICK PRACTICE 8-12

	P	S	CR	CP	G
(a) Performed services for cash.					
(b) Paid a creditor on account.					
(c) Corrected an error.					
(d) Purchased merchandise for cash.					
(e) Sold merchandise for cash.					
(f) Adjusted for supplies used.					
(g) Sold merchandise on account.					
(h) Purchased merchandise on account.					
(i) Owner withdrew merchandise.					
(j) Collected cash on account.					

Exercises

EXERCISE 8-1

Sales Journal
Page 1

	Date		Invoice No.	Customer's Name	P.R.	Accts. Rec. Dr. Sales Cr.		
1								1
2								2
3								3
4								4
5								5
6								6
7								7
8								8
9								9
10								10

General Ledger

ACCOUNT Accounts Receivable · ACCOUNT NO. 112

DATE	ITEM	P.R.	DEBIT	CREDIT	BALANCE DEBIT	BALANCE CREDIT

ACCOUNT Sales · ACCOUNT NO. 411

DATE	ITEM	P.R.	DEBIT	CREDIT	BALANCE DEBIT	BALANCE CREDIT

Accounts Receivable Ledger

NAME   Adams Co.

ADDRESS

Date		Item	P.R.	Debit	Credit	Balance

NAME   Brown Co.

ADDRESS

Date		Item	P.R.	Debit	Credit	Balance

NAME   Heard, Inc.

ADDRESS

Date		Item	P.R.	Debit	Credit	Balance

NAME   Mallory, Inc.

ADDRESS

Date		Item	P.R.	Debit	Credit	Balance

EXERCISE 8-2

General Journal   Page 1

	Date		Account Title	P.R.	Debit	Credit	
1							1
2							2
3							3
4							4
5							5
6							6
7							7
8							8
9							9
10							10
11							11
12							12
13							13
14							14
15							15
16							16
17							17
18							18
19							19
20							20
21							21
22							22
23							23
24							24
25							25
26							26
27							27
28							28
29							29
30							30
31							31
32							32
33							33
34							34
35							35

EXERCISE 8-3

General Journal

	Date	Account Title	P.R.	Debit	Credit	
1						1
2						2
3						3
4						4
5						5
6						6
7						7
8						8
9						9
10						10
11						11
12						12
13						13
14						14
15						15
16						16
17						17
18						18
19						19
20						20
21						21
22						22
23						23
24						24
25						25
26						26
27						27
28						28
29						29
30						30
31						31
32						32
33						33
34						34
35						35

EXERCISE 8-4

Cash Receipts Journal

Page 1

Date	Account Credited	P.R.	General Cr.	Sales Cr.	Accounts Rec. Cr.	Sales Discounts Dr.	Cash Dr.

Proof: _____

_____

EXERCISE 8-5

	Date		Account Title	P.R.	Debit	Credit	
1							1
2							2
3							3
4							4
5							5
6							6
7							7
8							8
9							9
10							10
11							11
12							12
13							13
14							14
15							15
16							16
17							17
18							18
19							19
20							20
21							21
22							22
23							23
24							24
25							25
26							26
27							27
28							28
29							29
30							30
31							31
32							32
33							33
34							34
35							35
36							36

EXERCISE 8-6

General Journal

Page 1

	Date		Account Title	P.R.	Debit	Credit	
1							1
2							2
3							3
4							4
5							5
6							6
7							7
8							8
9							9
10							10
11							11
12							12
13							13
14							14
15							15
16							16
17							17
18							18
19							19
20							20
21							21
22							22
23							23
24							24
25							25
26							26
27							27

EXERCISE 8-7

1. _____

_____

2., 3.   **General Journal**   Page 1

	Date	Account Title	P.R.	Debit	Credit	
1						1
2						2
3						3
4						4
5						5
6						6
7						7
8						8
9						9
10						10
11						11
12						12

EXERCISE 8-8

1., 2.   **Sales Journal**   Page 1

Date	Inv. No.	Customer's Name	P.R.	Accounts Receivable Dr.	Sales Cr.	Sales Tax Payable Cr.

EXERCISE 8-9

General Journal   Page 1

	Date	Account Title	P.R.	Debit	Credit	
1						1
2						2
3						3
4						4
5						5
6						6
7						7
8						8
9						9
10						10
11						11
12						12
13						13
14						14

EXERCISE 8-10

	P	S	CR	CP	G

(a) Collected cash on account.

(b) Purchased supplies for cash.

(c) Owner invested several noncash assets.

(d) Paid a creditor on account.

(e) Purchased merchandise for cash.

(f) Owner withdrew merchandise.

(g) Performed services on credit.

(h) Sold merchandise for cash.

(i) Corrected an error.

(j) Purchased equipment on credit.

(k) Paid utilities expense.

(l) Sold merchandise on credit.

(m) Purchased merchandise on credit.

(n) Adjusted for supplies used.

(o) Performed services for cash.

This page intentionally left blank.

Case Problems

PROBLEM 8-1A OR 8-1B

3., 4.

General Journal

Page 1

	Date		Account Title	P.R.	Debit	Credit	
1							1
2							2
3							3
4							4
5							5
6							6
7							7
8							8
9							9
10							10
11							11
12							12
13							13
14							14

Sales Journal

Page 1

	Date	Invoice No.	Customer's Name	P.R.	Accts. Rec. Dr. Sales Cr.	
1						1
2						2
3						3
4						4
5						5
6						6
7						7
8						8
9						9
10						10
11						11
12						12

PROBLEM 8-1A OR 8-1B (continued)

2., 4.   **General Ledger**

ACCOUNT Accounts Receivable   ACCOUNT NO. 112

DATE	ITEM	P.R.	DEBIT	CREDIT	BALANCE	
					DEBIT	CREDIT

ACCOUNT Sales   ACCOUNT NO. 411

DATE	ITEM	P.R.	DEBIT	CREDIT	BALANCE	
					DEBIT	CREDIT

ACCOUNT Sales Returns and Allowances   ACCOUNT NO. 411.1

DATE	ITEM	P.R.	DEBIT	CREDIT	BALANCE	
					DEBIT	CREDIT

PROBLEM 8-1A OR 8-1B (continued)

1., 3.   **Accounts Receivable Ledger**

NAME

ADDRESS

Date	Item	P.R.	Debit	Credit	Balance

NAME

ADDRESS

Date	Item	P.R.	Debit	Credit	Balance

NAME

ADDRESS

Date	Item	P.R.	Debit	Credit	Balance

NAME

ADDRESS

Date	Item	P.R.	Debit	Credit	Balance

NAME _____

ADDRESS _____

Date		Item	P.R.	Debit	Credit	Balance

5.

_____		
_____		
_____		

6.   The balance of the Accounts Receivable controlling account: _____

PROBLEM 8-2A OR 8-2B

3., 4.   **Sales Journal**   Page 1

Date	Inv. No.	Customer's Name	P.R.	Accounts Receivable Dr.	Sales Cr.	Sales Tax Payable Cr.

2., 4.   **General Ledger**

ACCOUNT Accounts Receivable   ACCOUNT NO. 112

DATE	ITEM	P.R.	DEBIT	CREDIT	BALANCE DEBIT	BALANCE CREDIT

ACCOUNT Sales Tax Payable   ACCOUNT NO. 212

DATE	ITEM	P.R.	DEBIT	CREDIT	BALANCE DEBIT	BALANCE CREDIT

ACCOUNT Sales   ACCOUNT NO. 411

DATE	ITEM	P.R.	DEBIT	CREDIT	BALANCE DEBIT	BALANCE CREDIT

PROBLEM 8-2A OR 8-2B (continued)

1., 3.   **Accounts Receivable Ledger**

NAME

ADDRESS

Date	Item	P.R.	Debit	Credit	Balance

NAME

ADDRESS

Date	Item	P.R.	Debit	Credit	Balance

NAME

ADDRESS

Date	Item	P.R.	Debit	Credit	Balance

NAME

ADDRESS

Date	Item	P.R.	Debit	Credit	Balance

PROBLEM 8-2A OR 8-2B (continued)

5.

The balance of the Accounts Receivable controlling account: _____

This page intentionally left blank.

PROBLEM 8-3A OR 8-3B

1., 2.

Cash Receipts Journal

Date	Account Credited	P.R.	General Cr.	Sales Cr.	Accounts Rec. Cr.	Sales Discounts Dr.	Cash Dr.

Proof: _____

_____

This page intentionally left blank.

PROBLEM 8-4A OR 8-4B

3., 4.   General Journal   Page 1

	Date		Account Title	P.R.	Debit	Credit	
1							1
2							2
3							3
4							4
5							5
6							6
7							7
8							8
9							9
10							10
11							11
12							12
13							13
14							14

Sales Journal   Page 1

	Date	Invoice No.	Customer's Name	P.R.	Accts. Rec. Dr. Sales Cr.	
1						1
2						2
3						3
4						4
5						5
6						6
7						7
8						8
9						9
10						10
11						11
12						12
13						13
14						14

Cash Receipts Journal   Page 1

Date	Account Credited	P.R.	General Cr.	Sales Cr.	Accounts Rec. Cr.	Sales Discounts Dr.	Cash Dr.

2., 3.   **General Ledger**

ACCOUNT Cash   ACCOUNT NO. 111

DATE	ITEM	P.R.	DEBIT	CREDIT	BALANCE DEBIT	BALANCE CREDIT

ACCOUNT Accounts Receivable   ACCOUNT NO. 112

DATE	ITEM	P.R.	DEBIT	CREDIT	BALANCE DEBIT	BALANCE CREDIT

PROBLEM 8-4A OR 8-4B (continued)

ACCOUNT Sales   ACCOUNT NO. 411

DATE	ITEM	P.R.	DEBIT	CREDIT	BALANCE DEBIT	BALANCE CREDIT

ACCOUNT Sales Returns and Allowances   ACCOUNT NO. 411.1

DATE	ITEM	P.R.	DEBIT	CREDIT	BALANCE DEBIT	BALANCE CREDIT

ACCOUNT Sales Discounts   ACCOUNT NO. 411.2

DATE	ITEM	P.R.	DEBIT	CREDIT	BALANCE DEBIT	BALANCE CREDIT

1., 3.   **Accounts Receivable Ledger**

NAME

ADDRESS

Date	Item	P.R.	Debit	Credit	Balance

NAME

ADDRESS

Date	Item	P.R.	Debit	Credit	Balance

NAME

ADDRESS

Date	Item	P.R.	Debit	Credit	Balance

PROBLEM 8-4A OR 8-4B (continued)

NAME

ADDRESS

Date	Item	P.R.	Debit	Credit	Balance

NAME

ADDRESS

Date	Item	P.R.	Debit	Credit	Balance

NAME

ADDRESS

Date	Item	P.R.	Debit	Credit	Balance

PROBLEM 8-4A OR 8-4B (continued)

5.

The balance of the Accounts Receivable controlling account: _____

PROBLEM 8-5A OR 8-5B

4., 5.

General Journal

Page ____

	Date		Account Title	P.R.	Debit	Credit	
1							1
2							2
3							3
4							4
5							5
6							6
7							7
8							8
9							9
10							10
11							11
12							12
13							13
14							14
15							15
16							16
17							17
18							18
19							19
20							20
21							21
22							22

Sales Journal

Page ____

	Date	Invoice No.	Customer's Name	P.R.	Accts. Rec. Dr. Sales Cr.	
1						1
2						2
3						3
4						4
5						5
6						6
7						7

PROBLEM 8-5A OR 8-5B (continued)

Purchases Journal

Page _____

	Date	Invoice No.	Account Credited	P.R.	Purchases Dr. Accts. Pay. Cr.	
1						1
2						2
3						3
4						4
5						5
6						6
7						7

Cash Receipts Journal

Page _____

Date	Account Credited	P.R.	General Cr.	Sales Cr.	Accounts Rec. Cr.	Sales Discounts Dr.	Cash Dr.

PROBLEM 8-5A OR 8-5B (continued)

Cash Payments Journal

Page ____

Date	Ck. No.	Account Debited	P.R.	General Dr.	Accounts Payable Dr.	Purchases Discounts Cr.	Cash Cr.

1., 5.

General Ledger

ACCOUNT Cash

ACCOUNT NO. 111

DATE	ITEM	P.R.	DEBIT	CREDIT	BALANCE DEBIT	BALANCE CREDIT

PROBLEM 8-5A OR 8-5B (continued)

ACCOUNT Accounts Receivable   ACCOUNT NO. 112

DATE	ITEM	P.R.	DEBIT	CREDIT	BALANCE	
					DEBIT	CREDIT

ACCOUNT Store Supplies   ACCOUNT NO. 113

DATE	ITEM	P.R.	DEBIT	CREDIT	BALANCE	
					DEBIT	CREDIT

ACCOUNT Office Supplies   ACCOUNT NO. 114

DATE	ITEM	P.R.	DEBIT	CREDIT	BALANCE	
					DEBIT	CREDIT

ACCOUNT Store Equipment   ACCOUNT NO. 121

DATE	ITEM	P.R.	DEBIT	CREDIT	BALANCE	
					DEBIT	CREDIT

ACCOUNT Office Equipment   ACCOUNT NO. 122

DATE	ITEM	P.R.	DEBIT	CREDIT	BALANCE	
					DEBIT	CREDIT

PROBLEM 8-5A OR 8-5B (continued)

ACCOUNT Accounts Payable ACCOUNT NO. 211

DATE	ITEM	P.R.	DEBIT	CREDIT	BALANCE DEBIT	BALANCE CREDIT

ACCOUNT Sales ACCOUNT NO. 411

DATE	ITEM	P.R.	DEBIT	CREDIT	BALANCE DEBIT	BALANCE CREDIT

ACCOUNT Sales Returns and Allowances ACCOUNT NO. 411.1

DATE	ITEM	P.R.	DEBIT	CREDIT	BALANCE DEBIT	BALANCE CREDIT

ACCOUNT Sales Discounts ACCOUNT NO. 411.2

DATE	ITEM	P.R.	DEBIT	CREDIT	BALANCE DEBIT	BALANCE CREDIT

ACCOUNT Purchases   ACCOUNT NO. 511

DATE		ITEM	P.R.	DEBIT	CREDIT	BALANCE	
						DEBIT	CREDIT

ACCOUNT Purchases Returns and Allowances   ACCOUNT NO. 511.1

DATE		ITEM	P.R.	DEBIT	CREDIT	BALANCE	
						DEBIT	CREDIT

ACCOUNT Purchases Discounts   ACCOUNT NO. 511.2

DATE		ITEM	P.R.	DEBIT	CREDIT	BALANCE	
						DEBIT	CREDIT

ACCOUNT Rent Expense   ACCOUNT NO. 611

DATE		ITEM	P.R.	DEBIT	CREDIT	BALANCE	
						DEBIT	CREDIT

ACCOUNT Salaries Expense   ACCOUNT NO. 612

DATE		ITEM	P.R.	DEBIT	CREDIT	BALANCE	
						DEBIT	CREDIT

PROBLEM 8-5A OR 8-5B (continued)

ACCOUNT Utilities Expense   ACCOUNT NO. 613

DATE	ITEM	P.R.	DEBIT	CREDIT	BALANCE DEBIT	BALANCE CREDIT

ACCOUNT Repairs Expense   ACCOUNT NO. 614

DATE	ITEM	P.R.	DEBIT	CREDIT	BALANCE DEBIT	BALANCE CREDIT

ACCOUNT Advertising Expense   ACCOUNT NO. 615

DATE	ITEM	P.R.	DEBIT	CREDIT	BALANCE DEBIT	BALANCE CREDIT

ACCOUNT Gas and Oil Expense   ACCOUNT NO. 616

DATE	ITEM	P.R.	DEBIT	CREDIT	BALANCE DEBIT	BALANCE CREDIT

ACCOUNT Miscellaneous Expense   ACCOUNT NO. 618

DATE	ITEM	P.R.	DEBIT	CREDIT	BALANCE DEBIT	BALANCE CREDIT

2., 4. **Accounts Receivable Ledger**

NAME

ADDRESS

	Date		Item	P.R.	Debit	Credit	Balance

NAME

ADDRESS

	Date		Item	P.R.	Debit	Credit	Balance

NAME

ADDRESS

	Date		Item	P.R.	Debit	Credit	Balance

NAME

ADDRESS

	Date		Item	P.R.	Debit	Credit	Balance

NAME

ADDRESS

	Date		Item	P.R.	Debit	Credit	Balance

3., 4.   **Accounts Payable Ledger**

NAME

ADDRESS

	Date		Item	P.R.	Debit	Credit	Balance

NAME

ADDRESS

	Date		Item	P.R.	Debit	Credit	Balance

NAME

ADDRESS

	Date		Item	P.R.	Debit	Credit	Balance

NAME

ADDRESS

	Date	Item	P.R.	Debit	Credit	Balance

NAME

ADDRESS

	Date	Item	P.R.	Debit	Credit	Balance

6.

The balance of the Accounts Receivable controlling account: _____

PROBLEM 8-5A OR 8-5B (continued)

The balance of the Accounts Payable controlling account: _____

This page intentionally left blank.

Critical Thinking Problems

Challenge Problem

4., 5.   **General Journal**   Page 14

	Date	Account Title	P.R.	Debit	Credit	
1						1
2						2
3						3
4						4
5						5
6						6
7						7
8						8
9						9
10						10
11						11
12						12
13						13
14						14
15						15
16						16
17						17
18						18
19						19
20						20
21						21
22						22
23						23
24						24
25						25
26						26
27						27
28						28
29						29
30						30
31						31
32						32

Challenge Problem (continued)

Sales Journal

	Date	Invoice No.	Customer's Name	P.R.	Accts. Rec. Dr. Sales Cr.	
1						1
2						2
3						3
4						4
5						5
6						6
7						7
8						8
9						9
10						10
11						11
12						12

Purchases Journal

	Date	Invoice No.	Account Credited	P.R.	Purchases Dr. Accts. Pay. Cr.	
1						1
2						2
3						3
4						4
5						5
6						6
7						7
8						8

Challenge Problem (continued)

Date	Account Credited	P.R.	General Cr.	Sales Cr.	Accounts Rec. Cr.	Sales Discounts Dr.	Cash Dr.

Proof: _____

_____

Challenge Problem (continued)

Cash Payments Journal

Date	Ck. No.	Account Debited	P.R.	General Dr.	Accounts Payable Dr.	Purchases Discounts Cr.	Cash Cr.

Proof: _____

_____

Challenge Problem (continued)

1., 6.

General Ledger

ACCOUNT **Cash**   ACCOUNT NO. **111**

DATE	ITEM	P.R.	DEBIT	CREDIT	BALANCE DEBIT	BALANCE CREDIT

ACCOUNT **Accounts Receivable**   ACCOUNT NO. **112**

DATE	ITEM	P.R.	DEBIT	CREDIT	BALANCE DEBIT	BALANCE CREDIT

ACCOUNT **Store Supplies**   ACCOUNT NO. **113**

DATE	ITEM	P.R.	DEBIT	CREDIT	BALANCE DEBIT	BALANCE CREDIT

ACCOUNT **Office Supplies**   ACCOUNT NO. **114**

DATE	ITEM	P.R.	DEBIT	CREDIT	BALANCE DEBIT	BALANCE CREDIT

Challenge Problem (continued)

ACCOUNT Prepaid Insurance ACCOUNT NO. 115

DATE	ITEM	P.R.	DEBIT	CREDIT	BALANCE DEBIT	BALANCE CREDIT

ACCOUNT Store Equipment ACCOUNT NO. 119

DATE	ITEM	P.R.	DEBIT	CREDIT	BALANCE DEBIT	BALANCE CREDIT

ACCOUNT Accumulated Depreciation—Store Equipment ACCOUNT NO. 119.1

DATE	ITEM	P.R.	DEBIT	CREDIT	BALANCE DEBIT	BALANCE CREDIT

ACCOUNT Office Equipment ACCOUNT NO. 120

DATE	ITEM	P.R.	DEBIT	CREDIT	BALANCE DEBIT	BALANCE CREDIT

ACCOUNT Accumulated Depreciation—Office Equipment ACCOUNT NO. 120.1

DATE	ITEM	P.R.	DEBIT	CREDIT	BALANCE DEBIT	BALANCE CREDIT

Challenge Problem (continued)

ACCOUNT **Accounts Payable**   ACCOUNT NO. 211

DATE		ITEM	P.R.	DEBIT	CREDIT	BALANCE	
						DEBIT	CREDIT

ACCOUNT **James Collier, Capital**   ACCOUNT NO. 312

DATE		ITEM	P.R.	DEBIT	CREDIT	BALANCE	
						DEBIT	CREDIT

ACCOUNT **James Collier, Drawing**   ACCOUNT NO. 313

DATE		ITEM	P.R.	DEBIT	CREDIT	BALANCE	
						DEBIT	CREDIT

ACCOUNT **Sales**   ACCOUNT NO. 411

DATE		ITEM	P.R.	DEBIT	CREDIT	BALANCE	
						DEBIT	CREDIT

ACCOUNT **Sales Returns and Allowances**   ACCOUNT NO. 411.1

DATE		ITEM	P.R.	DEBIT	CREDIT	BALANCE	
						DEBIT	CREDIT

Challenge Problem (continued)

ACCOUNT Sales Discounts   ACCOUNT NO. 411.2

DATE	ITEM	P.R.	DEBIT	CREDIT	BALANCE DEBIT	BALANCE CREDIT

ACCOUNT Purchases   ACCOUNT NO. 511

DATE	ITEM	P.R.	DEBIT	CREDIT	BALANCE DEBIT	BALANCE CREDIT

ACCOUNT Purchases Returns and Allowances   ACCOUNT NO. 511.1

DATE	ITEM	P.R.	DEBIT	CREDIT	BALANCE DEBIT	BALANCE CREDIT

ACCOUNT Purchases Discounts   ACCOUNT NO. 511.2

DATE	ITEM	P.R.	DEBIT	CREDIT	BALANCE DEBIT	BALANCE CREDIT

ACCOUNT Freight In   ACCOUNT NO. 512

DATE	ITEM	P.R.	DEBIT	CREDIT	BALANCE DEBIT	BALANCE CREDIT

Challenge Problem (continued)

ACCOUNT **Salaries Expense**   ACCOUNT NO. 611

DATE		ITEM	P.R.	DEBIT	CREDIT	BALANCE	
						DEBIT	CREDIT

ACCOUNT **Rent Expense**   ACCOUNT NO. 612

DATE		ITEM	P.R.	DEBIT	CREDIT	BALANCE	
						DEBIT	CREDIT

ACCOUNT **Utilities Expense**   ACCOUNT NO. 613

DATE		ITEM	P.R.	DEBIT	CREDIT	BALANCE	
						DEBIT	CREDIT

ACCOUNT **Advertising Expense**   ACCOUNT NO. 614

DATE		ITEM	P.R.	DEBIT	CREDIT	BALANCE	
						DEBIT	CREDIT

ACCOUNT **Telephone Expense**   ACCOUNT NO. 615

DATE		ITEM	P.R.	DEBIT	CREDIT	BALANCE	
						DEBIT	CREDIT

ACCOUNT **Repairs Expense**   ACCOUNT NO. 616

DATE		ITEM	P.R.	DEBIT	CREDIT	BALANCE	
						DEBIT	CREDIT

Challenge Problem (continued)

ACCOUNT Miscellaneous Expense   ACCOUNT NO. 622

DATE	ITEM	P.R.	DEBIT	CREDIT	BALANCE DEBIT	BALANCE CREDIT

2., 4.   **Accounts Receivable Ledger**

NAME   Aims Corp.

ADDRESS

Date	Item	P.R.	Debit	Credit	Balance

NAME   Hanks Co.

ADDRESS

Date	Item	P.R.	Debit	Credit	Balance

NAME   Illinois Central Products Co.

ADDRESS

Date	Item	P.R.	Debit	Credit	Balance

Challenge Problem (continued)

NAME   Leland Co.

ADDRESS

Date		Item	P.R.	Debit	Credit	Balance

NAME   McFarland Co.

ADDRESS

Date		Item	P.R.	Debit	Credit	Balance

NAME   Tom Larkin

ADDRESS

Date		Item	P.R.	Debit	Credit	Balance

NAME   Xavier Corp.

ADDRESS

Date		Item	P.R.	Debit	Credit	Balance

Challenge Problem (continued)

3., 4.   **Accounts Payable Ledger**

NAME   Adams Inc.

ADDRESS

	Date	Item	P.R.	Debit	Credit	Balance

NAME   Allan Co.

ADDRESS

	Date	Item	P.R.	Debit	Credit	Balance

NAME   Dunlop Co.

ADDRESS

	Date	Item	P.R.	Debit	Credit	Balance

NAME   Dwyar Products Co.

ADDRESS

	Date	Item	P.R.	Debit	Credit	Balance

Challenge Problem (continued)

NAME   Elgin Co.

ADDRESS

Date		Item	P.R.	Debit	Credit	Balance

NAME   Faulk Co.

ADDRESS

Date		Item	P.R.	Debit	Credit	Balance

NAME   McFadden Co.

ADDRESS

Date		Item	P.R.	Debit	Credit	Balance

NAME   Thompson Suppliers

ADDRESS

Date		Item	P.R.	Debit	Credit	Balance

NAME   Wall Supply, Inc.

ADDRESS

Date		Item	P.R.	Debit	Credit	Balance

Challenge Problem (continued)

7.

ACCOUNT TITLE	DEBIT	CREDIT

Challenge Problem (continued)

8.

_____						
_____						
_____						

9.

_____						
_____						
_____						

10.

The balance of the Accounts Receivable controlling account: _____.

The balance of the Accounts Payable controlling account: _____.

This page intentionally left blank.

Communications

Team Internet Project

Ethics

In the Real World

Practice Test Answers

True/False

1. T
2. F
3. T
4. T
5. F
6. T
7. T
8. T
9. F
10. T
11. F
12. F
13. T
14. F
15. T

Matching

1. g
2. k
3. a
4. l
5. e
6. h
7. f
8. n
9. j
10. d
11. o
12. i
13. b
14. m
15. c

Fill in the Blanks

1. net cash
2. COD
3. Sales
4. credit, merchandise
5. purchases
6. subsidiary, accounts receivable
7. accounts receivable, alphabetically
8. contra
9. temporary
10. receipts, cash
11. debits
12. accounts receivable, general, monthly
13. schedule
14. sales tax
15. cash

Multiple Choice

1. c
2. a
3. b
4. b
5. d
6. a
7. a
8. b
9. c
10. d
11. c
12. b
13. d
14. c
15. a

Writing/Short Answer

Answers will vary. Please discuss questions with your instructor.

The Perpetual Inventory System

Summary  Interactive Summary in English and Spanish

In Chapters 7 and 8, we recorded the cost of merchandise purchased in the Purchases account. We made no effort to keep an ongoing record of the cost of items sold or the amount of merchandise remaining on hand at any given time. This system is called the **periodic inventory system**.

In the appendix to Chapter 8, we introduced another inventory system—the **perpetual inventory system**. Under this system, an individual record for each inventory item is set up in a subsidiary ledger. When merchandise is purchased, an asset account entitled Merchandise Inventory is debited, and the individual inventory records are increased. When merchandise is sold, the Merchandise Inventory account is credited, and the individual inventory records are decreased. Thus, an ongoing, or perpetual, record is maintained for inventory items. The cost of merchandise sold is debited to an expense account entitled **Cost of Goods Sold**.

True/False

Please circle the correct answer.

T F   1. In the perpetual inventory system, the cost of merchandise purchased is debited to the Purchases account.

T F   2. The Cost of Goods Sold account is an expense account used to record the cost of merchandise sold to customers.

T F   3. The Merchandise Inventory account is credited for the selling price of merchandise sold to customers.

T F   4. In the perpetual inventory system, freight on incoming merchandise is debited to Merchandise Inventory.

T F   5. In the perpetual inventory system, cash discounts received for early payments of invoices are credited to the Purchases Discounts account.

T F   6. The Merchandise Inventory account is a controlling account.

T F   7. Only businesses with small amounts of inventory use the perpetual inventory system.

T F   8. In the perpetual inventory system, the cost of goods returned to a supplier is credited to the Merchandise Inventory account.

Matching

Please match each of the following terms with its definition.

a. Cost of Goods Sold
b. Merchandise Inventory

c. periodic inventory system
d. perpetual inventory system

_____ 1. An inventory system in which no attempt is made to keep ongoing records of goods sold or the amount of goods on hand at any given time.

_____ 2. An expense account debited for the cost of merchandise sold in a perpetual inventory system.

_____ 3. An asset account used to record the cost of merchandise purchased in a perpetual inventory system.

_____ 4. An inventory system in which ongoing records are kept showing the cost of items sold and the amount of inventory remaining on hand at any given time.

Fill In The Blanks

Please complete each sentence with the correct word.

1. In the _____ inventory system, records are maintained that show a continuous balance of goods on hand.

2. In the perpetual inventory system, the _____ account is debited when merchandise is purchased.

3. In the _____ inventory system, the cost of goods purchased is debited to the Purchases account, and no attempt is made to keep a continuous record of the cost of goods sold or the amount remaining on hand at any given time.

4. In the perpetual inventory system, freight charges on incoming merchandise are debited to the _____ account.

5. The _____ account is credited when merchandise is returned to a supplier in a perpetual inventory system.

6. In the perpetual inventory system, the cost of merchandise sold to customers is debited to the _____ account.

Multiple Choice

Please circle the correct answer.

1. Today, the perpetual inventory system is commonly used by
   a. small businesses.
   b. large businesses.
   c. businesses with a low amount of inventory on hand at year-end.
   d. any size business.

2. In the perpetual inventory system, the cost of merchandise purchased is debited to
   a. Purchases.
   b. Merchandise Inventory.
   c. Cost of Goods Sold.
   d. None of the above

3. Cost of Goods Sold is
   a. an expense account.
   b. an asset account.
   c. a revenue account.
   d. a liability account.

4. In the perpetual inventory system, freight charges on incoming merchandise are debited to
   a. Freight In.
   b. Transportation Expense.
   c. Cost of Goods Sold.
   d. Merchandise Inventory.

5. In the perpetual inventory system, the cost of goods returned to a supplier is
   a. credited to Purchases Returns and Allowances.
   b. credited to Cost of Goods Sold.
   c. debited to Merchandise Inventory.
   d. credited to Merchandise Inventory.

6. When merchandise is sold in a perpetual inventory system, the
   a. Merchandise Inventory account is credited for the cost of the merchandise.
   b. Merchandise Inventory account is debited for the cost of the merchandise.
   c. Cost of Goods Sold account is credited for the cost of the merchandise.
   d. Purchases account is debited for the cost of the merchandise.

7. In the perpetual inventory system, every sale of merchandise on account requires what two entries?
   a. (1) debit to Accounts Receivable/credit to Sales for the selling price; (2) debit to Cost of Goods Sold/credit to Merchandise Inventory for the cost
   b. (1) debit to Accounts Receivable/credit to Sales for the selling price; (2) debit to Cost of Goods Sold/credit to Purchases for the cost
   c. (1) debit to Accounts Receivable/credit to Sales for the selling price; (2) debit to Merchandise Inventory/credit to Cost of Goods Sold for the cost
   d. (1) debit to Accounts Receivable/credit to Merchandise Inventory for the selling price; (2) debit to Cost of Goods Sold/credit to Sales for the cost

Skills Review

Exercises

EXERCISE C-1

General Journal

	Date		Account Title	P.R.	Debit	Credit	
1							1
2							2
3							3
4							4
5							5
6							6
7							7
8							8
9							9
10							10
11							11
12							12
13							13
14							14
15							15
16							16
17							17
18							18
19							19
20							20
21							21
22							22
23							23
24							24
25							25
26							26
27							27
28							28
29							29
30							30
31							31

EXERCISE C-1 (continued)

General Journal

	Date		Account Title	P.R.	Debit	Credit	
32							32
33							33
34							34
35							35
36							36

EXERCISE C-2

General Journal

	Date		Account Title	P.R.	Debit	Credit	
1							1
2							2
3							3
4							4
5							5
6							6
7							7
8							8
9							9
10							10
11							11
12							12
13							13
14							14
15							15
16							16
17							17
18							18
19							19
20							20
21							21
22							22
23							23
24							24
25							25
26							26

EXERCISE C-3

Purchases Journal

	Date	Invoice No.	Account Credited	P.R.	Mer. Inv. Dr./ Accts. Pay. Cr.	
1						1
2						2
3						3
4						4
5						5
6						6
7						7
8						8

Cash Payments Journal

Date	Ck. No.	Account Debited	P.R.	General Dr.	Accounts Payable Dr.	Mer. Inv. Cr.	Cash Cr.

EXERCISE C-4

Sales Journal

	Date		Inv. No.	Customer's Name	P.R.	Accts. Rec. Dr./ Sales Cr.	Cost of Goods Sold Dr./ Mer. Inv. Cr.	
1								1
2								2
3								3
4								4
5								5
6								6
7								7
8								8

Cash Receipts Journal

Date	Account Credited	P.R.	General Cr.	Sales Cr.	Cost of Goods Sold Dr./ Mer. Inv. Cr.	Accounts Receivable Cr.	Sales Discounts Dr.	Cash Dr.

Case Problems

PROBLEM C-1

General Journal

Page 18

	Date		Account Title	P.R.	Debit	Credit	
1							1
2							2
3							3
4							4
5							5
6							6
7							7
8							8
9							9
10							10
11							11
12							12

Purchases Journal

Page 12

	Date	Invoice No.	Account Credited	P.R.	Mer. Inv. Dr./ Accts. Pay. Cr.	
1						1
2						2
3						3
4						4
5						5
6						6

Cash Payments Journal

Page 19

Date	Ck. No.	Account Debited	P.R.	General Dr.	Accounts Payable Dr.	Mer. Inv. Cr.	Cash Cr.

Sales Journal

	Date		Inv. No.	Customer's Name	P.R.	Accts. Rec. Dr./ Sales Cr.	Cost of Goods Sold Dr./ Mer. Inv. Cr.	
1								1
2								2
3								3
4								4
5								5
6								6
7								7
8								8

Cash Receipts Journal

Date	Account Credited	P.R.	General Cr.	Sales Cr.	Cost of Goods Sold Dr./ Mer. Inv. Cr.	Accounts Receivable Cr.	Sales Discounts Dr.	Cash Dr.

PROBLEM C-2

3.

General Ledger

	Date		Account Title	P.R.	Debit	Credit	
1							1
2							2
3							3
4							4
5							5
6							6
7							7
8							8
9							9
10							10
11							11
12							12
13							13
14							14
15							15
16							16
17							17
18							18
19							19
20							20
21							21
22							22
23							23
24							24
25							25
26							26
27							27
28							28
29							29

PROBLEM C-2 (continued)

Sales Journal

	Date	Inv. No.	Customer's Name	P.R.	Accts. Rec. Dr./ Sales Cr.	Cost of Goods Sold Dr./ Mer. Inv. Cr.	
1							1
2							2
3							3
4							4
5							5
6							6
7							7
8							8
9							9
10							10
11							11
12							12

Cash Receipts Journal

Date	Account Credited	P.R.	General Cr.	Sales Cr.	Cost of Goods Sold Dr./ Mer. Inv. Cr.	Accounts Receivable Cr.	Sales Discounts Dr.	Cash Dr.

PROBLEM C-2 (continued)

Purchases Journal

	Date		Invoice No.	Account Credited	P.R.	Mer. Inv. Dr./ Accts. Pay. Cr.		
1								1
2								2
3								3
4								4
5								5
6								6
7								7
8								8

Cash Payments Journal

Date		Ck. No.	Account Debited	P.R.	General Dr.	Accounts Payable Dr.	Mer. Inv. Cr.	Cash Cr.

PROBLEM C-2 (continued)

1., 5.   **General Ledger**

ACCOUNT Cash   ACCOUNT NO. 111

DATE	ITEM	P.R.	DEBIT	CREDIT	BALANCE DEBIT	BALANCE CREDIT

ACCOUNT Accounts Receivable   ACCOUNT NO. 112

DATE	ITEM	P.R.	DEBIT	CREDIT	BALANCE DEBIT	BALANCE CREDIT

ACCOUNT Merchandise Inventory   ACCOUNT NO. 113

DATE	ITEM	P.R.	DEBIT	CREDIT	BALANCE DEBIT	BALANCE CREDIT

PROBLEM C-2 (continued)

ACCOUNT Store Supplies   ACCOUNT NO. 114

DATE	ITEM	P.R.	DEBIT	CREDIT	BALANCE	
					DEBIT	CREDIT

ACCOUNT Office Supplies   ACCOUNT NO. 115

DATE	ITEM	P.R.	DEBIT	CREDIT	BALANCE	
					DEBIT	CREDIT

ACCOUNT Store Equipment   ACCOUNT NO. 121

DATE	ITEM	P.R.	DEBIT	CREDIT	BALANCE	
					DEBIT	CREDIT

ACCOUNT Office Equipment   ACCOUNT NO. 122

DATE	ITEM	P.R.	DEBIT	CREDIT	BALANCE	
					DEBIT	CREDIT

PROBLEM C-2 (continued)

ACCOUNT Accounts Payable   ACCOUNT NO. 211

DATE	ITEM	P.R.	DEBIT	CREDIT	BALANCE	
					DEBIT	CREDIT

ACCOUNT Sales   ACCOUNT NO. 411

DATE	ITEM	P.R.	DEBIT	CREDIT	BALANCE	
					DEBIT	CREDIT

ACCOUNT Sales Returns and Allowances   ACCOUNT NO. 411.1

DATE	ITEM	P.R.	DEBIT	CREDIT	BALANCE	
					DEBIT	CREDIT

ACCOUNT Sales Discounts   ACCOUNT NO. 411.2

DATE	ITEM	P.R.	DEBIT	CREDIT	BALANCE	
					DEBIT	CREDIT

PROBLEM C-2 (continued)

ACCOUNT Cost of Goods Sold   ACCOUNT NO. 601

DATE	ITEM	P.R.	DEBIT	CREDIT	BALANCE	
					DEBIT	CREDIT

ACCOUNT Salaries Expense   ACCOUNT NO. 611

DATE	ITEM	P.R.	DEBIT	CREDIT	BALANCE	
					DEBIT	CREDIT

ACCOUNT Rent Expense   ACCOUNT NO. 612

DATE	ITEM	P.R.	DEBIT	CREDIT	BALANCE	
					DEBIT	CREDIT

ACCOUNT Rent Expense   ACCOUNT NO. 612

DATE	ITEM	P.R.	DEBIT	CREDIT	BALANCE	
					DEBIT	CREDIT

PROBLEM C-2 (continued)

ACCOUNT Gas and Oil Expense   ACCOUNT NO. 614

DATE		ITEM	P.R.	DEBIT	CREDIT	BALANCE	
						DEBIT	CREDIT

ACCOUNT Repairs Expense   ACCOUNT NO. 615

DATE		ITEM	P.R.	DEBIT	CREDIT	BALANCE	
						DEBIT	CREDIT

ACCOUNT Miscellaneous Expense   ACCOUNT NO. 620

DATE		ITEM	P.R.	DEBIT	CREDIT	BALANCE	
						DEBIT	CREDIT

PROBLEM C-2 (continued)

Accounts Receivable Ledger

NAME Handy Andy's Food World

ADDRESS

	Date	Item	P.R.	Debit	Credit	Balance

NAME Kim Janicki

ADDRESS

	Date	Item	P.R.	Debit	Credit	Balance

NAME Lori Lawson's Natural Foods

ADDRESS

	Date	Item	P.R.	Debit	Credit	Balance

NAME Nika Hall

ADDRESS

	Date	Item	P.R.	Debit	Credit	Balance

PROBLEM C-2 (continued)

NAME Riverside Grocery

ADDRESS

Date		Item	P.R.	Debit	Credit	Balance

NAME Wilder Foods

ADDRESS

Date		Item	P.R.	Debit	Credit	Balance

3., 5.   **Accounts Payable Ledger**

NAME H.H. Farless Company

ADDRESS

Date		Item	P.R.	Debit	Credit	Balance

NAME J.J. Bakker Food Processors

ADDRESS

Date		Item	P.R.	Debit	Credit	Balance

NAME Sam DuPree Products Company

ADDRESS

Date		Item	P.R.	Debit	Credit	Balance

NAME Taylor Company

ADDRESS

Date		Item	P.R.	Debit	Credit	Balance

NAME Tyler Meat Packers

ADDRESS

Date		Item	P.R.	Debit	Credit	Balance

NAME White's Office Supply

ADDRESS

Date		Item	P.R.	Debit	Credit	Balance

6.

7.

Practice Test Answers

True/False

1. F
2. T
3. F
4. T
5. F
6. T
7. F
8. T

Matching

1. c
2. a
3. b
4. d

Fill in the Blanks

1. perpetual
2. Merchandise Inventory
3. periodic
4. Merchandise Inventory
5. Merchandise Inventory
6. Cost of Goods Sold

Multiple Choice

1. d
2. b
3. a
4. d
5. d
6. a
7. a

Work Sheet and Adjustments for a Merchandising Business

Chapter Summary

Interactive Summary in English and Spanish

The end-of-period activities for a merchandising business are similar to those of a service business. Both types of businesses determine needed adjustments at the end of the period. Adjusting entries are based on the *matching principle* of accounting, which states that the revenue for a period should be offset by the expenses necessary to generate that revenue.

We recorded several adjustments in this chapter. One of the new adjustments we looked at is for merchandise inventory. The cost of merchandise purchased during the accounting period is recorded in the Purchases account. However, the Purchases account only shows the amount purchased during the accounting period—not the value of the goods on hand at the end of an accounting period. Therefore, it is necessary to take an **inventory**, a physical count of the goods on hand, periodically and adjust the **Merchandise Inventory account** to reflect the latest inventory value.

The adjustment for merchandise inventory is relatively simple. The Merchandise Inventory account is reduced by the old inventory (**beginning merchandise inventory**) figure and increased by the **ending merchandise inventory** figure. The adjustment is accomplished by debiting the Income Summary account and crediting the Merchandise Inventory account for the value of the old inventory. Then, the new inventory figure is recorded by debiting the Merchandise Inventory account and crediting the Income Summary account.

Other adjustments typically needed by a merchandising business are those to record the cost of prepaid items consumed, depreciation of long-term assets, and **accrued salaries** (salaries that are unpaid and unrecorded at the end of an accounting period). Accrued salaries are also referred to as accrued wages.

This page intentionally left blank.

True/False

Please circle the correct answer.

T F 1. The matching principle states that every transaction should be recorded at cost.

T F 2. The chart of accounts shows the page numbers where each account is to be found in the general ledger.

T F 3. The first step in the end-of-period activities is to take a trial balance of the general ledger.

T F 4. Some adjusting entries for a merchandising firm are the same as those for a service business.

T F 5. The first step in adjusting the Merchandise Inventory account is to credit Income Summary and debit Merchandise Inventory for the beginning balance in the inventory account.

T F 6. The beginning balance in Merchandise Inventory represents the amount of inventory that was on hand at the beginning of the accounting period.

T F 7. The second step in adjusting the Merchandise Inventory account is to debit Merchandise Inventory and credit Income Summary for the ending inventory figure.

T F 8. In recording depreciation, each depreciation expense account is credited and each accumulated depreciation account is debited.

T F 9. An accumulated depreciation account is a contra asset account.

T F 10. A depreciation expense account is a temporary account that will be closed to Income Summary.

T F 11. Each accumulated depreciation account will be closed to Income Summary at the end of the period.

T F 12. A work sheet is an informal working paper.

T F 13. An adjusted trial balance is used to check the accuracy of the combined trial balance and adjustments before extending the amounts to the financial statement columns of the work sheet.

T F 14. If an account has a debit balance and a debit adjustment is made to it, the new balance is determined by subtracting the adjustment from the old balance.

T F 15. If an account has a balance and no adjustment is made to it, it may be left off the adjusted trial balance.

Matching

Please match each of the following terms with its definition.

a. adjusted trial balance
b. adjusting entries
c. chart of accounts
d. Income Summary
e. matching principle
f. Merchandise Inventory
g. 10-column work sheet
h. trial balance

_____ 1. An informal working paper that is used by accountants to summarize end-of-period data; it includes columns for entering adjustments and preparing an adjusted trial balance.

_____ 2. A listing of all accounts in the general ledger and the debit or credit balance of each.

_____ 3. The account that provides a record of the cost of goods on hand at a given time.

_____ 4. Entries made at the end of an accounting period to update certain accounts.

_____ 5. The principle of accounting that states that the revenue for an accounting period should be offset by the expenses necessary to generate that revenue.

_____ 6. The trial balance taken to show updated account balances after adjustments.

_____ 7. A clearing account used to summarize revenues and expenses.

_____ 8. The directory of accounts in the general ledger.

Fill in the Blanks

Please complete each sentence with the correct word or words.

1. End-of-period activities for a merchandising business are similar to those for a(n) _____ business.

2. The _____ states that the revenue earned during an accounting period should be offset by the _____ that were necessary to generate that revenue.

3. The first step in the end-of-period activities is to take a(n) _____ of the general ledger.

4. The second step is to determine needed _____.

5. The adjustment to _____ requires that a count be made to determine how much merchandise is unsold at the end of the period.

6. Merchandise Inventory is a(n) _____ account.

7. The first step in adjusting the Merchandise Inventory account requires a debit to _____ and a credit to _____ for the beginning balance in the Merchandise Inventory account.

8. The second step in adjusting the Merchandise Inventory account is to _____ Merchandise Inventory and _____ Income Summary for the amount of the inventory value at the end of the period.

9. The two-step procedure for adjusting Merchandise Inventory is preferred by accountants because both the _____ and _____ balances of inventory appear on the _____.

10. Many of the adjustments needed in a merchandising business are the same as those needed in a(n) _____ business.

11. An accumulated depreciation account does not relate to a single period; it is a(n) _____ account used to _____ depreciation over the useful life of the asset to which it relates.

12. Recording accrued salaries for the period is required by the _____ principle.

13. The _____ trial balance contains the updated balances that result from combining the original trial balance amounts and the adjustments.

14. If an account has a debit balance and the adjustment is a credit, the _____ between the two amounts is entered in the adjusted trial balance.

15. If an account has a credit balance and the adjustment is a credit, the two numbers are _____ and entered in the _____ column of the adjusted trial balance.

16. All _____ and _____ accounts and the owner's _____ and _____ accounts are extended to the Balance Sheet columns of the work sheet.

Multiple Choice

Please circle the correct answer.

1. All merchandise purchased during the accounting period is debited to the
   a. Purchases account.
   b. Accounts Receivable account.
   c. Merchandise Inventory account.
   d. Accounts Payable account.

2. The adjustment to Merchandise Inventory requires that
   a. a count of inventory be taken to determine the ending inventory amount.
   b. the beginning balance of inventory be debited to Income Summary and credited to Merchandise Inventory.
   c. the ending balance of inventory be debited to Merchandise Inventory and credited to Income Summary.
   d. All of the above

3. Super Stores had a balance of $1,500 in Store Supplies before adjustment. A count of the supplies on hand revealed that $400 of supplies were still unused. What is the adjusting entry needed at the end of the period?
   a. Debit Store Supplies Expense and credit Store Supplies for $1,100.
   b. Debit Store Supplies and credit Store Supplies Expense for $1,100.
   c. Debit Store Supplies and credit Store Supplies Expense for $400.
   d. Debit Store Supplies Expense and credit Store Supplies for $400.

4. An adjustment to record accrued salaries is required by the
   a. cost principle.
   b. matching principle.
   c. business entity principle.
   d. None of the above

5. Purchases Discounts and Accumulated Depreciation are both examples of
   a. accounts with debit balances.
   b. expense accounts.
   c. asset accounts.
   d. contra accounts.

6. Sales, Purchases Returns and Allowances, and Purchases Discounts are found in which column of the work sheet?
   a. Income Statement, Debit
   b. Income Statement, Credit
   c. Balance Sheet, Debit
   d. Balance Sheet, Credit

7. The owner's drawing account is found in which column of the work sheet?
   a. Income Statement, Debit
   b. Income Statement, Credit
   c. Balance Sheet, Debit
   d. Balance Sheet, Credit

Writing/Short Answer

1. **Reflect** Make a list, in words or simple phrases, of the most important and meaningful points in this chapter.

2. **Question** Think about the most confusing points or the material you do not understand in this chapter. Write down two or three questions that remain unanswered.

3. **Connect** Explain, in one or two sentences, the connection between the main points of this chapter and the major goals of the entire course.

4. **Summarize** Review this chapter's Joining the Pieces visual summary, and explain the concept(s) illustrated in a few sentences.

Skills Review

Quick Practice

QUICK PRACTICE 9-1

General Journal

Page 1

	Date	Account Title	P.R.	Debit	Credit	
1						1
2						2
3						3

QUICK PRACTICE 9-2 (5 MIN.)

General Journal

Page 1

	Date	Account Title	P.R.	Debit	Credit	
1						1
2						2
3						3

QUICK PRACTICE 9-3 (10 MIN.)

(a)

General Journal

Page 1

	Date	Account Title	P.R.	Debit	Credit	
1						1
2						2
3						3

(b)

General Journal

Page 1

	Date	Account Title	P.R.	Debit	Credit	
1						1
2						2
3						3

QUICK PRACTICE 9-4

General Journal

Page 1

	Date		Account Title	P.R.	Debit	Credit	
1							1
2							2
3							3
4							4
5							5
6							6

QUICK PRACTICE 9-5

General Journal

Page 1

	Date		Account Title	P.R.	Debit	Credit	
1							1
2							2
3							3
4							4
5							5
6							6
7							7

QUICK PRACTICE 9-6

Account Title	Trial Balance		Adjustments	
	Debit	Credit	Debit	Credit

This page intentionally left blank.

Account Title	Trial Balance				Adjustments			
	Debit		Credit		Debit		Credit	

	Adjusted Trial Balance		Income Statement		Balance Sheet	
	Debit	Credit	Debit	Credit	Debit	Credit

QUICK PRACTICE 9-8

1. _____   5. _____   9. _____

2. _____   6. _____   10. _____

3. _____   7. _____

4. _____   8. _____

QUICK PRACTICE 9-9

1. _____

2. _____

3. _____

4. _____

5. _____

6. _____

7. _____

Exercises

EXERCISE 9-1

Policy Number	Monthly Expiration	Expense for 20XX
(1)		
(2)		
(3)		

EXERCISE 9-2

(a) _____

(b) _____

(c) _____

EXERCISE 9-3

(a)

(b)

(c)

(d)

EXERCISE 9-4

(a)

(b)

(c)

(d)

(e)

(f)

EXERCISE 9-5

1. _____   5. _____   9. _____

2. _____   6. _____   10. _____

3. _____   7. _____   11. _____

4. _____   8. _____   12. _____

EXERCISE 9-6

Account Title	Trial Balance		Adjustments	
	Debit	Credit	Debit	Credit

EXERCISE 9-6 (continued)

	Adjusted Trial Balance		Income Statement		Balance Sheet	
	Debit	Credit	Debit	Credit	Debit	Credit

This page intentionally left blank.

Case Problems

PROBLEM 9-1A OR 9-1B

(a) _____

_____

_____

_____

(b) _____

_____

_____

_____

(c) _____

(d) _____

This page intentionally left blank.

PROBLEM 9-2A OR 9-2B

(a)

(b)

(c)

(d)

(e)

(f)

This page intentionally left blank.

This page intentionally left blank.

PROBLEM 9-3A OR 9-3B

Account Title	Trial Balance		Adjustments	
	Debit	Credit	Debit	Credit

	Adjusted Trial Balance		Income Statement		Balance Sheet	
	Debit	Credit	Debit	Credit	Debit	Credit

This page intentionally left blank.

This page intentionally left blank.

PROBLEM 9-4A OR 9-4B

Account Title	Trial Balance		Adjustments	
	Debit	Credit	Debit	Credit

PROBLEM 9-4A OR 9-4B (continued)

	Adjusted Trial Balance		Income Statement		Balance Sheet	
	Debit	Credit	Debit	Credit	Debit	Credit

This page intentionally left blank.

This page intentionally left blank.

Critical Thinking Problems

Challenge Problem

1., 2.

Account Title	Trial Balance		Adjustments	
	Debit	Credit	Debit	Credit

Challenge Problem (continued)

	Adjusted Trial Balance		Income Statement		Balance Sheet	
	Debit	Credit	Debit	Credit	Debit	Credit

This page intentionally left blank.

Communications

_____
_____
_____
_____
_____
_____
_____
_____
_____
_____
_____
_____
_____
_____
_____
_____

Team Internet Project

_____
_____
_____
_____
_____
_____
_____
_____
_____
_____
_____
_____
_____
_____
_____
_____
_____
_____
_____

Ethics

___

In the Real World

___

Practice Test Answers

True/False

1. F
2. F
3. T
4. T
5. F
6. T
7. T
8. F
9. T
10. T
11. F
12. T
13. T
14. F
15. F

Matching

1. g
2. h
3. f
4. b
5. e
6. a
7. d
8. c

Fill in the Blanks

1. service
2. matching principle, expenses
3. trial balance

4. adjustments
5. Merchandise Inventory
6. asset
7. Income Summary, Merchandise Inventory
8. debit, credit
9. beginning, ending, income statement
10. service
11. contra, accumulate
12. matching
13. adjusted
14. difference
15. added, Credit
16. asset, liability, capital, drawing

Multiple Choice

1. a
2. d
3. a
4. b
5. d
6. b
7. c

Writing/Short Answer

Answers will vary. Please discuss questions with your instructor.

Merchandise Inventory Adjustment and Work Sheet Using the Perpetual Inventory System

Summary  Interactive Summary in English and Spanish

Use of the perpetual inventory system allows for better inventory control because individual inventory records are maintained for all items a business sells. When new merchandise is purchased, the inventory records are increased. When merchandise is sold, the inventory records of the items sold are decreased. Thus, the inventory records always show the amount of inventory that *should* be on hand. To verify the accuracy of the perpetual, or "book," inventory, businesses periodically take a physical inventory count (usually at the end of the accounting period). The actual count of merchandise is then compared with the perpetual records to determine if there have been inventory losses from shoplifting, breakage, errors, employee theft, and the like.

If a difference is found between the actual inventory count and the perpetual inventory records, an adjusting entry is needed to reconcile the two amounts. Inventory shortages are common. The amount of a shortage is debited to an account entitled **Inventory Short and Over** and credited to Merchandise Inventory. Inventory overages are rare but may occur, usually due to error. An overage is debited to Merchandise Inventory and credited to Inventory Short and Over. A period-end debit balance (shortage) in the Inventory Short and Over account is listed with other expenses on the income statement; a credit balance (overage) is listed with other revenue.

The work sheet of a company using the perpetual inventory system is identical to the work sheet of a company using the periodic inventory system, except for the merchandise inventory adjustment. In the periodic system, the Merchandise Inventory account is always adjusted to reflect the latest inventory value. In the perpetual system, the Merchandise Inventory account is not adjusted unless there is a difference between the physical inventory count and the perpetual inventory records.

This page intentionally left blank.

Practice Test

True/False

Please circle the correct answer.

T   F   1. Use of the perpetual inventory system eliminates the need for a physical inventory count.

T   F   2. Factors such as shoplifting and employee theft can distort a perpetual inventory.

T   F   3. Inventory shortages are debited to an account entitled Inventory Short and Over.

T   F   4. Inventory overages are common.

T   F   5. A period-end debit balance in the Inventory Short and Over account is listed on the income statement with other expenses.

T   F   6. Work sheets are not used by firms using the perpetual inventory system.

Matching

Please match each of the following terms with its definition.

a. Inventory Short and Over
b. inventory shortage
c. period-end credit balance in the Inventory Short and Over account

d. period-end debit balance in the Inventory Short and Over account

_____   1. Occurs when the physical inventory count shows less inventory than the perpetual inventory records.

_____   2. An account used to record a difference between a physical inventory count and the perpetual inventory records.

_____   3. Reported as other income on the income statement.

_____   4. Reported as other expense on the income statement.

Fill in the Blanks

Please complete each sentence with the correct word or words.

1. An inventory _____ exists when a physical inventory shows less inventory than the perpetual inventory records.

2. The _____ account is used to record inventory shortages or overages.

3. A period-end credit balance in the Inventory Short and Over account means there is an inventory _____.

4. A period-end debit balance in the Inventory Short and Over account means there is an inventory

    _____.

5. A period-end debit balance in the Inventory Short and Over account is reported on the income

    statement as _____.

6. A period-end credit balance in the Inventory Short and Over account is reported on the income

    statement as _____.

Multiple Choice

Please circle the correct answer.

1. An inventory shortage
    a. occurs when a physical count shows less inventory than the perpetual records.
    b. occurs when a physical count shows more inventory than the perpetual records.
    c. does not exist in perpetual inventory systems because computers are used.
    d. is ignored unless the amount is significant.

2. The Inventory Short and Over account is
    a. a special type of asset account.
    b. another name for the Cash Short and Over account.
    c. used to record inventory shortages or overages.
    d. used to record discounts taken, or lost, on inventory purchases.

3. A period-end debit balance in the Inventory Short and Over account means
    a. an inventory shortage.
    b. an inventory overage.
    c. miscellaneous revenue.
    d. the perpetual system is not in use.

4. A period-end credit balance in the Inventory Short and Over account means
    a. an inventory shortage.
    b. an inventory overage.
    c. miscellaneous expense.
    d. shoplifting or employee theft occurred.

Skills Review

Exercises

EXERCISE D-1

General Journal Page 1

	Date		Account Title	P.R.	Debit			Credit			
1											1
2											2
3											3
4											4

EXERCISE D-2

General Journal Page 1

	Date		Account Title	P.R.	Debit			Credit			
1											1
2											2
3											3
4											4

Ingersol Company
Work Sheet
For Year Ended April 30, 20X2

Account Title	Trial Balance		Adjustments	
	Debit	Credit	Debit	Credit
Cash				
Accounts Receivable				
Merchandise Inventory				
Store Supplies				
Office Supplies				
Prepaid Insurance				
Store Equipment				
Accum. Depr.—Store Equipment				
Office Equipment				
Accum. Depr.—Office Equipment				
Accounts Payable				
Salaries Payable				
Notes Payable				
Jay Ingersol, Capital				
Jay Ingersol, Drawing				
Sales				
Sales Returns and Allowances				
Cost of Goods Sold				
Inventory Short and Over				
Sales Salaries Expense				
Advertising Expense				
Store Supplies Expense				
Depr. Exp.—Store Equipment				
Rent Expense				
Office Salaries Expense				
Depr. Exp.—Office Equipment				
Utilities Expense				
Office Supplies Expense				
Insurance Expense				
Miscellaneous Expense				
Net Income				

	Adjusted Trial Balance		Income Statement		Balance Sheet	
	Debit	Credit	Debit	Credit	Debit	Credit

This page intentionally left blank.

Practice Test Answers

True/False

1. F
2. T
3. T
4. F
5. T
6. F

Matching

1. b
2. a
3. c
4. d

Fill in the Blanks

1. shortage
2. Inventory Short and Over
3. overage
4. shortage
5. other expense
6. other income

Multiple Choice

1. a
2. c
3. a
4. b

Financial Statements and Closing Entries for a Merchandising Business

 **Chapter Summary** Interactive Summary in English and Spanish

Financial statements are prepared soon after the work sheet has been completed. All the information needed to prepare formal financial statements can be taken directly from the work sheet.

A *classified financial statement* is one divided into major sections. A **classified income statement** for a merchandising business usually has sections for revenue, cost of goods sold, operating expenses, income from operations, and other income and expenses. Revenue for a merchandising business is expressed as **net sales**. Net sales is calculated by deducting sales returns and allowances and sales discounts from sales. **Cost of goods sold** is the cost of merchandise sold to customers during the accounting period. For some merchandising businesses, the volume of sales may be too large to calculate the cost of goods as they are being sold. In such cases, cost of goods sold is usually determined at the end of an accounting period by using the formula shown below. The amount of net purchases in the formula is calculated by deducting purchases returns and allowances and purchases discounts from purchases and adding the freight cost for incoming merchandise.

	Beginning merchandise inventory
+	Net purchases of merchandise
=	Goods available for sale
−	Ending merchandise inventory
=	Cost of goods sold

Net sales less cost of goods sold yields **gross profit**. The total operating expenses are deducted from the gross profit to find the **income from operations**.

Two types of operating expenses are **general expenses** and **selling expenses**. **Operating expenses** are those incurred in the normal operations of the business. Nonoperating expenses are those that are not directly associated with the actual operations of the business. Interest paid on loans is an example of a nonoperating expense. Nonoperating expenses are usually referred to as **other expenses**. Similarly, nonoperating income, such as the interest received on loans, is usually called **other income**. Other income is added to the income from operations and other expenses are deducted from it to determine the net income.

A **classified balance sheet** has sections for assets, liabilities, and owner's equity as well as subsections for current assets and plant assets and current liabilities and long-term liabilities. **Current assets** include cash and any other asset that will be realized in cash, used up, sold, or expired within one year. Current assets are listed on the balance sheet in the order of their **liquidity**—how quickly they can be turned into cash or how quickly they will be used up or expire. **Plant assets** are assets that will be used in the business for more than one year. Plant assets are listed in the order of their **stability**—how long they will last.

Current liabilities are debts that are due for payment within one year. **Long-term liabilities** are debts that are not due for payment within one year.

A financial statement is a decision-making tool. It provides information necessary for decisions and judgments about a business. For maximum benefit, it is common to make certain analyses from the financial statements. In this chapter, we introduced financial statement analysis by presenting two very common analyses from the balance sheet: working capital and the current ratio. **Working capital** is the excess of a firm's current assets over its current liabilities. A strong working capital position indicates that a business is able to carry on current operations. The **current ratio** is obtained by dividing current assets by current liabilities. It gives an indication of the ability of a business to pay its short-term debts as they fall due.

After financial statements are prepared, the next step in the accounting cycle is to journalize adjusting and closing entries. Adjusting entries already appear on the work sheet. They simply need to be copied into the journal and then get posted to the general ledger.

The closing process involves making entries to close the temporary accounts. Revenue, expense, and cost accounts are closed to Income Summary, which, in turn, is closed to the owner's capital account. The owner's drawing account is closed directly to the owner's capital account.

After the adjusting and closing entries are journalized and posted, a post-closing trial balance is taken to ensure that the general ledger is still in balance. Only permanent accounts (assets, contra assets, liabilities, and owner's capital) appear on the post-closing trial balance—the temporary accounts have been closed.

In Chapters 4 and 9 we learned the proper accounting treatment for expenses that have been incurred but are unpaid when the accounting period ends. We learned that an expense account (such as Salaries Expense) is debited, and a liability account (such as Salaries Payable) is credited. In this chapter, we looked at the entry necessary to record the payment of an accrued expense in the next accounting period. We learned that to make this entry properly, we had to split the entry between the liability recorded at the end of the last accounting period and the amount of expense incurred in the new accounting period. However, some accountants do not like to refer to the records of the previous period and split the entry. A technique called **reversing entries** allows us to make a routine accounting entry to record the payment of an accrued expense, even though two accounting periods are involved. Reversing entries are made as of the first day of the next accounting period and are the exact opposite of the adjusting entries for accrued expenses.

Many businesses prepare **interim statements** for periods of less than 12 months, such as monthly or quarterly statements. However, adjusting and closing entries are not made until the end of the fiscal year.

True/False

Please circle the correct answer.

T   F   1. An income statement summarizes changes in the owner's capital for the period.

T   F   2. A classified income statement for a merchandising business has a section showing cost of goods sold.

T   F   3. Net sales for the period minus cost of goods sold equals net income.

T   F   4. Gross profit is the profit before subtracting the expenses of doing business.

T   F   5. Cost of goods sold is determined by adding net purchases to beginning inventory and subtracting ending inventory.

T   F   6. Net sales is calculated by taking the amount of sales and adding the amount of sales returns and allowances and the amount of sales discounts.

T   F   7. Operating expenses are expenses incurred in the normal operations of the business.

T   F   8. Interest expense is an example of an item that would be included in the section for other expenses on a classified income statement.

T   F   9. The statement of owner's equity is the link between the income statement and the balance sheet.

T   F   10. The principal objective of the balance sheet is to provide information about the results of the company's operations for the period.

T   F   11. Current assets include cash and those assets that will be realized in cash, sold, used up, or expired within one year.

T   F   12. Current liabilities are those that must be paid within one year.

T   F   13. Working capital is the same as cash.

T   F   14. Adjusting and closing entries do not need to be journalized or posted when using a work sheet.

T   F   15. Reversing entries are made on the last day of an accounting period.

Matching

Please match each of the following terms with its definition.

a. classified balance sheet
b. classified income statement
c. cost of goods sold
d. current assets
e. current liabilities
f. current ratio
g. gross profit
h. income from operations

i. liquidity
j. long-term liabilities
k. net sales
l. operating expenses
m. other expenses
n. plant assets
o. reversing entries
p. working capital

_____ 1. Expenses incurred in the normal operations of the business.

_____ 2. The cost of merchandise sold to customers during the accounting period.

_____ 3. The profit before subtracting the expenses of doing business.

_____ 4. The amount obtained by subtracting the amount of sales returns and allowances and the amount of sales discounts from the amount of sales.

_____ 5. Cash and any other asset that will be realized in cash, used up, sold, or expired within one year.

_____ 6. The excess of a firm's current assets over its current liabilities.

_____ 7. Refers to how quickly an asset can be turned into cash, used up, sold, or expired.

_____ 8. An income statement divided into sections for revenue, cost of goods sold, operating expenses, income from operations, and other income and expenses.

_____ 9. Debts that are due for payment within one year.

_____ 10. A balance sheet divided into subsections for current and plant assets and current and long-term liabilities.

_____ 11. Gross profit minus operating expenses.

_____ 12. Debts that are not due for payment within one year.

_____ 13. Expenses that are not directly associated with the actual running of the business.

_____ 14. Entries made as of the first day of a new accounting period to offset certain adjusting entries.

_____ 15. The ratio obtained by dividing current assets by current liabilities.

_____ 16. Assets that are expected to be used in the business for more than one year.

Fill in the Blanks

Please complete each sentence with the correct word or words.

1. A classified income statement is divided into sections as follows: _____, cost of goods sold, _____, income from operations, and other income and expenses.

2. Gross profit is determined by taking net sales for the period and subtracting _____.

3. Gross profit minus _____ equals income from operations.

4. Net sales is calculated by subtracting the amount of _____ and the amount of _____ from the amount of sales.

5. Adding _____ to beginning merchandise inventory gives the goods available for sale.

6. Cost of goods sold is determined by computing the _____ and subtracting ending merchandise inventory.

7. Interest expense is an example of _____.

8. Cash is an example of a(n) _____ asset.

9. Accounts payable is an example of a(n) _____.

10. _____ is computed by subtracting current liabilities from current assets.

11. The current ratio is calculated by dividing current assets by _____.

12. The adjusting entries on the work sheet must be _____ and _____.

13. The Income Summary account will have _____ adjusting entries and _____ closing entries posted to it before it is closed.

14. The _____ is taken to assure that the general ledger is in balance to begin the new period.

15. Adjustments for accrued expenses are often _____ at the start of a new accounting period.

Multiple Choice

Please circle the correct answer.

1. Which of the following represents the divisions found in a classified income statement?
   a. Revenue, assets, liabilities, and owner's equity
   b. Revenue, cost of goods sold, operating expenses, income from operations, and other income and expenses
   c. Revenue and expenses
   d. Assets, liabilities, and owner's equity

2. Net sales for the period is computed by
   a. subtracting the amount of sales returns and allowances and the amount of sales discounts from the amount of sales.
   b. adding the amount of purchases returns and allowances and the amount of purchases discounts to the amount of sales.
   c. adding the amount of sales returns and allowances and the amount of sales discounts to the amount of sales.
   d. footing the Sales account.

3. Cost of goods sold is
   a. the cost of operating a merchandising business.
   b. the cost of merchandise sold by the business.
   c. the cost of purchases made during the period.
   d. the cost of purchases plus the beginning inventory of the period.

4. The three figures needed to determine cost of goods sold are
   a. purchases, purchases returns and allowances, and purchases discounts.
   b. purchases, freight in, and purchases returns and allowances.
   c. beginning inventory, purchases, and freight in.
   d. beginning inventory, net purchases, and ending inventory.

5. Gross profit is
   a. revenues minus expenses.
   b. revenues minus cost of goods sold and operating expenses.
   c. revenues minus all costs and expenses.
   d. revenues minus cost of goods sold.

6. Some examples of operating expenses are
   a. salaries, utilities, and rent.
   b. insurance, interest, and supplies used.
   c. salaries, utilities, and the owner's withdrawals.
   d. utilities, supplies used, and accounts payable.

7. An example of other expenses is
   a. rent expense.
   b. depreciation expense.
   c. interest expense.
   d. salaries expense.

8. Current assets include such assets as
   a. cash, accounts receivable, and prepaid insurance.
   b. cash, equipment, and land.
   c. cash, buildings, and owner's capital.
   d. cash, merchandise inventory, and office furniture.

9. Plant assets include such assets as
   a. cash, accounts receivable, and prepaid insurance.
   b. buildings, equipment, and accounts receivable.
   c. land, buildings, and cash.
   d. land, buildings, and equipment.

10. Current assets are generally listed on the balance sheet according to their
    a. stability.
    b. cost.
    c. liquidity.
    d. durability.

11. Some examples of current liabilities include
    a. accounts payable and mortgages payable.
    b. accounts payable and salaries payable.
    c. salaries payable and long-term notes payable.
    d. only accounts payable.

12. Working capital analysis attempts to answer which of the following questions?
    a. Does the business have enough capital to operate?
    b. Does the business have enough capital to continue growing?
    c. Does the business have enough capital to pay its current debts on time?
    d. All of the above

13. Working capital is
    a. current assets divided by current liabilities.
    b. current liabilities divided by current assets.
    c. current assets minus current liabilities.
    d. current liabilities minus current assets.

14. The current ratio is
    a. current assets divided by current liabilities.
    b. current liabilities divided by current assets.
    c. current assets minus current liabilities.
    d. current liabilities minus current assets.

15. Before it is closed, the Income Summary account will have four entries posted to it. They are
    a. beginning inventory and revenues on the debit side and ending inventory and expenses on the credit side.
    b. ending inventory and revenues on the debit side and beginning inventory and expenses on the credit side.
    c. beginning inventory and expenses on the debit side and ending inventory and revenues on the credit side.
    d. None of the above

Writing/Short Answer

1. **Reflect** Make a list, in words or simple phrases, of the most important and meaningful points in this chapter.

2. **Question** Think about the most confusing points or the material you do not understand in this chapter. Write down two or three questions that remain unanswered.

3. **Connect** Explain, in one or two sentences, the connection between the main points of this chapter and the major goals of the entire course.

4. **Summarize** Review this chapter's Joining the Pieces visual summary, and explain the concept(s) illustrated in a few sentences.

Skills Review

Quick Practice

QUICK PRACTICE 10-1

1. _____

2. _____

3. _____

4. _____

5. _____

6. _____

7. _____

8. _____

QUICK PRACTICE 10-2

Kendall Kandlemakers																
Income Statement (Partial)																
For Year Ended December 31, 20XX																

QUICK PRACTICE 10-3

<table>
<tr><td colspan="10" align="center">Kendall Kandlemakers
Income Statement (Partial)
For Year Ended December 31, 20XX</td></tr>
<tr><td></td><td></td><td></td><td></td><td></td><td></td><td></td><td></td><td></td><td></td></tr>
<tr><td></td><td></td><td></td><td></td><td></td><td></td><td></td><td></td><td></td><td></td></tr>
<tr><td></td><td></td><td></td><td></td><td></td><td></td><td></td><td></td><td></td><td></td></tr>
<tr><td></td><td></td><td></td><td></td><td></td><td></td><td></td><td></td><td></td><td></td></tr>
<tr><td></td><td></td><td></td><td></td><td></td><td></td><td></td><td></td><td></td><td></td></tr>
<tr><td></td><td></td><td></td><td></td><td></td><td></td><td></td><td></td><td></td><td></td></tr>
<tr><td></td><td></td><td></td><td></td><td></td><td></td><td></td><td></td><td></td><td></td></tr>
<tr><td></td><td></td><td></td><td></td><td></td><td></td><td></td><td></td><td></td><td></td></tr>
<tr><td></td><td></td><td></td><td></td><td></td><td></td><td></td><td></td><td></td><td></td></tr>
</table>

QUICK PRACTICE 10-4

<table>
<tr><td colspan="10" align="center">Kendall Kandlemakers
Income Statement (Partial)
For Year Ended December 31, 20XX</td></tr>
<tr><td></td><td></td><td></td><td></td><td></td><td></td><td></td><td></td><td></td><td></td></tr>
<tr><td></td><td></td><td></td><td></td><td></td><td></td><td></td><td></td><td></td><td></td></tr>
<tr><td></td><td></td><td></td><td></td><td></td><td></td><td></td><td></td><td></td><td></td></tr>
<tr><td></td><td></td><td></td><td></td><td></td><td></td><td></td><td></td><td></td><td></td></tr>
<tr><td></td><td></td><td></td><td></td><td></td><td></td><td></td><td></td><td></td><td></td></tr>
<tr><td></td><td></td><td></td><td></td><td></td><td></td><td></td><td></td><td></td><td></td></tr>
<tr><td></td><td></td><td></td><td></td><td></td><td></td><td></td><td></td><td></td><td></td></tr>
<tr><td></td><td></td><td></td><td></td><td></td><td></td><td></td><td></td><td></td><td></td></tr>
<tr><td></td><td></td><td></td><td></td><td></td><td></td><td></td><td></td><td></td><td></td></tr>
<tr><td></td><td></td><td></td><td></td><td></td><td></td><td></td><td></td><td></td><td></td></tr>
<tr><td></td><td></td><td></td><td></td><td></td><td></td><td></td><td></td><td></td><td></td></tr>
<tr><td></td><td></td><td></td><td></td><td></td><td></td><td></td><td></td><td></td><td></td></tr>
<tr><td></td><td></td><td></td><td></td><td></td><td></td><td></td><td></td><td></td><td></td></tr>
</table>

Kendall Kandlemakers																		
Income Statement (Partial)																		
For Year Ended December 31, 20XX																		

Kendall Kandlemakers
Income Statement
For Year Ended December 31, 20XX

QUICK PRACTICE 10-7

1.

Income Summary

2.

General Journal

Page 1

	Date		Account Title	P.R.	Debit	Credit	
1							1
2							2
3							3
4							4
5							5
6							6
7							7
8							8
9							9
10							10
11							11
12							12
13							13
14							14
15							15
16							16
17							17
18							18
19							19
20							20
21							21
22							22

3. _____

QUICK PRACTICE 10-8

1. _____

2. _____

3. _____

4. _____

5. _____

6. _____

7. _____

8. _____

QUICK PRACTICE 10-9

(a) _____

(b) _____

Exercises

EXERCISE 10-1

EXERCISE 10-2

(a)

(b)

(c)

(d)

EXERCISE 10-3

(a)

(b)

(c)

EXERCISE 10-4

1.

EXERCISE 10-4 (continued)

2.

3.

4.

General Journal

	Date		Account Title	P.R.	Debit	Credit	
1							1
2							2
3							3
4							4
5							5
6							6
7							7
8							8
9							9
10							10
11							11
12							12
13							13
14							14
15							15
16							16
17							17
18							18
19							19
20							20
21							21
22							22
23							23
24							24
25							25
26							26
27							27
28							28
29							29
30							30
31							31
32							32

EXERCISE 10-5

EXERCISE 10-6

1. _____   5. _____   9. _____

2. _____   6. _____   10. _____

3. _____   7. _____

4. _____   8. _____

EXERCISE 10-7

(a) _____

(b) _____

EXERCISE 10-8

Income Summary

Case Problems

This page intentionally left blank.

1.

PROBLEM 10-2A OR 10-2B(continued)

2.

(a) _____

(b) _____

1.

2.

PROBLEM 10-3A OR 10-3B (continued)

3.

This page intentionally left blank.

PROBLEM 10-4A OR 10-4B

	Date	Account Title	P.R.	Debit	Credit	
1						1
2						2
3						3
4						4
5						5
6						6
7						7
8						8
9						9
10						10
11						11
12						12
13						13
14						14
15						15
16						16
17						17
18						18
19						19
20						20
21						21
22						22
23						23
24						24
25						25
26						26
27						27
28						28
29						29
30						30
31						31
32						32

This page intentionally left blank.

PROBLEM 10-5A OR 10-5B

General Journal

Page _____

	Date		Account Title	P.R.	Debit	Credit	
1							1
2							2
3							3
4							4
5							5
6							6
7							7
8							8
9							9
10							10
11							11
12							12
13							13
14							14
15							15
16							16
17							17
18							18
19							19
20							20
21							21
22							22
23							23
24							24
25							25
26							26
27							27
28							28
29							29
30							30
31							31
32							32

This page intentionally left blank.

General Journal

	Date		Account Title	P.R.	Debit	Credit	
1							1
2							2
3							3
4							4
5							5
6							6
7							7
8							8
9							9
10							10
11							11
12							12
13							13
14							14
15							15
16							16
17							17
18							18
19							19
20							20
21							21
22							22
23							23
24							24
25							25
26							26
27							27
28							28
29							29
30							30
31							31
32							32

This page intentionally left blank.

Critical Thinking Problems

Challenge Problem

1., 6., 7.   **General Ledger**

ACCOUNT Cash   ACCOUNT NO. 111

DATE	ITEM	P.R.	DEBIT	CREDIT	BALANCE DEBIT	BALANCE CREDIT

ACCOUNT Accounts Receivable   ACCOUNT NO. 112

DATE	ITEM	P.R.	DEBIT	CREDIT	BALANCE DEBIT	BALANCE CREDIT

ACCOUNT Merchandise Inventory   ACCOUNT NO. 113

DATE	ITEM	P.R.	DEBIT	CREDIT	BALANCE DEBIT	BALANCE CREDIT

ACCOUNT Office Supplies   ACCOUNT NO. 114

DATE	ITEM	P.R.	DEBIT	CREDIT	BALANCE DEBIT	BALANCE CREDIT

Challenge Problem (continued)

ACCOUNT Store Supplies   ACCOUNT NO. 115

DATE	ITEM	P.R.	DEBIT	CREDIT	BALANCE DEBIT	BALANCE CREDIT

ACCOUNT Prepaid Insurance   ACCOUNT NO. 116

DATE	ITEM	P.R.	DEBIT	CREDIT	BALANCE DEBIT	BALANCE CREDIT

ACCOUNT Office Equipment   ACCOUNT NO. 118

DATE	ITEM	P.R.	DEBIT	CREDIT	BALANCE DEBIT	BALANCE CREDIT

ACCOUNT Accumulated Depreciation—Office Equipment   ACCOUNT NO. 118.1

DATE	ITEM	P.R.	DEBIT	CREDIT	BALANCE DEBIT	BALANCE CREDIT

ACCOUNT Store Equipment   ACCOUNT NO. 119

DATE	ITEM	P.R.	DEBIT	CREDIT	BALANCE DEBIT	BALANCE CREDIT

Challenge Problem (continued)

ACCOUNT Accumulated Depreciation—Store Equipment   ACCOUNT NO. 119.1

DATE	ITEM	P.R.	DEBIT	CREDIT	BALANCE DEBIT	CREDIT

ACCOUNT Delivery Equipment   ACCOUNT NO. 120

DATE	ITEM	P.R.	DEBIT	CREDIT	BALANCE DEBIT	CREDIT

ACCOUNT Accumulated Depreciation—Delivery Equipment   ACCOUNT NO. 120.1

DATE	ITEM	P.R.	DEBIT	CREDIT	BALANCE DEBIT	CREDIT

ACCOUNT Accounts Payable   ACCOUNT NO. 211

DATE	ITEM	P.R.	DEBIT	CREDIT	BALANCE DEBIT	CREDIT

ACCOUNT Salaries Payable   ACCOUNT NO. 212

DATE	ITEM	P.R.	DEBIT	CREDIT	BALANCE DEBIT	CREDIT

ACCOUNT Notes Payable   ACCOUNT NO. 221

DATE	ITEM	P.R.	DEBIT	CREDIT	BALANCE DEBIT	CREDIT

Challenge Problem (continued)

ACCOUNT John Hatfield, Capital   ACCOUNT NO. 311

DATE	ITEM	P.R.	DEBIT	CREDIT	BALANCE DEBIT	BALANCE CREDIT

ACCOUNT John Hatfield, Drawing   ACCOUNT NO. 312

DATE	ITEM	P.R.	DEBIT	CREDIT	BALANCE DEBIT	BALANCE CREDIT

ACCOUNT Income Summary   ACCOUNT NO. 315

DATE	ITEM	P.R.	DEBIT	CREDIT	BALANCE DEBIT	BALANCE CREDIT

ACCOUNT Sales   ACCOUNT NO. 411

DATE	ITEM	P.R.	DEBIT	CREDIT	BALANCE DEBIT	BALANCE CREDIT

ACCOUNT Sales Returns and Allowances   ACCOUNT NO. 411.1

DATE	ITEM	P.R.	DEBIT	CREDIT	BALANCE DEBIT	BALANCE CREDIT

Challenge Problem (continued)

ACCOUNT **Sales Discounts**   ACCOUNT NO. 411.2

DATE		ITEM	P.R.	DEBIT	CREDIT	BALANCE	
						DEBIT	CREDIT

ACCOUNT **Purchases**   ACCOUNT NO. 511

DATE		ITEM	P.R.	DEBIT	CREDIT	BALANCE	
						DEBIT	CREDIT

ACCOUNT **Purchases Returns and Allowances**   ACCOUNT NO. 511.1

DATE		ITEM	P.R.	DEBIT	CREDIT	BALANCE	
						DEBIT	CREDIT

ACCOUNT **Purchases Discounts**   ACCOUNT NO. 511.2

DATE		ITEM	P.R.	DEBIT	CREDIT	BALANCE	
						DEBIT	CREDIT

ACCOUNT **Freight In**   ACCOUNT NO. 512

DATE		ITEM	P.R.	DEBIT	CREDIT	BALANCE	
						DEBIT	CREDIT

Challenge Problem (continued)

ACCOUNT Sales Salaries Expense   ACCOUNT NO. 611

DATE	ITEM	P.R.	DEBIT	CREDIT	BALANCE DEBIT	BALANCE CREDIT

ACCOUNT Store Supplies Expense   ACCOUNT NO. 612

DATE	ITEM	P.R.	DEBIT	CREDIT	BALANCE DEBIT	BALANCE CREDIT

ACCOUNT Advertising Expense   ACCOUNT NO. 613

DATE	ITEM	P.R.	DEBIT	CREDIT	BALANCE DEBIT	BALANCE CREDIT

ACCOUNT Depreciation Expense—Store Equipment   ACCOUNT NO. 614

DATE	ITEM	P.R.	DEBIT	CREDIT	BALANCE DEBIT	BALANCE CREDIT

ACCOUNT Depreciation Expense—Delivery Equipment   ACCOUNT NO. 615

DATE	ITEM	P.R.	DEBIT	CREDIT	BALANCE DEBIT	BALANCE CREDIT

Challenge Problem (continued)

ACCOUNT Rent Expense

ACCOUNT NO. 616

DATE		ITEM	P.R.	DEBIT	CREDIT	BALANCE	
						DEBIT	CREDIT

ACCOUNT Office Salaries Expense

ACCOUNT NO. 617

DATE		ITEM	P.R.	DEBIT	CREDIT	BALANCE	
						DEBIT	CREDIT

ACCOUNT Office Supplies Expense

ACCOUNT NO. 618

DATE		ITEM	P.R.	DEBIT	CREDIT	BALANCE	
						DEBIT	CREDIT

ACCOUNT Utilities Expense

ACCOUNT NO. 619

DATE		ITEM	P.R.	DEBIT	CREDIT	BALANCE	
						DEBIT	CREDIT

ACCOUNT Depreciation Expense—Office Equipment

ACCOUNT NO. 620

DATE		ITEM	P.R.	DEBIT	CREDIT	BALANCE	
						DEBIT	CREDIT

Challenge Problem (continued)

ACCOUNT Insurance Expense   ACCOUNT NO. 621

DATE		ITEM	P.R.	DEBIT	CREDIT	BALANCE	
						DEBIT	CREDIT

ACCOUNT Miscellaneous Expense   ACCOUNT NO. 622

DATE		ITEM	P.R.	DEBIT	CREDIT	BALANCE	
						DEBIT	CREDIT

ACCOUNT Interest Expense   ACCOUNT NO. 623

DATE		ITEM	P.R.	DEBIT	CREDIT	BALANCE	
						DEBIT	CREDIT

Challenge Problem (continued)

2.

Hatfield's Department Store								
Income Statement								
For Year Ended December 31, 20X2								

Challenge Problem (continued)

3.

Hatfield's Department Store											
Statement of Owner's Equity											
For Year Ended December 31, 20X2											

Challenge Problem (continued)

4.

	Hatfield's Department Store Balance Sheet December 31, 20X2												

Challenge Problem (continued)

5. _____

_____

6.

General Journal   Page 1

	Date		Account Title	P.R.	Debit	Credit	
1							1
2							2
3							3
4							4
5							5
6							6
7							7
8							8
9							9
10							10
11							11
12							12
13							13
14							14
15							15
16							16
17							17
18							18
19							19
20							20
21							21
22							22
23							23
24							24
25							25
26							26
27							27
28							28
29							29

Challenge Problem (continued)

7.

	Date		Account Title	P.R.	Debit	Credit	
1							1
2							2
3							3
4							4
5							5
6							6
7							7
8							8
9							9
10							10
11							11
12							12
13							13
14							14
15							15
16							16
17							17
18							18
19							19
20							20
21							21
22							22
23							23
24							24
25							25
26							26
27							27
28							28
29							29
30							30
31							31
32							32

Challenge Problem (continued)

8.

Hatfield's Department Store		
Post-Closing Trial Balance		
December 31, 20X2		
Account Title	Debit	Credit

9. **General Journal** Page 3

	Date	Account Title	P.R.	Debit	Credit	
1						1
2						2
3						3
4						4
5						5
6						6
7						7
8						8

Challenge Problem (continued)

10. Comments on the financial condition of the company:

_____

_____

_____

_____

_____

_____

_____

_____

_____

_____

_____

_____

_____

_____

_____

_____

_____

This page intentionally left blank.

Communications

_____

_____

_____

_____

_____

_____

_____

_____

_____

_____

_____

_____

_____

_____

_____

_____

Team Internet Project

_____

_____

_____

_____

_____

_____

_____

_____

_____

_____

_____

_____

_____

_____

_____

_____

_____

_____

Ethics

In the Real World

Practice Test Answers

True/False

1. F
2. T
3. F
4. T
5. T
6. F
7. T
8. T
9. T
10. F
11. T
12. T
13. F
14. F
15. F

Matching

1. l
2. c
3. g
4. k
5. d
6. p
7. i
8. b
9. e
10. a
11. h
12. j
13. m
14. o
15. f
16. n

Fill in the Blanks

1. revenue, operating expenses
2. cost of goods sold
3. operating expenses
4. sales returns and allowances, sales discounts
5. net purchases
6. goods available for sale
7. other expenses
8. current
9. current liability
10. Working capital
11. current liabilities
12. journalized, posted
13. four
14. post-closing trial balance
15. reversed

Multiple Choice

1. b
2. a
3. b
4. d
5. d
6. a
7. c
8. a
9. d
10. c
11. b
12. d
13. c
14. a
15. c

Writing/Short Answer

Answers will vary. Please discuss questions with your instructor.

Mills Sporting Goods Store

1., 6., 10., 11., 18., 22., 23.   **General Ledger**

ACCOUNT Cash   ACCOUNT NO. 111

DATE	ITEM	P.R.	DEBIT	CREDIT	BALANCE DEBIT	BALANCE CREDIT

ACCOUNT Accounts Receivable   ACCOUNT NO. 112

DATE	ITEM	P.R.	DEBIT	CREDIT	BALANCE DEBIT	BALANCE CREDIT

ACCOUNT Office Supplies   ACCOUNT NO. 113

DATE	ITEM	P.R.	DEBIT	CREDIT	BALANCE	
					DEBIT	CREDIT

ACCOUNT Store Supplies   ACCOUNT NO. 114

DATE	ITEM	P.R.	DEBIT	CREDIT	BALANCE	
					DEBIT	CREDIT

ACCOUNT Merchandise Inventory   ACCOUNT NO. 115

DATE	ITEM	P.R.	DEBIT	CREDIT	BALANCE	
					DEBIT	CREDIT

ACCOUNT Prepaid Insurance   ACCOUNT NO. 116

DATE	ITEM	P.R.	DEBIT	CREDIT	BALANCE	
					DEBIT	CREDIT

ACCOUNT Office Equipment   ACCOUNT NO. 121

DATE	ITEM	P.R.	DEBIT	CREDIT	BALANCE	
					DEBIT	CREDIT

ACCOUNT Accumulated Depreciation—Office Equipment   ACCOUNT NO. 121.1

DATE	ITEM	P.R.	DEBIT	CREDIT	BALANCE	
					DEBIT	CREDIT

ACCOUNT Store Equipment   ACCOUNT NO. 122

DATE	ITEM	P.R.	DEBIT	CREDIT	BALANCE	
					DEBIT	CREDIT

ACCOUNT Accumulated Depreciation—Store Equipment   ACCOUNT NO. 122.1

DATE	ITEM	P.R.	DEBIT	CREDIT	BALANCE	
					DEBIT	CREDIT

ACCOUNT Delivery Equipment   ACCOUNT NO. 123

DATE		ITEM	P.R.	DEBIT	CREDIT	BALANCE	
						DEBIT	CREDIT

ACCOUNT Accumulated Depreciation—Delivery Equipment   ACCOUNT NO. 123.1

DATE		ITEM	P.R.	DEBIT	CREDIT	BALANCE	
						DEBIT	CREDIT

ACCOUNT Accounts Payable   ACCOUNT NO. 211

DATE		ITEM	P.R.	DEBIT	CREDIT	BALANCE	
						DEBIT	CREDIT

ACCOUNT Cindi Mills, Capital   ACCOUNT NO. 311

DATE	ITEM	P.R.	DEBIT	CREDIT	BALANCE DEBIT	BALANCE CREDIT

ACCOUNT Cindi Mills, Drawing   ACCOUNT NO. 312

DATE	ITEM	P.R.	DEBIT	CREDIT	BALANCE DEBIT	BALANCE CREDIT

ACCOUNT Income Summary   ACCOUNT NO. 313

DATE	ITEM	P.R.	DEBIT	CREDIT	BALANCE DEBIT	BALANCE CREDIT

ACCOUNT Sales

ACCOUNT NO. 411

DATE		ITEM	P.R.	DEBIT	CREDIT	BALANCE	
						DEBIT	CREDIT

ACCOUNT Sales Returns and Allowances

ACCOUNT NO. 412

DATE		ITEM	P.R.	DEBIT	CREDIT	BALANCE	
						DEBIT	CREDIT

ACCOUNT Sales Discounts

ACCOUNT NO. 413

DATE		ITEM	P.R.	DEBIT	CREDIT	BALANCE	
						DEBIT	CREDIT

ACCOUNT Purchases

ACCOUNT NO. 511

DATE		ITEM	P.R.	DEBIT	CREDIT	BALANCE	
						DEBIT	CREDIT

ACCOUNT Purchases Returns and Allowances   ACCOUNT NO. 512

DATE	ITEM	P.R.	DEBIT	CREDIT	BALANCE DEBIT	CREDIT

ACCOUNT Purchases Discounts   ACCOUNT NO. 513

DATE	ITEM	P.R.	DEBIT	CREDIT	BALANCE DEBIT	CREDIT

ACCOUNT Freight In   ACCOUNT NO. 514

DATE	ITEM	P.R.	DEBIT	CREDIT	BALANCE DEBIT	CREDIT

ACCOUNT Salaries Expense   ACCOUNT NO. 611

DATE	ITEM	P.R.	DEBIT	CREDIT	BALANCE DEBIT	CREDIT

ACCOUNT Rent Expense   ACCOUNT NO. 612

DATE		ITEM	P.R.	DEBIT	CREDIT	BALANCE	
						DEBIT	CREDIT

ACCOUNT Utilities Expense   ACCOUNT NO. 613

DATE		ITEM	P.R.	DEBIT	CREDIT	BALANCE	
						DEBIT	CREDIT

ACCOUNT Office Supplies Expense   ACCOUNT NO. 614

DATE		ITEM	P.R.	DEBIT	CREDIT	BALANCE	
						DEBIT	CREDIT

ACCOUNT Store Supplies Expense   ACCOUNT NO. 615

DATE		ITEM	P.R.	DEBIT	CREDIT	BALANCE	
						DEBIT	CREDIT

ACCOUNT Insurance Expense   ACCOUNT NO. 616

DATE	ITEM	P.R.	DEBIT	CREDIT	BALANCE DEBIT	BALANCE CREDIT

ACCOUNT Depreciation Expense—Office Equipment   ACCOUNT NO. 617

DATE	ITEM	P.R.	DEBIT	CREDIT	BALANCE DEBIT	BALANCE CREDIT

ACCOUNT Depreciation Expense—Store Equipment   ACCOUNT NO. 618

DATE	ITEM	P.R.	DEBIT	CREDIT	BALANCE DEBIT	BALANCE CREDIT

ACCOUNT Depreciation Expense—Delivery Equipment   ACCOUNT NO. 619

DATE	ITEM	P.R.	DEBIT	CREDIT	BALANCE DEBIT	BALANCE CREDIT

NAME   Henry Galvin

ADDRESS

Date	Item	P.R.	Debit	Credit	Balance

NAME   Lee Maddox

ADDRESS

Date	Item	P.R.	Debit	Credit	Balance

NAME   Neagle Co.

ADDRESS

Date	Item	P.R.	Debit	Credit	Balance

NAME   Smitz, Inc.

ADDRESS

Date		Item	P.R.	Debit	Credit	Balance

3., 6., 18.   **Accounts Payable Ledger**

NAME   W. Bedford Co.

ADDRESS

Date		Item	P.R.	Debit	Credit	Balance

NAME   Jones Co.

ADDRESS

Date		Item	P.R.	Debit	Credit	Balance

NAME   Lemke Brothers

ADDRESS

Date		Item	P.R.	Debit	Credit	Balance

NAME   Wohlers, Inc.

ADDRESS

Date		Item	P.R.	Debit	Credit	Balance

	Date		Account Title	P.R.	Debit	Credit	
1							1
2							2
3							3
4							4
5							5
6							6
7							7
8							8
9							9
10							10
11							11
12							12
13							13
14							14
15							15
16							16
17							17
18							18
19							19
20							20
21							21
22							22
23							23
24							24
25							25
26							26
27							27
28							28
29							29
30							30
31							31
32							32
33							33
34							34
35							35
36							36

	Date		Account Title	P.R.	Debit	Credit	
1							1
2							2
3							3
4							4
5							5
6							6
7							7
8							8
9							9
10							10
11							11
12							12
13							13
14							14
15							15
16							16
17							17
18							18
19							19
20							20
21							21
22							22
23							23
24							24
25							25
26							26
27							27
28							28
29							29
30							30
31							31
32							32
33							33
34							34

	Date		Account Title	P.R.	Debit	Credit	
1							1
2							2
3							3
4							4
5							5
6							6
7							7
8							8
9							9
10							10
11							11
12							12
13							13
14							14
15							15
16							16
17							17
18							18
19							19
20							20
21							21
22							22
23							23
24							24
25							25
26							26
27							27
28							28
29							29
30							30
31							31
32							32
33							33
34							34

	Date		Account Title	P.R.	Debit	Credit	
1							1
2							2
3							3
4							4
5							5
6							6
7							7
8							8
9							9
10							10
11							11
12							12
13							13
14							14
15							15
16							16
17							17
18							18
19							19
20							20
21							21
22							22
23							23
24							24
25							25
26							26
27							27
28							28
29							29
30							30
31							31
32							32
33							33
34							34
35							35
36							36
37							37

	Date		Account Title	P.R.	Debit	Credit	
1							1
2							2
3							3
4							4
5							5
6							6
7							7
8							8
9							9
10							10
11							11
12							12
13							13
14							14
15							15
16							16
17							17
18							18
19							19
20							20
21							21
22							22
23							23
24							24
25							25
26							26
27							27
28							28
29							29
30							30
31							31
32							32

	Date		Invoice No.	Customer's Name	P.R.		Accts. Rec. Dr. Sales Cr.					
1												1
2												2
3												3
4												4
5												5
6												6
7												7
8												8
9												9
10												10
11												11
12												12
13												13
14												14
15												15

4., 5., 16., 17.   **Purchases Journal**   Page 10

	Date		Invoice No.	Account Credited	P.R.		Purchases Dr. Accts. Pay. Cr.					
1												1
2												2
3												3
4												4
5												5
6												6
7												7
8												8
9												9
10												10
11												11
12												12
13												13

Date	Account Credited	P.R.	General Cr.	Sales Cr.	Accounts Rec. Cr.	Sales Discounts Dr.	Cash Dr.

Date	Ck. No.	Account Debited	P.R.	General Dr.	Accounts Payable Dr.	Purchases Discounts Cr.	Cash Cr.

This page intentionally left blank.

7., 9.

	Mills Sporting Goods Store								
	Work Sheet								
	For Month Ended January 31, 20X1								
Account Title	Trial Balance				Adjustments				
	Debit		Credit		Debit		Credit		

	Adjusted Trial Balance		Income Statement		Balance Sheet	
	Debit	Credit	Debit	Credit	Debit	Credit

8.

Mills Sporting Goods Store					
Schedule of Accounts Receivable					
January 31, 20X1					

Mills Sporting Goods Store
Schedule of Accounts Payable
January 31, 20X1

12.

	Mills Sporting Goods Store															
	Post-Closing Trial Balance															
	January 31, 20X1															
Account Title	Debit					Credit				

13.

Mills Sporting Goods Store															
Income Statement															
For Month Ended January 31, 20X1															

14.

Mills Sporting Goods Store										
Statement of Owner's Equity										
For Month Ended January 31, 20X1										

15.

Mills Sporting Goods Store											
Balance Sheet											
January 31, 20X1											

19., 21.

	Mills Sporting Goods Store					
	Work Sheet					
	For Month Ended February 28, 20X1					

Account Title	Trial Balance		Adjustments	
	Debit	Credit	Debit	Credit

	Adjusted Trial Balance		Income Statement		Balance Sheet	
	Debit	Credit	Debit	Credit	Debit	Credit

20.

Mills Sporting Goods Store						
Schedule of Accounts Receivable						
February 28, 20X1						

Mills Sporting Goods Store

Schedule of Accounts Payable

February 28, 20X1

24.

Mills Sporting Goods Store				
Post-Closing Trial Balance				
February 28, 20X1				
Account Title	Debit		Credit	

25.

Mills Sporting Goods Store
Income Statement
For Month Ended February 28, 20X1

26.

Mills Sporting Goods Store										
Statement of Owner's Equity										
For Month Ended February 28, 20X1										

27.

Mills Sporting Goods Store															
Balance Sheet															
February 28, 20X1															

Accounting for Payroll

Employee Earnings and Deductions

Chapter Summary  Interactive Summary in English and Spanish

An **independent contractor** is an individual who performs a task for hire and has no permanent relationship with the hiring party. An **employee** works for others and is under the continuing control of those others. Almost all businesses have employees and, therefore, must make regular payments to them. These payments are referred to as payroll expense, wages expense, or salaries expense. Payroll expense is often a significant portion of the operating expenses of a business. Therefore, good control must be exercised over the payroll system.

The term **wage** is usually used to describe an amount paid by the hour. The term **salary** is usually used to describe an amount paid by the week, month, or year. In practice, the terms *wage* and *salary* are used interchangeably. Some employees are paid by a **piece-rate plan**, one in which they receive so much per unit produced.

Wage earners are typically covered by the **Fair Labor Standards Act**, commonly referred to as the Wages and Hours Law. Under this act, covered workers are entitled to a **minimum wage** and **overtime pay** for hours worked in excess of 40 in any workweek. Overtime means that an employee must be paid at least **time-and-a-half** (one and one-half times the regular rate) for overtime hours. Some companies have gone beyond this minimum and pay double time (two times the regular rate) for weekend and holiday work. Additionally, some companies pay overtime for any hours in excess of 8 in a day, even though total hours may not reach 40 for a week.

Gross earnings is the total amount that an employee earns before any amount is deducted by the employer. Gross earnings may be calculated on a weekly, biweekly, semimonthly, or monthly basis, depending on how often employees are paid. Gross earnings of a **salaried employee** are usually stated on an annual basis and then divided by the number of pay periods in the year to find the amount of gross earnings for each period. Gross earnings of an **hourly worker** are calculated by multiplying the number of hours worked by the hourly rate, including one and one-half or two times the hourly rate for overtime hours worked.

A **payroll deduction** is an amount that the employer withholds from the gross earnings of the employee. Payroll deductions are of two types: (1) required deductions and (2) optional deductions. The two required deductions are income taxes and **Federal Insurance Contributions Act (FICA)** taxes. Income taxes are collected by the federal government and may also be collected by state and local governments.

When an employee is hired, he or she fills out an **Employee's Withholding Allowance Certificate (Form W-4)**. On FormW-4, the employee indicates the **withholding allowances** (or exemptions) claimed. The amount of income tax withheld is then determined based on the employee's gross earnings, marital status, and number of withholding allowances, using an approach called the **wage bracket method**. Amounts to be withheld can be found in computer programs or in the **Employer's Tax Guide (Circular E)**.

FICA taxes, more commonly known as Social Security taxes, are used to finance (1) federal Old-Age, Survivors, and Disability Insurance (OASDI) and (2) federal Hospital Insurance (**HI**), or Medicare. The FICA tax rate is actually in two parts, one for OASDI and one for HI. All wages are subject to the HI rate, but there is a limit to the OASDI wages taxed, called the **OASDI taxable wage base**.

Optional deductions include union dues, insurance premiums, loan repayments, and deductions for various types of savings and retirement plans. The employer incurs a liability for each of these deductions and must remit them to the appropriate agency in a timely manner and according to contract terms.

Net earnings (net pay) are the result of subtracting all deductions from gross earnings. Another name for net earnings is take-home pay.

Employers use two basic means to record payroll information: the payroll register and the employee's earnings record. The **payroll register** is a form that summarizes gross earnings, deductions, and net pay for all employees for a pay period. The payroll register can be prepared manually or be a part of a computerized system. There are many commercial software programs available to handle payroll inexpensively and effectively. After all data are entered in the payroll register, a check of its totals, or **cross-footing**, occurs.

The payroll register is an auxiliary record. To account for the payroll, it is necessary to make a journal entry to record the total gross earnings, totals of the various deductions, and total net earnings for the pay period. The payroll register serves as the source document for the journal entry to record the payroll: to debit the **Salaries Expense account** for gross earnings; credit liability accounts for the deductions, such as the **FICA Tax Payable— OASDI account**, the **FICA Tax Payable—HI account**, and the **Federal Income Tax Payable account**; and credit the **Salaries Payable account** for net earnings.

An **employee's earnings record** has two parts: a heading that includes information about the employee, and a body that includes the employee's gross earnings, deductions, and net earnings for each pay period of the year.

True/False

Please circle the correct answer.

T   F   1. An employee is under the direct control of an employer on a continuing basis.

T   F   2. Payroll accounting applies to everyone who does any work for a firm, whether he or she is an employee or an independent contractor.

T   F   3. Salaried employees work for a fixed amount for a definite period of time, such as a week or a month.

T   F   4. All salaried employees are covered by the overtime provisions of the Fair Labor Standards Act.

T   F   5. The Fair Labor Standards Act requires overtime pay for covered employees at a minimum of one and one-half times the regular hourly rate for any hours worked beyond the normal 40 hours per week.

T   F.   6. Overtime pay beyond 8 hours a day is a matter of company policy, not federal law, if an employee works 40 or fewer hours during a week.

T   F   7. A piece-rate plan pays workers a certain rate per unit produced.

T   F   8. Gross earnings are the amount that is left after deductions.

T   F   9. The federal government requires withholdings for federal income taxes and Social Security taxes.

T   F   10. Deductions other than income taxes and FICA taxes are optional, not required.

T   F   11. The same rate applies to both the OASDI and HI parts of the FICA tax.

T   F   12. Net earnings is gross earnings minus all deductions.

T   F   13. Employers are required to keep a record called the payroll register for each employee during a calendar year.

T   F   14. The Salaries Expense account is debited for the amount of net earnings.

T   F   15. The payroll register and the employee's earnings record serve different purposes in a payroll system.

Matching

Please match each of the following terms with its definition.

a. cross-footing
b. employee
c. employee's earnings record
d. Employer's Tax Guide (Circular E)
e. Fair Labor Standards Act
f. FICA
g. Form W-4
h. gross earnings
i. independent contractor
j. minimum wage

k. net earnings
l. OASDI taxable wage base
m. overtime pay
n. payroll register
o. piece-rate plan
p. salary
q. wage
r. wage bracket method
s. withhold
t. withholding allowance or exemption

_____ 1. A person under the direct control of an employer on a continuing basis.

_____ 2. A person who agrees to perform and complete a specific job or task and is left to choose the ways and methods of completing that job or task.

_____ 3. A fixed amount paid to employees for a certain period of time, such as a week or a month.

_____ 4. A fixed hourly rate paid to employees.

_____ 5. An act passed by Congress that established standards for minimum wages, overtime pay, child labor, and required payroll record keeping.

_____ 6. An amount set by Congress that is the least that can be paid per hour to employees who are covered under the Fair Labor Standards Act.

_____ 7. A minimum of one and one-half times the regular rate of pay for more than 40 hours of work per week.

_____ 8. A method of payment in which workers are paid for each unit produced rather than so much per hour worked.

_____ 9. An employee's earnings before any amounts are deducted by the employer.

_____ 10. To deduct amounts from an employee's earnings before they are paid.

_____ 11. The law that requires employees and employers to pay taxes to fund the Social Security system.

_____ 12. The maximum amount of an employee's earnings during a calendar year that is subject to OASDI taxes.

_____ 13. An amount of earnings that is not subject to taxation.

_____ 14. A form filled out by every employee showing marital status and number of withholding allowances claimed.

_____ 15. An Internal Revenue Service publication containing federal income tax tables.

_____ 16. A method that uses government tax tables to determine the amount of income tax to withhold from each employee's gross earnings.

_____ 17. Gross earnings minus various deductions.

_____ 18. A summary of the gross earnings, deductions, and net pay for all employees for a specific payroll period.

_____ 19. The addition of columns of figures in different ways to check the accuracy of the totals.

_____ 20. A form that contains basic employee information and a summary of payroll data for that employee for a calendar year.

Fill in the Blanks

Please complete each sentence with the correct word or words.

1. A(n) _____ is a person who agrees to perform and complete a specific job or task and is left to choose the ways and methods of doing so.

2. The Fair Labor Standards Act applies only to firms engaged in _____.

3. The amounts taken from an employee's wages or salary before he or she is paid are called _____.

4. FICA taxes are paid by both the _____ and the _____.

5. The federal government's main source of revenue is the _____.

6. A withholding allowance is also called a(n) _____.

7. Most employers use the _____ method to determine the amount of income tax to be withheld from employee earnings.

8. Most states also require an employer to withhold _____ from the earnings of employees.

9. Net earnings is _____ minus _____.

10. In recording employee earnings and deductions, separate _____ should be maintained for the earnings and for each _____.

11. The _____ amount of payroll is debited to the Salaries Expense account.

12. Social Security taxes deducted from the employees' pay are credited to the _____ and the _____ accounts.

13. The amount of _____ is credited to the Salaries Payable account.

Multiple Choice

Please circle the correct answer.

1. An example of an independent contractor is
   a. a certified public accountant who does auditing and tax work for clients.
   b. a teacher.
   c. a receptionist.
   d. a factory production worker.

2. The number of paychecks received per year by a person who is paid semimonthly is
   a. 12.
   b. 24.
   c. 26.
   d. 52.

3. The federal income tax withheld from an employee's pay depends on which of the following three factors?
   a. Gross earnings, marital status, and occupation
   b. Net pay, exemptions, and marital status
   c. Gross earnings, marital status, and exemptions
   d. None of the above

4. In order for an employer to withhold amounts other than required deductions from an employee's pay,
   a. the union must give permission.
   b. the employee must give permission.
   c. the supervisor must give permission.
   d. the employer may not deduct anything other than taxes.

5. An individual earnings record must be maintained for each employee. This record shows
   a. the name, address, and Social Security number of the employee.
   b. the employee's gross earnings and deductions for each payroll period.
   c. the employee's year-to-date gross earnings and deductions.
   d. All of the above

6. The Salaries Expense account is debited to record
   a. the total amount of net pay.
   b. the total amount of deductions.
   c. the total amount of gross earnings.
   d. None of the above

7. The journal entry to record a payroll would include a debit to
   a. FICA Tax Payable—OASDI.
   b. Federal Income Tax Payable.
   c. Union Dues Payable.
   d. None of the above

Writing/Short Answer

1. **Reflect** Make a list, in words or simple phrases, of the most important and meaningful points in this chapter.

2. **Question** Think about the most confusing points or the material you do not understand in this chapter. Write down two or three questions that remain unanswered.

3. **Connect** Explain, in one or two sentences, the connection between the main points of this chapter and the major goals of the entire course.

4. **Summarize** Review this chapter's Joining the Pieces visual summary, and explain the concept(s) illustrated in a few sentences.

Skills Review

Quick Practice

QUICK PRACTICE 11-1

Amy Hassan _____

_____

_____

Rick Jiminez _____

_____

_____

QUICK PRACTICE 11-2

Total hours = _____

Regular earnings = _____

Overtime earnings = _____

Gross earnings = _____

QUICK PRACTICE 11-3

	FICA	
Employee	**OASDI**	**HI**
Jose Rios	_____	_____
Lori Sweat	_____	_____

QUICK PRACTICE 11-4

_____

_____

QUICK PRACTICE 11-5

Gross Earnings: _____

Deductions:

   OASDI _____

   HI _____

   Federal income tax _____

   Medical insurance _____

Total deductions _____

Net earnings _____

QUICK PRACTICE 11-6

General Journal

Page 1

	Date		Account Title	P.R.	Debit	Credit	
1							1
2							2
3							3
4							4
5							5
6							6
7							7
8							8
9							9
10							10
11							11
12							12

QUICK PRACTICE 11-7

General Journal

Page 2

	Date		Account Title	P.R.	Debit	Credit	
1							1
2							2
3							3
4							4
5							5
6							6
7							7
8							8
9							9
10							10
11							11
12							12

Exercises

EXERCISE 11-1

Bob Darby _____

_____

_____

Sam Jones _____

_____

_____

Joy Smith _____

_____

_____

Ben White _____

_____

_____

EXERCISE 11-2

Total hours = _____

Regular earnings = _____

Overtime earnings = _____

Gross earnings = _____

EXERCISE 11-3

Employee	FICA	
	OASDI	HI
David Mack	_____	_____
Jules Caray	_____	_____
Megan Slats	_____	_____
Kevin Sharp	_____	_____

EXERCISE 11-4

Employee	Amount of Withholding
(a)	_____
(b)	_____
(c)	_____
(d)	_____
(e)	_____

EXERCISE 11-5

Gross earnings:

   Regular earnings   _____

   Overtime earnings   _____

     Gross earnings   _____

Less Deductions:

  FICA—OASDI   _____

  FICA—HI   _____

  Federal income tax   _____

  Medical insurance   _____

     Total deductions   _____

Net earnings   _____

EXERCISE 11-6

General Journal

Page 1

	Date		Account Title	P.R.	Debit	Credit	
1							1
2							2
3							3
4							4
5							5
6							6
7							7
8							8
9							9
10							10
11							11
12							12
13							13
14							14
15							15
16							16
17							17
18							18

Case Problems

PROBLEM 11-1A OR 11-1B

Employee	Regular Pay	Overtime Pay	Gross Earnings	FICA		Fed. Inc. Tax	Net Pay
				OASDI	HI		

PROBLEM 11-2A

1. *(Left side)*

Fox Facts
Payroll Register
For Week Ended December 12, 20X3

Name	Status	Cumulative Earnings	Tot. Hrs.	Earnings Regular	Earnings Overtime	Earnings Total	Taxable Earnings Unemployment	Taxable Earnings FICA OASDI	Taxable Earnings FICA HI
Allen, Robert	M-2	37 2 0 0 00	40	3 8 0 00		3 8 0 00			
Bowen, Clarence	M-1	52 0 0 0 00	40	4 2 5 00		4 2 5 00			
Carlson, Wally	M-2	21 3 0 0 00	45	4 0 0 00	7 5 00	4 7 5 00			
Goodman, Mary	S-1	31 6 0 0 00	42	3 2 0 00	2 4 00	3 4 4 00			
Heuy, Jim	S-0	3 8 0 0 00	20	1 2 5 00		1 2 5 00			
Jones, Stan	M-3	27 6 0 0 00	40	3 6 0 00		3 6 0 00			
Totals									

(Right side)

	Deductions Federal Income Tax	State Income Tax	Medical Insurance	Savings Bonds	Union Dues	Total	FICA OASDI	HI	Payments Ck. No.	Net Amount	Expense Account Debited Sales Salaries Expense	Office Salaries Expense
Allen			3 8 00	2 5 00					201			3 8 0 00
Bowen			3 8 00	5 0 00					202			4 2 5 00
Carlson			3 8 00	2 5 00					203			4 7 5 00
Goodman			1 8 00						204		3 4 4 00	
Heuy									205			1 2 5 00
Jones			3 8 00	2 5 00					206		3 6 0 00	

PROBLEM 11-2A (continued)

2., 3.   **General Journal**   Page 1

	Date		Account Title	P.R.	Debit	Credit	
1							1
2							2
3							3
4							4
5							5
6							6
7							7
8							8
9							9
10							10
11							11
12							12
13							13
14							14
15							15
16							16
17							17
18							18
19							19
20							20
21							21
22							22
23							23
24							24
25							25
26							26
27							27
28							28
29							29
30							30
31							31
32							32

1.

(Left side)

NATHAN'S BONES PAYROLL REGISTER

Name	Status	Cumulative Earnings	Tot. Hrs.	EARNINGS Regular	EARNINGS Overtime	EARNINGS Total	TAXABLE EARNINGS Unemployment	TAXABLE EARNINGS FICA OASDI	TAXABLE EARNINGS FICA HI
Alexander, Mary	S-1	18 3 5 0 00	35	2 8 0 00		2 8 0 00			
Burnett, Barbara	M-1	25 4 0 0 00	44	2 9 0 00	4 3 52	3 3 3 52			
Dye, Jan	M-2	36 4 2 0 00	40	3 9 0 00		3 9 0 00			
Gill, Lora	M-3	29 6 0 0 00	38	3 2 3 00		3 2 3 00			
Taylor, Glenn	S-0	27 5 1 0 00	43	3 5 0 00	3 9 38	3 8 9 38			
Zasada, Albert	M-2	17 3 0 0 00	30	2 7 0 00		2 7 0 00			
Totals									

FOR WEEK ENDED FOR WEEK ENDED OCTOBER 15, 20X3

(Right side)

DEDUCTIONS Federal Income Tax	DEDUCTIONS State Income Tax	DEDUCTIONS Medical Insurance	DEDUCTIONS Savings Bonds	DEDUCTIONS Union Dues	DEDUCTIONS FICA OASDI	DEDUCTIONS FICA HI	PAYMENTS Total	PAYMENTS Ck. #	PAYMENTS Net Amount	EXPENSE ACCT. DEBITED Sales Salaries Expense	EXPENSE ACCT. DEBITED Office Salaries Expense
								201		2 8 0 00	
								202		3 3 3 52	
								203		3 9 0 00	
								204			3 2 3 00
								205		3 8 9 38	
								206			2 7 0 00

PROBLEM 11-2B (continued)

2., 3.

	Date	Account Title	P.R.	Debit	Credit	
1						1
2						2
3						3
4						4
5						5
6						6
7						7
8						8
9						9
10						10
11						11
12						12
13						13
14						14
15						15
16						16
17						17
18						18
19						19
20						20
21						21
22						22
23						23
24						24
25						25
26						26
27						27
28						28
29						29
30						30
31						31
32						32

PROBLEM 11-3A OR 11-3B

1.

(Left side)

PAYROLL REGISTER

Name	Status	Cumulative Earnings	Tot. Hrs.	EARNINGS			TAXABLE EARNINGS		
				Regular	Overtime	Total	Unemploy-ment	OASDI	HI

(Right side)

FOR WEEK ENDED _____

DEDUCTIONS							PAYMENTS		EXPENSE ACCT. DEBITED	
FICA		Federal Income Tax	State Income Tax	Medical Insurance	Savings Bonds	Union Dues	Ck. #	Net Amount	Sales Salaries Expense	Office Salaries Expense
OASDI	HI					Total				

660 PART III | Accounting for Payroll

2.   **General Journal**   Page 1

	Date		Account Title	P.R.	Debit	Credit	
1							1
2							2
3							3
4							4
5							5
6							6
7							7
8							8
9							9
10							10
11							11
12							12
13							13
14							14
15							15
16							16
17							17
18							18
19							19
20							20
21							21
22							22
23							23
24							24
25							25
26							26
27							27
28							28
29							29
30							30
31							31
32							32

PROBLEM 11-4A OR 11-4B

1., 2.
General Journal
Page 1

	Date	Account Title	P.R.	Debit	Credit	
1						1
2						2
3						3
4						4
5						5
6						6
7						7
8						8
9						9
10						10
11						11
12						12
13						13
14						14
15						15
16						16
17						17
18						18
19						19
20						20
21						21
22						22
23						23
24						24
25						25
26						26
27						27
28						28
29						29
30						30
31						31
32						32

Critical Thinking Problems

Challenge Problem

1. Weekly salary   _____

   Commission on total sales   _____

   Bonus on yearly salary   _____

       Gross earnings for year   _____

2. Federal Income tax on salary   _____

   Federal Income tax on commission and bonus   _____

       total federal income tax for year   _____

3. FICA Tax

       OASDI   _____

       HI   _____

       Total FICA taxes for year   _____

This page intentionally left blank.

Communications

_____
_____
_____
_____
_____
_____
_____
_____
_____
_____
_____
_____
_____
_____
_____
_____

Team Internet Project

_____
_____
_____
_____
_____
_____
_____
_____
_____
_____
_____
_____
_____
_____
_____

Ethics

_____

_____

_____

_____

_____

_____

_____

_____

_____

_____

_____

_____

_____

_____

_____

_____

_____

In the Real World

_____

_____

_____

_____

_____

_____

_____

_____

_____

_____

_____

_____

_____

_____

_____

_____

_____

Practice Test Answers

True/False

1. T
2. F
3. T
4. F
5. T
6. T
7. T
8. F
9. T
10. T
11. F
12. T
13. F
14. F
15. T

Matching

1. b
2. i
3. p
4. q
5. e
6. j
7. m
8. o
9. h
10. s
11. f
12. l
13. t
14. g
15. d
16. r
17. k
18. n
19. a
20. c

Fill in the Blanks

1. independent contractor
2. interstate commerce
3. payroll deductions
4. employee, employer
5. income tax
6. exemption
7. wage bracket
8. state income taxes
9. gross earnings, deductions
10. accounts, deduction
11. gross
12. FICA Tax Payable—OASDI, FICA Tax Payable—HI
13. net earnings

Multiple Choice

1. a
2. b
3. c
4. b
5. d
6. c
7. d

Writing/Short Answer

Answers will vary. Please discuss questions with your instructor.

Accounting for Payroll

Employer Taxes and Reports

Chapter Summary  Interactive Summary in English and Spanish

Payroll taxes are not only a deduction from the gross earnings of employees. The employer has expenses for payroll taxes as well as a responsibility to submit a variety of reports about these taxes. Just as individuals have Social Security numbers, all employers of at least one employee in this country must have an **employer identification number** (**EIN**). The EIN is listed on all payroll reports filed by the employer.

Employers are obligated to pay FICA tax, federal unemployment tax, and state unemployment tax. All three payroll taxes of the employer are debited to an operating expense account entitled **Payroll Tax Expense**. Each is credited to the appropriate liability account. The FICA Tax Payable—OASDI and FICA Tax Payable—HI accounts are the same accounts used to record the amounts withheld from the employees' earnings. In fact, the employer must match the amounts that were deducted from employees' earnings for FICA tax. The **FUTA Tax Payable account** and the **SUTA Tax Payable account** are used to record liabilities for the two types of unemployment tax. When any tax or other deduction is paid to the government or appropriate party, the liability account is debited and the Cash account is credited.

The **Federal Unemployment Tax Act** (**FUTA**) requires the payment of taxes to the federal government to provide benefits for workers during periods of unemployment. This tax cannot be withheld from the pay of employees, as it is an expense of the employer. The current rate of the FUTA tax is 6.2% of the first $7,000 of wages paid to each employee during a calendar year. An employer can take a credit of 5.4% for timely contributions to state unemployment funds. This leaves an effective rate for federal unemployment tax of 0.8%.

The **State Unemployment Tax Act** (**SUTA**) requires payments to the state government to provide benefits to workers during periods of unemployment. The rate varies among the states and from employer to employer since a **merit-rating system** is used to reward employers with more stable employment.

All three taxes must be reported and paid on a regular basis. FICA and federal income taxes are reported on **Form 941, Employer's Quarterly Federal Tax Return** every three months. If the total of both taxes for the quarter is $2,500 or less, payment is sent in with Form 941. If the total exceeds $2,500, the taxes must be deposited in a Federal Reserve or other authorized bank on a monthly or semiweekly basis. The time period that applies depends on the **lookback period**, which is the 12-month period ending on June 30 of the prior year. If total taxes for the lookback period were $50,000 or less, the employer becomes a monthly depositor this year. If total taxes for the lookback period were over $50,000, semiweekly deposits are made this year. Another time period applies to an employer that owes $100,000 or more per day—that amount must be deposited on the next day. When the taxes are deposited, **Form 8109, Federal Tax Deposit Coupon** is completed to accompany the deposit.

Federal unemployment taxes are remitted quarterly, as long as the amount to be deposited is more than $500. Once a year, **Form 940, Employer's Annual Federal Unemployment Tax Return** is filed to summarize FUTA deposits for the year. State unemployment tax forms and payment guidelines vary from state to state.

Employers must also prepare an annual report to employees, **Form W-2, Wage and Tax Statement**, which must be in the hands of employees by January 31. This form summarizes that employee's earnings and deductions for the past year. The employer files **Form W-3, Transmittal of Wage and Tax Statements**, annually to accompany the federal government's copies of all W-2 forms.

Most state governments require employers to carry **workers' compensation insurance** to provide protection for employees who suffer a job-related illness or injury. The employer usually pays the entire cost of this insurance. The Workers' Compensation Insurance Expense account is debited to record the estimated cost of the insurance. At the end of the year, the amount in the expense account is adjusted to the actual cost through an adjusting entry.

True/False

Please circle the correct answer.

T   F   1.   An EIN is assigned to both employers and employees.

T   F   2.   The Payroll Tax Expense account is an operating expense account for a business.

T   F   3.   The FICA tax paid by the employer is a different amount from the deduction made from the earnings of the employees.

T   F   4.   The amount of federal income tax withheld from an employee's gross earnings must be matched by an equal contribution by the employer.

T   F   5.   The rate for FUTA tax depends on the merit rating of the employer.

T   F   6.   Employers are required to deposit FICA taxes and federal income taxes withheld at a bank when the amount is $2,500 or more for a quarter.

T   F   7.   The lookback period for 2008 ends on June 30, 2007.

T   F   8.   Employers report FICA taxes and federal income taxes withheld to the government quarterly on Form 941.

T   F   9.   Both federal and state unemployment taxes are withheld from employees' salaries.

T   F   10.   Form 940 is filed quarterly to report federal unemployment taxes.

T   F   11.   Form W-2 summarizes the earnings and required deductions of an employee for the previous year.

T   F   12.   The Workers' Compensation Expense account is adjusted annually for the exact amount of the expense.

Matching

Please match each of the following terms with its definition.

a. employer identification number
b. Federal Unemployment Tax Act
c. Form 940
d. Form 941
e. Form 8109
f. Form W-2
g. Form W-3

h. FUTA Tax Payable account
i. lookback period
j. merit-rating system
k. Payroll Tax Expense account
l. State Unemployment Tax Act
m. SUTA Tax Payable account
n. workers' compensation insurance

_____ 1. An identifying number each business with one or more employees must have.

_____ 2. The operating expense account that is debited for the payroll taxes of the employer.

_____ 3. The liability account that is credited to record the amount owed to the federal government for unemployment taxes.

_____ 4. The liability account that is credited to record the amount owed to the state government for unemployment taxes.

_____ 5. A law that requires employers to pay taxes to the federal government to assist unemployed workers.

_____ 6. A law that requires employers to pay taxes to the state governments to assist unemployed workers.

_____ 7. A system of assigning unemployment tax rates based on an employer's record of providing stable employment.

_____ 8. The employer's quarterly federal tax return that summarizes the federal income taxes withheld and the employer and employees' shares of the FICA tax due for the quarter.

_____ 9. The reference time to determine if the employer must make monthly, semiweekly, or next-day deposits of taxes.

_____ 10. The form that accompanies any deposit of federal taxes by the employer.

_____ 11. The employer's annual federal unemployment tax return that must be filed by January 31 of each year.

_____ 12. A form given by the employer to the employee and to the IRS by January 31 of each year. It contains a summary of the employee's earnings for the past year and the amount of taxes withheld for that employee.

_____ 13. A form that accompanies the W-2 forms sent to the federal government.

_____ 14. Insurance that must be carried by an employer to provide benefits to employees for job-related illnesses or injuries.

Fill in the Blanks

Please complete each sentence with the correct word or words.

1. The employer must deduct FICA taxes from employee earnings and pay a(n) _____ amount.

2. There are two FICA tax rates: _____ for OASDI and _____ for HI.

3. State unemployment tax rates can vary for each employer under a(n) _____ system.

4. Federal and state _____ taxes are paid only by employers.

5. To record the employer's payroll taxes, debit the _____ account and credit each tax liability account.

6. The next-day deposit rule for FICA taxes and federal income taxes withheld applies when a firm accumulates a tax liability of _____ or more for that day.

7. Form 941 is used to report _____ taxes and _____ taxes withheld and is filed _____.

8. The employer must furnish each employee with a(n) _____ by January 31 of each year.

9. Form W-3 is sent to the _____ along with copies of the employees' W-2 forms.

10. If a credit is due for overestimated workers' compensation insurance, debit the Workers' Compensation Insurance _____ account.

Multiple Choice

Please circle the correct answer.

1. The employer must pay three payroll taxes. They are
   a. FICA, FUTA, and SUTA.
   b. FICA, state income tax withholding, and federal income tax withholding.
   c. FICA, federal income tax withholding, and workers' compensation insurance.
   d. None of the above

2. If an employer owes less than $500 for FICA taxes and federal income taxes withheld, the deposit must be made
   a. at the end of the quarter.
   b. at the end of the month.
   c. within 15 days after the end of the month.
   d. at the end of the year.

3. The lookback period for 2009 is
   a. January 1, 2008 to December 31, 2008.
   b. July 1, 2007 to June 30, 2008.
   c. July 1, 2008 to June 30, 2009.
   d. None of the above

4. Form 941 must be filed by employers
   a. weekly.
   b. quarterly.
   c. annually.
   d. monthly.

5. Form 940 is an annual tax return used to report
   a. federal income taxes withheld.
   b. FICA taxes.
   c. federal unemployment taxes.
   d. state unemployment taxes.

6. A deposit of federal unemployment taxes must be made whenever
   a. the amount exceeds $500 for the quarter.
   b. the amount exceeds $500 at the end of the month.
   c. the amount exceeds $3,000 for the day.
   d. Form 940 is due.

7. By January 31 of each year, every employee must receive
   a. Form 8109.
   b. Form W-2.
   c. Form W-3.
   d. Form 941.

8. If the estimated premium for workers' compensation insurance is $750 and the actual expense is $755, the adjusting entry will include
   a. a debit to Workers' Compensation Insurance Payable for $5.
   b. a debit to Workers' Compensation Insurance Receivable for $5.
   c. a credit to Workers' Compensation Insurance Expense for $5.
   d. None of the above

Writing/Short Answer

1. **Reflect** Make a list, in words or simple phrases, of the most important and meaningful points in this chapter.

2. **Question** Think about the most confusing points or the material you do not understand in this chapter. Write down two or three questions that remain unanswered.

3. **Connect** Explain, in one or two sentences, the connection between the main points of this chapter and the major goals of the entire course.

4. **Summarize** Review this chapter's Joining the Pieces visual summary, and explain the concept(s) illustrated in a few sentences.

Skills Review

Quick Practice

QUICK PRACTICE 12-1

	FICA Taxable Earnings		FUTA Taxable Earnings	SUTA Taxable Earnings	
	OASDI	HI			
	_____	_____	_____	_____	
Rate	_____	_____	_____	_____	
Total Tax Owed	_____	_____	_____	_____	_____

QUICK PRACTICE 12-2

	FICA Taxable Earnings		FUTA Taxable Earnings	SUTA Taxable Earnings	
	OASDI	HI			
	_____	_____	_____	_____	
Rate	_____	_____	_____	_____	
Total Tax Owed	_____	_____	_____	_____	_____

QUICK PRACTICE 12-3

	FICA Taxable Earnings		FUTA Taxable Earnings	SUTA Taxable Earnings	
	OASDI	HI			
	_____	_____	_____	_____	
Rate	_____	_____	_____	_____	
Total Tax Owed	_____	_____	_____	_____	_____

QUICK PRACTICE 12-4

General Journal

Page 1

	Date		Account Title	P.R.	Debit	Credit	
1							1
2							2
3							3
4							4
5							5
6							6
7							7
8							8

QUICK PRACTICE 12-5

	FICA Taxable Earnings		FUTA Taxable Earnings	SUTA Taxable Earnings	
	OASDI	HI			
	_____	_____	_____	_____	
Rate	_____	_____	_____	_____	
Total Tax Owed	_____	_____	_____	_____	_____

General Journal

Page 1

	Date		Account Title	P.R.	Debit	Credit	
1							1
2							2
3							3
4							4
5							5
6							6
7							7
8							8

QUICK PRACTICE 12-6

General Journal

Page 1

	Date		Account Title	P.R.	Debit	Credit	
1							1
2							2
3							3
4							4
5							5
6							6
7							7
8							8

QUICK PRACTICE 12-7

General Journal

Page 1

	Date		Account Title	P.R.	Debit	Credit	
1							1
2							2
3							3
4							4
5							5
6							6
7							7
8							8

QUICK PRACTICE 12-8

General Journal

Page 1

	Date		Account Title	P.R.	Debit	Credit	
1							1
2							2
3							3
4							4
5							5
6							6
7							7
8							8

General Journal   Page 1

	Date		Account Title	P.R.	Debit	Credit	
1							1
2							2
3							3
4							4
5							5
6							6
7							7
8							8

Exercises

EXERCISE 12-1

Employee	FICA Taxable Earnings		FUTA Taxable Earnings	SUTA Taxable Earnings
	OASDI	HI		
Burns, Jim	_____	_____	_____	_____
Carrol, Helen	_____	_____	_____	_____
Harold, Barbara	_____	_____	_____	_____
Total Taxable Earnings	_____	_____	_____	_____
Rate	_____	_____	_____	_____
Total Tax Owed	_____	_____	_____	_____

EXERCISE 12-2

General Journal
Page 1

	Date	Account Title	P.R.	Debit	Credit	
1						1
2						2
3						3
4						4
5						5
6						6
7						7
8						8
9						9
10						10

EXERCISE 12-3

	FICA Taxable Earnings		FUTA Taxable Earnings	SUTA Taxable Earnings
	OASDI	HI		
	_____	_____	_____	_____
Rate	_____	_____	_____	_____
Total Tax Owed	_____	_____	_____	_____

General Journal
Page 1

	Date		Account Title	P.R.	Debit	Credit	
1							1
2							2
3							3
4							4
5							5
6							6
7							7
8							8

EXERCISE 12-4

	FICA Taxable Earnings		FUTA Taxable Earnings	SUTA Taxable Earnings
	OASDI	HI		
	_____	_____	_____	_____
Rate	_____	_____	_____	_____
Total Tax Owed	_____	_____	_____	_____

General Journal
Page 1

	Date		Account Title	P.R.	Debit	Credit	
1							1
2							2
3							3
4							4
5							5
6							6
7							7
8							8

EXERCISE 12-5

General Journal

Page 1

	Date		Account Title	P.R.	Debit					Credit					
1															1
2															2
3															3
4															4
5															5
6															6
7															7
8															8

EXERCISE 12-6

(a)

(b)

(c)

EXERCISE 12-7

General Journal

Page 1

		Date		Account Title	P.R.	Debit						Credit						
(a)	1																	1
	2																	2
	3																	3
	4																	4
	5																	5
	6																	6
(b)	7																	7
	8																	8
	9																	9
	10																	10
	11																	11
	12																	12
(c)	13																	13
	14																	14
	15																	15
	16																	16
	17																	17

Case Problems

PROBLEM 12-1A OR 12-1B

1.

Employee	FICA Taxable Earnings		FUTA Taxable Earnings	SUTA Taxable Earnings
	OASDI	HI		
_____	_____	_____	_____	_____
_____	_____	_____	_____	_____
_____	_____	_____	_____	_____
_____	_____	_____	_____	_____
_____	_____	_____	_____	_____
_____	_____	_____	_____	_____
Total Taxable Earnings	_____	_____	_____	_____
Rate	_____	_____	_____	_____
Total Tax Owed	_____	_____	_____	_____ |_____

2.

General Journal   Page 1

	Date	Account Title	P.R.	Debit	Credit	
1						1
2						2
3						3
4						4
5						5
6						6
7						7
8						8
9						9
10						10

This page intentionally left blank.

PROBLEM 12-2A OR 12-2B

1.

Month	FICA Taxable Earnings		FUTA Taxable Earnings	SUTA Taxable Earnings
	OASDI	HI		
_____	_____	_____	_____	_____
Rate	_____	_____	_____	_____
Total Tax Owed	_____	_____	_____	_____	_____
_____	_____	_____	_____	_____
Rate	_____	_____	_____	_____
Total Tax Owed	_____	_____	_____	_____	_____
_____	_____	_____	_____	_____
Rate	_____	_____	_____	_____
Total Tax Owed	_____	_____	_____	_____	_____

2., 3., 4.   **General Journal**   Page 1

	Date		Account Title	P.R.	Debit	Credit	
1							1
2							2
3							3
4							4
5							5
6							6
7							7
8							8
9							9
10							10
11							11
12							12
13							13
14							14
15							15
16							16
17							17
18							18
19							19
20							20
21							21
22							22
23							23
24							24
25							25
26							26
27							27
28							28
29							29
30							30
31							31
32							32
33							33
34							34

PROBLEM 12-3A OR 12-3B

2. <div style="text-align:center">**General Journal**</div> Page 6

	Date		Account Title	P.R.	Debit	Credit	
1							1
2							2
3							3
4							4
5							5
6							6
7							7
8							8
9							9
10							10
11							11
12							12
13							13
14							14
15							15
16							16
17							17
18							18
19							19
20							20
21							21
22							22
23							23
24							24
25							25
26							26
27							27
28							28
29							29
30							30
31							31
32							32

General Journal

Page 7

	Date		Account Title	P.R.	Debit	Credit	
1							1
2							2
3							3
4							4
5							5
6							6
7							7
8							8
9							9
10							10
11							11
12							12
13							13
14							14
15							15
16							16
17							17
18							18
19							19
20							20
21							21
22							22
23							23
24							24
25							25
26							26
27							27
28							28
29							29
30							30
31							31
32							32

PROBLEM 12-3A OR 12-3B (continued)

1., 2.

ACCOUNT FICA Tax Payable—OASDI   ACCOUNT NO. 215

DATE	ITEM	P.R.	DEBIT	CREDIT	BALANCE DEBIT	BALANCE CREDIT

ACCOUNT FICA Tax Payable—HI   ACCOUNT NO. 216

DATE	ITEM	P.R.	DEBIT	CREDIT	BALANCE DEBIT	BALANCE CREDIT

ACCOUNT Federal Income Tax Payable   ACCOUNT NO. 217

DATE	ITEM	P.R.	DEBIT	CREDIT	BALANCE DEBIT	BALANCE CREDIT

ACCOUNT State Income Tax Payable   ACCOUNT NO. 218

DATE	ITEM	P.R.	DEBIT	CREDIT	BALANCE DEBIT	BALANCE CREDIT

ACCOUNT FUTA Tax Payable   ACCOUNT NO. 219

DATE		ITEM	P.R.	DEBIT	CREDIT	BALANCE	
						DEBIT	CREDIT

ACCOUNT SUTA Tax Payable   ACCOUNT NO. 220

DATE		ITEM	P.R.	DEBIT	CREDIT	BALANCE	
						DEBIT	CREDIT

ACCOUNT Union Dues Payable   ACCOUNT NO. 221

DATE		ITEM	P.R.	DEBIT	CREDIT	BALANCE	
						DEBIT	CREDIT

ACCOUNT Payroll Tax Expense   ACCOUNT NO. 551

DATE		ITEM	P.R.	DEBIT	CREDIT	BALANCE	
						DEBIT	CREDIT

PROBLEM 12-4A OR 12-4B

(a)

(c)

(d)

General Journal

		Date	Account Title	P.R.	Debit	Credit	
(b)	1						1
	2						2
	3						3
	4						4
	5						5
	6						6
(c)	7						7
	8						8
	9						9
	10						10
	11						11
(d)	12						12
	13						13
	14						14
	15						15
	16						16

This page intentionally left blank.

Critical Thinking Problems

Challenge Problem

Month	FICA Taxable Earnings		FUTA Taxable Earnings	SUTA Taxable Earnings
	OASDI	HI		
January				
Rate				
Total Tax Owed				
February				
Rate				
Total Tax Owed				
March				
Rate				
Total Tax Owed				
April				
Rate				
Total Tax Owed				
May				
Rate				
Total Tax Owed				
June				
Rate				
Total Tax Owed				

Challenge Problem (continued)

Month	FICA Taxable Earnings		FUTA Taxable Earnings	SUTA Taxable Earnings
	OASDI	HI		
July				
Rate				
Total Tax Owed				
August				
Rate				
Total Tax Owed				
September				
Rate				
Total Tax Owed				
October				
Rate				
Total Tax Owed				
November				
Rate				
Total Tax Owed				
December				
Rate				
Total Tax Owed				

Challenge Problem (continued)

	Date		Account Title	P.R.	Debit	Credit	
1							1
2							2
3							3
4							4
5							5
6							6
7							7
8							8
9							9
10							10
11							11
12							12
13							13
14							14
15							15
16							16
17							17
18							18
19							19
20							20
21							21
22							22
23							23
24							24
25							25
26							26
27							27
28							28
29							29
30							30
31							31
32							32
33							33

This page intentionally left blank.

Communications

Team Internet Project

Ethics

_____
_____
_____
_____
_____
_____
_____
_____
_____
_____
_____
_____
_____
_____
_____
_____
_____

In the Real World

_____
_____
_____
_____
_____
_____
_____
_____
_____
_____
_____
_____
_____
_____
_____

Practice Test Answers

True/False

1. F
2. T
3. F
4. F
5. F
6. T
7. T
8. T
9. F
10. F
11. T
12. T

Matching

1. a
2. k
3. h
4. m
5. b
6. l
7. j
8. d
9. i
10. e
11. c
12. f
13. g
14. n

Fill in the Blanks

1. matching
2. 6.2%, 1.45%
3. merit-rating
4. unemployment
5. Payroll Tax Expense
6. $100,000
7. FICA, federal income, quarterly
8. W-2 form
9. federal government
10. Receivable

Multiple Choice

1. a
2. a
3. b
4. b
5. c
6. a
7. b
8. d

Writing/Short Answer

Answers will vary. Please discuss questions with your instructor.

Carlson Company

(Left side)

CARLSON COMPANY PAYROLL REGISTER

Name	Status	Cumulative Earnings	Tot. Hrs.	EARNINGS			TAXABLE EARNINGS		
				Regular	Overtime	Total	Unemploy-ment	FICA OASDI	FICA HI

FOR WEEK ENDED _____

DEDUCTIONS								PAYMENTS		EXPENSE ACCT. DEBITED	
FICA OASDI	FICA HI	Federal Income Tax	State Income Tax	Medical Insurance	Savings Bonds	Union Dues	Total	Ck. #	Net Amount	Sales Salaries Expense	Office Salaries Expense

(Right side)

701

CARLSON COMPANY PAYROLL REGISTER

Name	Status	Cumulative Earnings	Tot. Hrs.	EARNINGS			TAXABLE EARNINGS			
				Regular	Overtime	Total	Unemploy- ment	OASDI	FICA	HI

FOR WEEK ENDED _____

FICA		DEDUCTIONS						PAYMENTS		EXPENSE ACCT. DEBITED	
OASDI	HI	Federal Income Tax	State Income Tax	Medical Insurance	Savings Bonds	Union Dues	Total	Ck. #	Net Amount	Sales Salaries Expense	Office Salaries Expense

(Right side)

	Date		Account Title	P.R.	Debit	Credit	
1							1
2							2
3							3
4							4
5							5
6							6
7							7
8							8
9							9
10							10
11							11
12							12
13							13
14							14
15							15
16							16
17							17
18							18
19							19
20							20
21							21
22							22
23							23
24							24
25							25
26							26
27							27
28							28
29							29
30							30
31							31
32							32
33							33
34							34
35							35
36							36

	Date		Account Title	P.R.	Debit					Credit					
1															1
2															2
3															3
4															4
5															5
6															6
7															7
8															8
9															9
10															10
11															11
12															12
13															13
14															14
15															15
16															16
17															17
18															18
19															19
20															20
21															21
22															22
23															23
24															24
25															25
26															26
27															27
28															28
29															29
30															30
31															31
32															32
33															33
34															34
35															35
36															36